In life it is key as followers of Christ to have daily interaction with the Lord. Just like relationships on earth you have to spend time and effort to grow them. The Lodestar Guidance daily devotional book is a great quiet time or small group tool to help you continue to grow your relationship with the Lord.

—Quin Houff
NASCAR Cup Series Driver

Forty-eight years ago Steve Wingfield was instrumental in leading me to faith in Christ. It is truly an honor to have had a small part in this devotional. My prayer for each of you is that our wonderful Lord and Savior will use this book to draw you closer unto Him. As you are drawn near to Jesus, I pray you might see yourself in the mirror of His glory and allow His word to do a work in your heart and life, molding you into His image.

—Dr. Don Paxton
Sr. Pastor Rosedale Baptist, Abingdon, VA

Steve Wingfield is my friend and I value his investment in my life and my family's life. He walks his talk and I know these daily devotions will help you be a better you! It is a must read!

—Josh Reume
Owner Reume Brothers Racing, #33 Driver NASCAR Truck Series

Steve Wingfield has put encouraging spiritual wisdom in a profoundly simple book—to help us grow daily!

—Bobb Biehl
Executive Mentor

In these days of civil unrest, Covid-19 pandemic, and economic uncertainties, everyone is challenged to the core of our beings. Life is a hard ball game and only the strong and courageous survive. My friend and fellow evangelist, Steve Wingfield has written a powerful new book that I highly recommend. This new book will refresh and inspire you to accept and meet the daily challenges of living for Christ in a godless age. It will help you personally, your family and friends in your business. I believe it will develop Christ honoring character in each of us.

—Dr. Tim Robnett
President, ETeamGlobal

Steve Wingfield is a tremendous motivator, both verbally and in his writings! Every time I have had the pleasure to be around him, I leave encouraged and ready to fight the devil if needed! He's the definition of "radical for Jesus" in every sense of the word! These devotionals and prayers will lift up your spirit and increase your faith and understanding of the word of God! Get this book and buy some more for your friends!

—Jason Crabb
Grammy Award-winning Christian Artist

Everyone must get accurate direction for their life from God and that helps them accomplish God's purpose for their life. This book is the beginning of the process—not the end—it points you to find two things. First, you get God's purpose for your life, everyone must know God's promise, "For I know the thoughts that I think toward you, says the Lord, thoughts of peace and not of evil, to give you a future and a hope (Jeremiah 29:11). After you get God's plan for your life, the next step is to "do it." My life verse is 1 Thess. 5:24 "Faithful is he that calleth you, who also will do it."

— Elmer L. Towns
Co-founder, Liberty University

Dr. Steve Wingfield is a gifted evangelist, who communicates the message of the gospel of Christ with a profound conviction. It was a joy to sing at many Steve Wingfield Crusades and witness firsthand the Lord using him to bring many to Christ. What a powerful preacher! I highly recommend *Guiding Principles* as a must read. It will strengthen your spiritual life by building godly character.

—Babbie Mason
Christian singer, songwriter, and author

It's easier to preach for an hour than to inspire in a minute; Steve Wingfield can do both. This is his collection of spiritual espresso shots that will provide life-changing wisdom in memorable chunks that will lodge every morning in your soul. Short is sweet; enjoy this thematic assemblage of God-sourced wisdom that will refine your daily pursuits in service to the God of Eternity.

—Bob Shank
Founder, "Master's Program"

Steve Wingfield's Lodestar Guidance Devotional will encourage you with hope and wisdom to strengthen your relationship with God. You will want to start your day with this practical and inspiring devotional that provides a biblical perspective on the big issues of life. This devotional will help you in your daily spiritual journey as each page provides biblical principles for victorious Christin living.

—David L. Jones
Executive Director
Palau Foundation for World Evangelism

GUIDING PRINCIPLES

TO LIVE, LEARN, AND LEAD

BY

STEVE WINGFIELD

J. WESTIN
BOOKS

J. Westin Books
100 Missionary Ridge
Birmingham, AL 35242
An imprint of Iron Stream Media
IronStreamMedia.com

Library of Congress Cataloging-in-Publication Data 2020918648.

ISBN-13: 978-1-56309-483-5
Ebook ISBN: 978-1-56309-488-0

1 2 3 4 5—24 23 22 21 20

GUIDING PRINCIPLES
is dedicated to my friend Paul Weaver.

In 2019, Paul gifted Lodestar Guidance to Wingfield Ministries, Inc. I am thankful for Paul and the investment he has made in my life and ministry. Paul took a small leather shop and grew it to become the leading leather business in America. He had the vision to develop Lodestar Guidance as an investment in the employees of Weaver Leather. From my observation of many visits to the company, his investment has reaped tenfold dividends. The culture that Lodestar Guidance has helped create at Weaver Leather, Inc. is an amazing thing to behold. All business owners should consider making such an investment in their employees.

ACKNOWLEDGEMENTS

I am grateful to God for the many companies and individuals who have chosen to use Lodestar Guidance. I am convinced this program has the power to change our world if we will implement these guiding principles as a way of life.

Elaine Starner for taking my material and making it better.

Once again, I am amazed at God's divine appointments. While speaking at a prayer breakfast in Franklin, TN, I met Paul Shepherd, president of Shepherd Literary Services, who said he would like to publish my next book.

Each daily devotional has an accompanying prayer written by my family, mentors, partners in ministry, and friends.

Last but not least, I am thankful for my wife Barbara and our children, Michelle and husband Howard and their children Phin, Lars, Katie Anne, Field Jude, and J.R. and our son David and wife Havilah and their children Selah and Jubal. They all continue to be a great encouragement to me as I seek to follow hard after Christ.

Most of all, I am thankful for the night Jesus rescued me and accepted me into his fold.

May God bless these writings and use this devotional for the advancement of His kingdom.

GUIDING PRINCIPLES is a compilation of devotionals spanning a timeframe of one year that can be used in conjunction with the Lodestar Guidance program, a character-building program that has been in existence for over eight years.

What is a *lodestar*? It is a navigational star, such as Polaris, the North Star, a star that leads or guides so you know where you are. For followers of Christ, it is Jesus. He will always lead us to truth.

I encourage you to visit LodestarGuidance.com to learn more about this groundbreaking program and choose the membership that best suits your home, small group, Sunday school class, or business. Additionally, please consider sponsoring this program for use in your local school.

Below is the list of Lodestar Guidance principles in alphabetical order. You may find it best to study one principle per week or by topic, depending on which principle you are currently studying.

Accountability	Gratefulness	Productivity
Attitude	Honesty	Punctuality
Boldness	Humility	Resourcefulness
Compassion	Influence	Respect
Courage	Initiative	Rest
Decisiveness	Innovation	Restraint
Dependability	Integrity	Self-awareness
Determination	Joyfulness	Self-control
Development	Kindness	Sensitivity
Diligence	Likability	Sincerity
Discernment	Loyalty	Stewardship
Discretion	Motivation	Teachable
Empathy	Motives	Thoroughness
Fairness	Orderliness	Transparency
Flexibility	Ownership	Trustworthiness
Focus	Passion	Wisdom
Forgiveness	Patience	
Generosity	Peace	

It is my earnest prayer that God will use this material to help each of us become more like the Master. May Philippians 1:6 be a reality in each of our lives. "Being confident of this, that he who began a good work in you will carry it on to completion until the day of Christ Jesus." —Steve Wingfield

GUIDING PRINCIPLES

ACCOUNTABILITY

Accountability is a choice. Brave men are accountable.
—Paul Weaver

DAY 1

Two are better than one, because they have a good return for their labor: if either of them falls down, one can help the other up. . . . A cord of three strands is not quickly broken.

—Ecclesiastes 4:9–10, 12

ACCOUNTABILITY IS BEING WILLINGLY ANSWERABLE and responsible for your behavior. For a number of years, I have been involved in a group of six men, an accountability group. At times, they'll ask me hard questions or I'll ask them hard questions. I'm also accountable to my wife, to my family, and to a board of directors. I don't want to be a lone wolf out there, because being accountable—being willing to answer for and take responsibility for our actions—helps us to grow and have healthy relationships.

God has made us to live in relationships with others. In the Garden of Eden, at the beginning of our history, God not only created a companion for Adam, he also walked in relationship with Adam and Eve. God's ideal of relationship is meant to expand our lives and help us. Throughout the New Testament especially, God urges us to tend our relationships, caring for each other and helping each other. Romans 12:5 says that all who are in Christ are a part of the same body and "each member belongs to all the others."

Relationships are crucial to our business lives, our spiritual lives, and our personal lives. And it's only when we're willing to be answerable and take responsibility for our behavior that these bonds created by God for our good can stay strong and productive.

Lord Jesus, guide me as I nurture my relationships with others. Amen.

Prayers on ACCOUNTABILITY by Dr. Robert Coleman.

Day 2

Do not lie to each other, since you have taken off your old self with its practices and have put on the new self, which is being renewed in knowledge in the image of its Creator.
—Colossians 3:9–10

In my accountability group, the last question we will ask of each other is, "Have you lied to me?" Truth is the foundation of accountability. Without that foundation, accountability crumbles and ceases to exist. When accountability is lacking, we start operating in secrecy; and when we're operating in secrecy, we slide into areas in which we compromise our integrity. This is true in our workplace, in our homes, and in our social circles. I don't want to have secrets; I want to live openly and honestly. I want to be known as a person of integrity, and to guard my integrity, I will have to be accountable for my actions.

In Colossians 3:9–10, we read that we're not to lie to each other. Sometimes we also lie to ourselves and cannot even admit it. We're to strip off our old wicked deeds and put on the new nature God has planted in us. That means stripping off the untruths and excuses and putting on truth every day. Many times, this is a fierce battle for us. But in this striving to mature and grow more like Him, we will be helped tremendously if we are willing to be accountable to others who are seeking the same goals we are and who can encourage and support us.

Heavenly Father, help me to be open and honest with the people who depend on me. Amen.

Day 3

So then, each of us will give an account of ourselves to God.
—Romans 14:12

IT IS IMPORTANT FOR US ALL TO REALIZE THIS: Every one of us, whether a follower of Christ or not, is accountable to God because we can have no secrets from Him. We cannot hide any activity or secret motives from His eyes. He sees and knows it all. He is the Creator who made our hearts, observes and understands everything we do (Psalm 33:15).

There is no place for excuses or shifting the blame when we stand before God. Whether or not we've lived with accountability in our earthly lives, we will certainly have to give an account to God someday for whatever we've done. I don't have to live in fear over that because His great kindness and mercy have provided a way for us to be able to stand before Him with clear records. His forgiveness is for all who confess their sin. This is the greatest accountability relationship we can have, and we can have it *right now.* If we are willing to take responsibility and acknowledge our sin to Him, He "is faithful and just and will forgive us our sins and purify us from all unrighteousness" (1 John 1:9). He not only forgives, He cleanses us, too! In that relationship, there's responsibility. There's truth. There's cleansing and growth. That's the greatest accountability relationship you can have, my friend.

In light of the grace you grant me, Holy Spirit, spur me on to be full of integrity and accountable before God. Amen.

Day 4

Therefore encourage one another and build each other up, just as in fact you are doing.

—1 Thessalonians 5:11

MANY TIMES IN THE LETTERS OF THE NEW TESTAMENT to early, young Christians we read "Make every effort to . . ." Have you ever felt as though your efforts just aren't enough? Accountability will strengthen us, my friend.

Being in accountable relationships helps us grow. We can share our struggles, our weaknesses, and our failings with people we trust. We can also celebrate in those relationships and nurture our good choices and strengths. We give and receive encouragement. We help each other keep a clear focus on our mission to represent Jesus well. As 1 Thessalonians 5:11 says, we build each other up.

Accountable relationships strengthen us in another way. You know that every time you use a muscle, you strengthen it. Every time we decide to take responsibility for our actions instead of making excuses, we are increasing our accountability to *ourselves*. We're bolstering our will to make the right choices and follow the right path. We are exercising the "muscle" of accountability. Accountability helps us to grow into God's best for our lives, and His best includes strength.

Lord Jesus, help me to practice accountability each day as regularly as I eat and drink. Amen.

Steve Wingfield

Day 5

He makes the whole body fit together perfectly. As each part does its own special work, it helps the other parts grow, so that the whole body is healthy and growing and full of love.

—Ephesians 4:16 (NLT)

THE SPIRIT OF GOD, LIVING IN US, has given each of us certain gifts. We're to use these gifts well to serve each other. Do you know what your gift is? The "gifts" we've been given aren't necessarily what the world sees as talents and abilities. Those are gifts, too, but the Spirit also gifts people to be encouragers, to be kind to those who need kindness, to be givers in many varied ways, to see truth in situations, to show hospitality, to be sensitive to those who always feel on the "outside." There are many, many ways the Spirit works through individual lives. And when all these individual parts of one body are doing the special work the Spirit has given them, we help each other grow, and "the whole body is healthy and growing and full of love."

Accountability relationships can help us determine and develop those gifts. Some people are very aware of their gifts; others find it difficult to look at their personality and life and see what God is doing. Relationships that build each other up help us to see ourselves from other perspectives. Sometimes the Holy Spirit works through others to speak to us.

God created each one of us to fill certain roles in His plan. Step into that role. Be an accountable steward of the gift you've been given.

Holy Spirit, guide me to recognize my gift and bring it forward with all the love and diligence of Jesus. Amen.

DAY 6

Carry each other's burdens, and in this way you will fulfill the law of Christ.
—Galatians 6:2

WHAT IS OUR RESPONSIBILITY TO OTHERS IN ACCOUNTABILITY RELATIONSHIPS? The truth must always be the foundation. On that foundation, we build each other up. The purpose for all who belong to the body of Christ is to fulfill Jesus' commandment to all disciples at every time in history: Love each other as I have loved you.

Colossians 3 gives us specific guidelines. We're to have mercy when a person stumbles. We're to be kind and humble, gentle and patient. We're to forgive, just as God forgave us. We're to teach and counsel each other in wisdom given from God and keep Him at the center of our worship. And everything we do and say, we do as a representative of the Lord Jesus (3:12–17).

In our accountability relationships, we are Jesus' representative. We love each other as He loves us and them. We work for their good, as He does. We help them walk in God's best path, just as their heavenly Shepherd does.

Pray for the Spirit of Jesus to guide you in your accountability relationships. Friends, we have been entrusted with His mission. Accountability in all areas of our lives will help us and others accomplish the work He's given us, the greatest work of which is loving each other.

Nurture my relationships, dear Lord, so that I might be seen as an accountable follower of God. Amen.

Steve Wingfield

DAY 7

Let each of you look not only to his own interests, but also to the interests of others.
—Philippians 2:4 (ESV)

IN HEBREWS 10 WE READ THESE WORDS: "And let us consider how we may spur one another on toward love and good deeds, not giving up meeting together" (Hebrews 10:24–25). My friend, take today to consider how accountability can make you stronger and help you grow toward God's best for you. Accountability is important in leadership and character. But as a man or woman of God, relationships that nurture and guard you as Jesus the Great Shepherd nurtures and guards you are of utmost importance. In turn, you will be representing Jesus the Shepherd to others as they are willing to be accountable to you.

If you don't have such a connection to a small group, ask God for guidance on finding an accountability relationship. Ask Him for the courage to follow through and build those connections. His love is great and lasts forever. He wants to give you the best for your life. He'll answer those prayers.

Heavenly Father, fill me with the desire to meet with my fellow believers, stirring one another up to good deeds and accountability. Amen.

Notes and Prayers

_____

_____

_____

_____

_____

_____

_____

_____

_____

_____

_____

_____

_____

_____

_____

_____

_____

_____

_____

_____

Steve Wingfield

ATTITUDE

Our Creator gave us control over the mind,
but he tells us to guard it because everything we do flows from it.
—Paul Weaver

DAY 1

Do not conform to the pattern of this world, but be transformed by the renewing of your mind. Then you will be able to test and approve what God's will is—his good, pleasing and perfect will.

—Romans 12:2

ATTITUDE IS ONE OF THE MOST IMPORTANT QUALITIES OF ANYONE'S LIFE. It can be defined as the capacity to stay positive and optimistic despite the circumstances. Attitude is something you choose. My dad would not put up with a bad attitude. If we grumbled or complained, he would just tell us to get over it. "*Can't* never did anything. You try."

Abraham Lincoln said, "You can be excited about the fact that thorns have roses, or you can be upset about the fact that roses have thorns." The beautiful rose and the irritating thorn are both there. What do we choose to see?

What we see in every circumstance of life is determined by our attitude.

The Bible tells us that we are responsible for our attitude. We need to be positive and optimistic, not only in what we say but also in how we think. To live as followers of Jesus Christ, to "shine as bright stars" in this world, we need to *choose* how we think, feel, and talk about every situation in our daily lives.

Lord, forgive me for my bad attitude and the things I did to develop it. Guide me to make good choices today so I will have a better attitude to face tomorrow and the future. Amen.

Prayers on ATTITUDE by Dr. Elmer Towns.

Day 2

Anxiety in a man's heart weighs him down, but a good word makes him glad.
—Proverbs 12:25 (ESV)

YOUR CHOICE OF ATTITUDE WILL AFFECT YOUR PERSONAL LIFE, your relationships, and your business life. If you choose to live with a positive and optimistic outlook, I promise you'll see rewarding benefits in your life.

A person with a bad attitude will be known as someone who is always arguing, complaining, or blaming someone else. They are stuck in a world of worry and disenchantment. Pessimistic and unable to see hope, they don't make progress in either their personal lives or relationships. Advancement in business does not come to those with bad attitudes.

That's not the kind of reputation you want to have, my friend.

The right attitude will help you make better decisions. It will increase your productivity. You won't be stuck. You'll emphasize and build on the positive. You'll be seen as a person who comes into a situation and says, "Let's get the job done and move on to where we've got to go." You want to be known as a person who can see good even in bad situations and find opportunity in problems.

That positive and optimistic outlook is a benefit to any type of business environment and essential to healthy and stable relationships. In every area of life, how you think changes who you are.

Lord, when I look to you, I get a good outlook on life. You give me forgiveness when I confess so I can change. You give me a positive vison in life when I surrender all to Christ. You give me options to step out in faith to obey Your Word. Amen.

Steve Wingfield

DAY 3

Do everything without grumbling or arguing.
—Philippians 2:14

YOU PROBABLY KNOW SOMEONE WHO IS ALWAYS COMPLAINING, arguing, grumbling, and expecting the worst from each situation—maybe even *looking* for the worst in situations. You've experienced how those people cast clouds over any situation or conversation. It's unpleasant to work with people who have that mindset. It's uncomfortable to even be around them briefly.

God got really tired of hearing the Israelites complaining in the wilderness. Scripture tells us He was very angry with them for their constant complaining, in spite of everything He was doing for them. He was guiding, providing, and protecting—doing miraculous things for them. But that's not what they chose to think about. Their thoughts and conversations were focused on what they did not have. Psalm 78:33 tells us the sad story of their years: they ended their lives "in futility and terror."

Attitudes are expressed in our speech and our actions, and our attitude will affect every day of our lives. Grumbling and complaining have no place in the thoughts and conversations of those who represent Christ.

It is wise to listen to our own words and check our own thoughts. Many thoughts come marching through our heads every day; which ones do we allow to stay? Those thoughts will be the ones that determine who we are and what kind of day we have today.

Lord, forgive me when I have complained about things. I will trust You next time. Focus my eyes on following You today, so I can have the same optimism You have. Amen.

Day 4

Rejoice always, pray continually, give thanks in all circumstances; for this is God's will for you in Christ Jesus. Do not quench the Spirit.

—1 Thessalonians 5:16–19

IN CONTRAST TO THE VERSES ABOUT COMPLAINING, arguing, and grumbling, there are many Scriptures that turn us toward the proper attitude. These verses take us to an even higher level than our Lodestar definition of attitude: a positive and optimistic outlook.

Philippians 4 tells us to rejoice in everything. It is repeated for emphasis, in case we weren't paying attention the first time. Verse 6 tells us not to worry about anything, to pray, to cultivate a thankful heart. Verse 7 talks about having a peaceful mind and heart. And verse 8 is about choosing to dwell on what is good and true and lovely and praiseworthy.

That certainly presents a different picture than one of constant complaining, worry, and expecting the worst, doesn't it? It's the picture of a life with a heart and mind guarded by peace.

How do we find such a life? The key is in the 1 Thessalonians verse above: Don't say No to the Spirit; say YES! The Spirit of Christ lives in you. His will is that this is the way you think, and that your life displays these attitudes. Ask Him to help you choose His will in the attitude you carry into today. Then follow His lead.

Lord, I thank You that things are not as bad as they could be. I thank You for who I am . . . what I have . . . where I live and the friends I have. I thank You that tomorrow will be better because I follow Jesus and I look to You for daily guidance. Amen.

Steve Wingfield

Day 5

I remain confident of this: I will see the goodness of the LORD in the land of the living.

—Psalm 27:13

ARE YOU CONFIDENT YOU WILL SEE THE GOODNESS OF THE LORD? Knowing God has a purpose for us and that He is always working for our good, we have a reason to rejoice, and to rejoice always (Philippians 4:4). We know that regardless of the circumstances we will see the goodness of the Lord.

"In the morning, LORD, you hear my voice; in the morning I lay my requests before you and wait expectantly" (Psalm 5:3). God is always working for our good. He is always with us. We are loved and treasured by Him. He died for us to make us His own. He will never forsake us.

Paul Weaver wrote, "When dark days and long nights are our fate for a period of time, we have a choice to make. We can become bitter and declare that life is unfair and that our loving heavenly Father is actually an angry and ruthless God, or we can ask for direction, motivation, and healing that can make us better, not bitter. It's our choice."

If God is for us, then we can be confident we will see the goodness of the Lord in all circumstances of our lives. Our attitude makes our choice to wait expectantly and look for His goodness. This will change your day, I guarantee it.

Lord, I praise You for all the good things You have given me in life. Thank You for all the lessons You have taught me from my past problems and trials. I know You will handle future difficulties the way you have handled them in the past. Amen.

Day 6

Finally, brothers and sisters, whatever is true, whatever is noble, whatever is right, whatever is pure, whatever is lovely, whatever is admirable—if anything is excellent or praiseworthy—think about such things.

—Philippians 4:8

You've heard the maxim that "You are what you eat." You've probably proven the truth of that statement in your own experience. What we feed our bodies has a huge effect on how we look, feel, and act. The same can be said about what we feed our minds. Our minds have this great capacity to gobble up things we see, hear, and read. And what our minds gobble up, in turn, has a huge effect on how we think, on our attitude, on our outlook, and on our behavior. So, be careful of what you feed your mind.

Romans 12:2 says that renewing our minds will transform us. As you seek to renew your mind, two things are life-changing: the Scriptures and the encouragement of others. Find friends who will "feed" the proper diet to your mind, who will encourage you, build you up, and who are confident of seeing the goodness of the Lord. Soak your mind with Scriptures. Know what God has promised. Know what He says about events in this world. Know what He says about who you are and who He is. The Spirit in you works through the Scriptures. He'll renew your mind and transform you.

Think on these things, my friend.

Lord, thank you for who I am today. I am the product of all my experiences and things you have taught me. Help me remember past lessons, and help me build on them in the future. "I can do all this through him who gives me strength" (Philippians 4:13). *Amen.*

DAY 7

That is why we labor and strive, because we have put our hope in the living God, who is the Savior of all people, especially of those who believe.

—1 Timothy 4:10

As a FOLLOWER OF JESUS CHRIST, you have one thing the rest of the world does not—your hope in a living God! If all we can hope for is what is within our own power and our own resources, we can't hope for a great deal. In spite of all the self-help and self-empowerment advice available today, we still too easily give up or take wrong turns. When we place our hope in other people, or institutions, or ideas, we are often disappointed and disillusioned.

If you put your trust and hope in God, your hope is held by a God who is alive and who acts in the lives of His people. He loves you. His love is not conditional and does not end. He has a plan for His creation. He has a plan for you, and He will accomplish His plan. Your Shepherd holds you by the hand, leads you, protects you, and provides for you. He has promised to provide everything you need. God is for His children!

In whatever situations we face today, when our hope rests in this living God, we will be able to stay positive and optimistic despite any circumstances.

Lord, thank You for the hope You have given me in the past, and how it has helped me reach today. Thank You for present hope in the future and guide me as I apply it daily. I know You will have new hope for me tomorrow. I look forward to a brighter day. Amen.

Notes and Prayers

_____

_____

_____

_____

_____

_____

_____

_____

_____

_____

_____

_____

_____

_____

_____

_____

_____

_____

_____

_____

_____

Steve Wingfield

BOLDNESS

As leaders, we need clear visions and total commitment to our ideas, or we will lack the boldness to see our goals through to the end.

—Paul Weaver

DAY 1

But the Lord stood at my side and gave me strength, so that through me the message might be fully proclaimed and all the Gentiles might hear it. And I was delivered from the lion's mouth.

—2 Timothy 4:17

BOLDNESS CAN BE DEFINED AS THE CONFIDENCE AND COURAGE to do what is right, regardless of circumstances or the opinions of others. In his letter to Timothy, Paul wrote about a time when he was dragged into court because his preaching had created such an uproar in the city. All of his friends and associates disappeared. Because he knew the Lord was with him, he delivered the gospel message anyway.

The better you know Christ, the more you trust His promises and the more you will have the confidence that He's standing with you. This is what gives boldness. This is where we find our courage to do the right thing, even when we're staring into the lion's mouth. As a matter of fact, Christ's presence turns the tables on that lion. Proverbs 28:1 says the righteous are as bold as a lion.

Now, you may not be there yet, but I promise you that this is the key to the spirit-led boldness we want to have as leaders. Work on your relationship with Him. The stronger that relationship is, the more encouragement you'll have to be confident and courageous.

Dear Jesus, thank You for standing with me when all others have deserted me. Help me to fully trust You for deliverance when fear and doubt threaten to overpower me. Amen.

Prayers on BOLDNESS by Delphos Howard.

Day 2

For the Spirit God gave us does not make us timid, but gives us power, love and self-discipline.

—2 Timothy 1:7

As a follower of Christ, I want to represent Him well. I want to be able to say what I need to say, when I need to say it. I want the courage and wisdom to make hard but wise decisions. I want to have that kind of boldness. But sometimes boldness puts us in an uncomfortable position. Maybe it's even more than uncomfortable—maybe it's downright dangerous. Maybe saying what needs to be said will put your job at risk. Or it might threaten important relationships that you've worked hard to develop. Or it might make you the target of ridicule and criticism or even attack.

For me, boldness comes when I know that I'm in the center of God's will and I'm representing Christ. Our confidence of that comes as we maintain our relationship with Him. The Spirit of Christ in us gives us this confidence and courage. Those who are led by the Spirit are children of God, and the Spirit "gives us power, love and self-discipline."

The Spirit living in us is described in Isaiah 11:2—a spirit of wisdom, understanding, counsel, strength, knowledge, and the fear of the Lord. Which of those qualities are you in need of today? The Spirit in you will provide them. He is with you to help you.

You and I don't want to be timid and fearful. We want to be bold. We represent our King, and He will always be with us and provide what we need in every situation today.

Heavenly Father, may Your Spirit fill me with boldness so that my words and actions always represent You truthfully, lovingly, and powerfully. Amen.

Day 3

Who is going to harm you if you are eager to do good? But even if you should suffer for what is right, you are blessed. "Do not fear their threats; do not be frightened." But in your hearts revere Christ as Lord.

—1 Peter 3:13–15

IN THE DAYS WHEN ROMANIA WAS STILL UNDER COMMUNIST RULE and the government persecuted Christians, I stood in a local official's office with my friend, a local pastor. He had been jailed before, beaten, and threatened. The communists had tried to kill him. Yet in that office when he was warned against preaching, he pounded his hand on the table and declared, "We will obey God!" After the revolution, standing in a city square where thousands of revolutionists had been mowed down, I had the privilege of presenting the gospel on live national television. I can't say I wasn't a little nervous—there were still many soldiers all around with their guns—but what a privilege that was, to stand and boldly declare Christ the Lord to Romania.

When Jesus is Lord in our lives, He is the one to whom we're accountable. He is the one we represent. It is His truth that is truth and reality for us. The Jesus we follow is King. We are citizens of His kingdom. He holds all authority. He has all our loyalty and our lives are devoted to Him and His truth. When we truly revere Him as Lord over all, it changes everything—including how we speak and act. We can be bold; we are living in His kingdom, acting in and on His truth, because our King Jesus is almighty God.

Lead me, Sovereign Lord, to proclaim the gospel to others and share your truth courageously. Amen.

DAY 4

Therefore, since we have such a hope, we are very bold.

—2 Corinthians 3:12

PETER CARTWRIGHT WAS A TRAVELING METHODIST PREACHER in the nineteenth century. He was what we call a fire-and-brimstone preacher, delivering riveting sermons on God's wrath and eternal punishment. He never backed down from preaching the gospel, and he baptized thousands of people; his passion was that others would experience the forgiveness he himself had found.

The story is told about one service in which General Andrew Jackson, the future president of the United States, was in attendance. Jackson was known for his quick temper, and others had advised Cartwright to be careful of what he said in his sermon. Those in charge of the meeting did not want to offend the general. Boldly, Cartwright preached the necessity for repentance—and pointed out that even General Jackson would go to hell if he did not turn to God.

Now, fire-and-brimstone preaching might not be the best way to win souls for Christ. Both Peter and Paul advised that we should share the gospel with gentleness and respect. But Cartwright's boldness sprang out of his absolute belief in God's Word and his love of Jesus Christ.

C. H. Spurgeon said, "Christ's people must have bold, unflinching, lion-like hearts, loving Christ first, and his truth next, and Christ and his truth beyond all the world."

Love Christ and His truth beyond anything else in this world, and you'll find that lion-hearted boldness, my friend. You'll have the confidence and courage to do what's right, regardless of the circumstances or the opposition.

Blessed Jesus, show me how to love You above all else; and fill my heart with Your truth, that I may boldly declare Your Word to the world around me. Amen.

DAY 5

I pray that out of his glorious riches he may strengthen you with power through his Spirit in your inner being.

—Ephesians 3:16

GOD WANTS TO USE THE GIFTS HE'S GIVEN YOU. He has a purpose for those gifts, and He's promised to equip you in your inner being with the power to use them well. We are weak and powerless without His power. Paul wrote in 2 Corinthians 4 that we are like jars of clay holding a treasure. Our weakness gives room for His strength to work. When we depend not on our own strength and intellect but on His promises, then God's power shines through.

What are those promises? As you represent Him, His strength will work through you. He'll give you wisdom so that you use your intellect well. He said He will always stand with you. He said He will supply everything you need for living a life according to His will.

When the hard decisions are necessary or when boldness is required to move forward, then we rely on Him to shine through our lives. God can be glorified in our weakness. That is the purpose of followers of Christ—to glorify God in everything we do. Our boldness, directed by His spirit, can do just that, even though it requires us to step out of our comfort zone.

This is my prayer for you, my friend, that out of His glorious resources He will strengthen you through His spirit in your inner being.

Omnipotent God, thank You for giving me power to fulfill Your promises in my life. Lead me to glorify You as Your strength works through me. Amen.

DAY 6

All scripture is God-breathed and is useful for teaching, rebuking, correcting and training in righteousness so that the servant of God may be thoroughly equipped for every good work.

—2 Timothy 3:16–17

HAVE YOU NOTICED HOW OFTEN OUR THOUGHTS have returned to God's promises, truth, and His Word? One of the most important things you can do as you follow Christ is to saturate yourself with the Word of God. Dwight L. Moody has said, "When we find a man meditating on the words of God, my friends, that man is full of boldness and is successful."

The Spirit uses the Word to mold us, to guide us, and to protect us. In the Word, we find truth. We hear God's promises to us—promises we can depend on. The Word gives us hope; it gives us a proper perspective; it provides guidance. The Word gives us a solid foundation on which to stand. With such a foundation, knowing our King is Lord of all and He is with us always, how can we be timid about living as citizens of His kingdom? The words of an old hymn sum it up:

> *Standing on the promises of Christ the Lord,*
> *Bound to Him eternally by love's strong cord,*
> *Overcoming daily with the Spirit's sword,*
> *Standing on the promises of God.*

> *Standing on the promises I shall not fall,*
> *List'ning every moment to the Spirit's call,*
> *Resting in my Savior as my All in all,*
> *Standing on the promises of God.*

Father, may Your living Word implant truth in my heart and guide me to boldly live for You. Amen.

Steve Wingfield

Day 7

Always be prepared to give an answer to everyone who asks you to give the reason for the hope that you have. But do this with gentleness and respect.

—1 Peter 3:15

WE DON'T WANT TO BE BOLD IN OUR LEADERSHIP SIMPLY FOR THE SAKE OF BEING BOLD. That can quickly degrade into pride, stubbornness, ruthlessness, selfishness, boastfulness, and a generally grating personality. All of these character traits in leadership are one thing when controlled by our own egos but quite another when controlled by the spirit of Christ.

We have only to read the gospels and the book of Acts to see the difference the Spirit made in Peter—the bold, brash disciple who yet crumpled under pressure and miserably deserted Jesus when He was on trial. You'll remember the breakfast Jesus fixed for the disciples after a long night of fishing. In intimate moments with Peter, Jesus reestablished their relationship. I like to imagine that Jesus also encouraged Peter and told him, "Hang in there, Peter. I've got a big job for you coming up soon. You will be the main speaker, and thousands will hear my Good News."

Baptized with the Spirit, Peter became a bold, fearless apostle who preached to thousands in the middle of a religious festival. Always carry the message of Christ, he wrote, but do it with gentleness and respect, which the Spirit alone can equip you with. It is this lion-like, courageous, Spirit-tempered boldness that you and I want to have, my friend.

Holy Spirit, thank You for showing me the lionhearted Christ-like qualities I need in my life. Help me develop those qualities with compassion so that I may represent Christ well and share hope and peace with others. Amen.

Notes and Prayers

_____

_____

_____

_____

_____

_____

_____

_____

_____

_____

_____

_____

_____

_____

_____

_____

_____

_____

_____

_____

_____

Steve Wingfield

COMPASSION

When we are genuinely interested in people, they will almost always allow us to see their joys as well as their difficulties.

—Paul Weaver

DAY 1

Rejoice with those who rejoice; mourn with those who mourn.

—Romans 12:15

COMPASSION IS A LIFESTYLE. Defined, compassion is a willingness to bear the pain of others and invest whatever is necessary to heal their hurts. To know anyone's pain, you have to get in there with them to find out what's going on in their life. This is a choice we all must make. A person who has no compassion is seen as aloof and selfish. Such a self-absorbed person often develops bitterness. Mother Teresa said that "if we have no peace, it is because we have forgotten we belong to each other." We were created to be connected to each other and live in relationships.

So, compassion as a lifestyle means, first of all, that we make choices that keep us connected to others. We open ourselves to others, and we're willing not only to rejoice with those who rejoice but also to share the pain of those who are suffering.

Lord, fill me with the desire to show others that I care and will walk with them in their pain. Open my heart to the struggles and pain around me and give me an opportunity to serve those in need. Give me the wisdom to know what to say to those who are broken hearted and hurting, Lord. Let me point to You in all times of trouble, because You are the true Comforter. Lord, I want to show compassion to others the way You have shown compassion to me. In the name above every name, Jesus Christ my Lord, amen.

Prayers on COMPASSION by Scott Dawson.

DAY 2

But if anyone has the world's goods and sees his brother in need, yet closes his heart against him, how does God's love abide in him?

—1 John 3:17 (ESV)

COMPASSION ALSO MEANS THAT WHERE AND WHEN WE CAN, we are willing to invest whatever we have to aid someone else's healing. Compassion *acts*. We can't fix everyone's situation or rescue everyone in trouble. But we can always show kindness. Sharing financially is not always the necessary or best way to show compassion. The most necessary thing is opening our hearts. At times, just our presence is enough. We may be able to help by giving our time. Jesus said that something as simple as a cup of cold water can be a significant gift of compassion.

The guiding principle is not "What is best for my interests?" but rather, "How can I help this person in trouble or in pain? What does she need?" Compassionate living looks beyond yourself. It gives you the opportunity to touch other people where they are.

Open my eyes, heavenly Father, that I might see where my kindness and my time are most needed. As I look for people to invest in, keep my motives pure so that I may glorify You. Everything I have belongs to You, Lord, so if I can show compassion by being a provider to someone around me, show me the way. I want to help those in need, the way You have compassionately helped me in times of need. Lord, let my actions display a compassionate heart. I close by praying this prayer in the name above every name, Jesus Christ my Lord, amen.

Steve Wingfield

Day 3

Therefore, as God's chosen people, holy and dearly loved, clothe yourselves with compassion.

—Colossians 3:12

COMPASSION WILL MAKE YOU A BETTER PERSON. It's what servant leadership is all about. As a compassionate person, you will look at others and see beyond what they can do for the team or for you personally. You will see each person as an individual who carries joys and sorrows that have nothing to do with associations. You will celebrate and suffer with them. Your connection with the people you know and lead will go beyond thoughts of strategies, abilities, and productivity. It is a connection of the heart.

Compassionate leadership nurtures the whole person, not just what each person brings. Living in connection like this is not only healthy, it benefits everyone. Compassion, like smiles and kindness, is contagious. A compassionate leader spreads this trait throughout the network of those he or she leads and is involved with.

The most important reason to live with compassion is because we are men and women of God. We do not bring compassion to the workplace only because it benefits our organization or to our families because it only benefits ourselves. We live with compassion because God's people are always on the mission of healing and investing in others.

Holy Spirit, when I wake in the morning, clothe me in compassion for those around me. If there is any way that I have wronged another, or acted selfishly, reveal that to me so I can repent. Be with me as I go out, so all of my words and actions will display the love and compassion You have shown me. I pray this in the name above every name, Jesus Christ my Lord, amen.

Day 4

Shout for joy, you heavens; rejoice, you earth; break into song, you mountains! For the LORD comforts his people and will have compassion on his afflicted ones.

—Isaiah 49:13

OUR GOD IS A COMPASSIONATE GOD. He often instructed the Israelites to be especially kind and generous to those in need. "Don't be hardhearted or tightfisted toward the poor; give generously to those in need" (Deuteronomy 15:7). The Psalms celebrate his deep and unending compassion. "He has compassion on all he has made." (Psalm 145:9). Proverbs advises that our treatment of the poor is a serious matter.

Oppressing the poor insults their Creator. Helping them honors him (Proverbs 14:31). Helping the poor is like lending to the Lord, and He will repay you (Proverbs 19:17). God gives special instructions to take care of widows and orphans. We have been recipients of His great compassion and mercy. Now that we are His children, we are to imitate our Father and let His compassion and mercy flow through us into the world around us.

Thank You, Lord Jesus, for the compassion You have shown to me all my life. In times of affliction, You had compassion on me. You are my Shepherd, and with Your watchful eye You take care of me. Lord, open my heart. Let me recognize when others have a heart for You, so that I may rejoice with them. Fill my life with compassionate people and allow me to display the compassion You have continually shown to me. In the name above every name, Jesus Christ my Lord, amen.

Steve Wingfield

DAY 5

Jesus had compassion on them.

—Matthew 20:34

JESUS' GREAT COMPASSION marked His three years of teaching and ministry. He was often besieged by crowds of sick and the demon-possessed, and He healed them. At one house, the place was so full that people couldn't get through to see Jesus. On the day Jesus learned that Herod had beheaded His cousin John, Jesus wanted to get away by Himself and pray—but the crowds followed Him, and His compassion compelled Him to spend the rest of the day healing and teaching. He performed the miracle of the loaves and fishes because He had compassion on the people who had nothing to eat. He wept over Jerusalem because so many refused His message. While His body was wracked with pain as He was dying on the cross, it was His compassion that reached out, forgave, and reassured the thief dying next to Him.

Jesus saw the crowds and every hurting individual who came to Him as "harassed and helpless, like sheep without a shepherd" (Matthew 9:36). We don't have to look far to see more sheep who are not yet in the care of the Great Shepherd. We are Christ's representatives now in this world. Will we point everyone to the Shepherd? After all, it was His great compassion for them that took Him to the cross.

Father, help me to reflect Your unending kindness in my own actions today. Nothing comes together without You. When I think of how kind You have been to me, it gives me such joy and gladness. Lord, help me to share Your wonderful name with others, both in my actions and words. In the name above every name, Jesus Christ my Lord, amen.

Day 6

[The King] will reply, "Truly I tell you, whatever you did not do for one of the least of these, you did not do for me."

—Matthew 25:45

IN MATTHEW 25, JESUS TALKS TO HIS DISCIPLES ABOUT THE END OF THIS AGE, His return, and His judgment. When Jesus divides the people according to what they've done, every act He mentions is an act of compassion: feeding the poor, giving drink to the thirsty, taking in a stranger, providing clothes for those in need, caring for the sick, or visiting those in prison. The dividing criteria is not whether people have followed a set of rules, whether they have done great things, or whether or not they've been in church every Sunday. The judgment comes based on whether or not they have shown compassion.

Jesus is so concerned about those who are in need, He says He identifies with them. He takes it personally when we show compassion or when we fail to do so. It's kind of like a big brother on the playground telling a bully, "If you mess with my little brother, you're messin' with *me!*"

Acts of compassion are acts done—or not done—to the Lord Himself. How important it is to our Lord that we invest in the healing of others in this world!

Heavenly Father, remind me today how compassion, not personal success, is what I should value most. Teach me to put others before myself, because it pleases You. Show me those I should serve. Give me a compassionate heart to serve them gladly. Let my actions be selfless and kind. Remind me that when I serve others, I am serving You. In the name above every name, Jesus Christ my Lord, amen.

Steve Wingfield

Day 7

You, dear children, are from God and have overcome them, because the one who is in you is greater than the one who is in the world.

—1 John 4:4

Our mission is to represent Christ well in this world. The devil's mission is to prevent that! Satan does not want the world to see the compassionate God of mercy who died to save them and give them life. He will derail our mission whenever he can.

What are we to do? Hang on to the Vine! Stay close to Christ.

When we hang tightly onto the Vine, He holds us tightly, and the life of the Vine flows through us and bears His fruit. His Spirit lives in you, my friend. His Spirit is greater than the enemy who wants to keep us from our mission of healing and pointing people home to God.

You can depend on Jesus' promise. Remain in Him, and He'll remain in you, and then His Spirit in you can bear much fruit. Compassion will be one of those fruits.

Dear God, guide me so that I may be rich in kindness and overflowing with love. Prevent me from casting judgment on those in need, and instead fill my heart with compassion for even my worst of enemies. Let me always remember that I was once Your enemy Lord, yet You had compassion for me. Open my heart and fill it with love for You and for others. As I go forth, show me Your will and Your ways. Continue to fill me with compassion daily. In the name above every name, Jesus Christ my Lord, amen.

Notes and Prayers

_____

_____

_____

_____

_____

_____

_____

_____

_____

_____

_____

_____

_____

_____

_____

_____

_____

_____

_____

Steve Wingfield

COURAGE

Be a leader of courage today, and you and your team will gain confidence and even more courage.

—Paul Weaver

DAY 1

Do not be terrified by them, for the LORD your God, who is among you, is a great and awesome God.

—Deuteronomy 7:21

DAVID IS JUST A KID when his dad sends him to take food to his brothers who are fighting a battle. He gets to the army encampment and finds the troops of Israel hiding in their tents. A giant from the enemy's army taunts and intimidates them. David says, "I will fight him." Saul meets David and advises, "You can't go without protection. Take my armor."

"No," replies David. "The Lord has delivered a bear and a lion into my hands." So, he picks up five stones, and says confidently, "Today they are going to know that there is a mighty God in Israel."

The point is this: David sees a mighty God. Everybody else is looking at and listening to the big giant. If we will operate like David, we will find we have courage, too. If we know we are in the hands of a mighty God and that nobody can defeat us as we are in Christ, we will have courage to do the right thing.

Heavenly Father, sometimes the challenges facing me seem like they tower over me, but You've allowed them to be in front of me to see whether I'm ready to believe You can use me to accomplish something humanly impossible. Please allow me to exercise courage like David's today, to make my commitments based on the size of my God instead of the size of my enemies. He couldn't do it without You; neither can I.

Prayers on COURAGE by Bob Shank.

Day 2

By faith [Moses] left Egypt, not fearing the king's anger; he persevered because he saw him who is invisible.

—Hebrews 11:27

WHEN GOD FIRST TALKS TO MOSES about leading the Israelites out of Egypt, Moses has his excuses. The people won't believe him. He's not a good speaker, and God's asking him to go up against the most powerful man in the country. He's been living in the wilderness for forty years. He killed a man and had to run for his life. Moses listens to God's plan, but he certainly has reason to feel fear, and he makes excuses. But he follows God's commands and becomes one of the greatest leaders in the Bible. Why? He kept his eyes on the Lord. At one point in the Israelites' forty years of travel, Moses tells God, "I need assurance that you will always be with us. If you're not going to go with us, then don't make us go any farther."

God's promise that He will never leave us nor forsake us is one I claim often and a promise that gives me courage to go onward. We keep our eyes on Him, and we depend on His promise to always be with us. That's how we find courage for whatever we face.

Give me the gift of faith today—to think, speak, and act with the confidence that I'm not alone, that You are actively involved in everything I'm involved in. I believe You, all the time. Amen.

Day 3

Have I not commanded you? Be strong and courageous. Do not be afraid; do not be discouraged, for the LORD your God will be with you wherever you go.
—Joshua 1:9

COURAGE IS NOT A PRODUCT OF EMOTIONS. It is a choice we make, whether or not we will do what is right in spite of what we might feel. Often one person's courage will spur others to be courageous. As Moses' assistant, Joshua has seen the wonders God performed for the people of Israel. He is one of the spies sent into the Promised Land to check on the land and the people they're going up against when they move in. The group returns with good news and bad news. "It's a bountiful land, but the people are giants who will squash us."

Joshua and Caleb say, "But the Lord will be with us. We can do this. We must do this."

Joshua moves into leadership after the death of Moses, and he lives on the promises. Be strong. Be courageous. The Lord will never leave you nor forsake you. The Lord will go ahead of you. Don't be afraid.

Joshua goes forward and moves the Israelites into the Promised Land. There are obstacles and battles, yes. But his courage comes from confidence in what God has promised. Joshua even leads the people into battle with Jericho with no weapons because God has promised them victory if they follow his instructions. Deciding to trust and act on God's promises will give us courage to move forward.

Lord, help me to hear Your voice the way Moses and Joshua did. I want to be strong and courageous. Give me the strength and confidence to do it, and to do it faithfully. I will trust You today. Amen.

Day 4

When they saw the courage of Peter and John and realized that they were unschooled, ordinary men, they were astonished and they took note that these men had been with Jesus.

—Acts 4:13

When I think of courage, I think of Peter. At Pentecost, Peter begins preaching boldly to thousands of people. His preaching has such an impact that the established religious authorities grow alarmed and try to silence him. He and John are arrested and spend the night in jail. When they're brought before the Sanhedrin council the next day, Peter preaches to them! When they are ordered to stop talking about Jesus, Peter and John say boldly, "We're going to obey God, not men."

The council is astonished at the unmovable stand Peter and John take. "And they took note that these men had been with Jesus."

Being able to live courageously comes from leaning on our Lord, focusing on Him, and listening to His assurance. He said that following Him will be costly. It will require bravery and courage. He has promised He will never leave us. He'll always be with us. But we have to be with Him, too. *We* can't leave *Him*. We've got to spend time with him, in His Word, in prayer, in listening for what He has to say to us. If we want to live with courage, we've got to be with Jesus.

I have no reason to be timid or fearful, Lord. Help me remember that today. Help me live my life day by day, knowing that You know my story and will take me into my future as part of Your plan. My job is to do what You have for me to do, today. Amen.

DAY 5

Now all glory to God, who is able, through his mighty power at work within us, to accomplish infinitely more than we might ask or think.

—Ephesians 3:20 (NLT)

THE ACCOUNT IN ACTS OF PETER AND JOHN BEFORE THE SANHEDRIN GIVES US AN IMPORTANT DETAIL. "Then Peter, filled with the Spirit…" Peter is the same man who had been too afraid to say, "Yes, I know Jesus." He had vowed to go to the death with Jesus, but he backed down from that vow when faced with not a giant, but a servant girl. He was afraid, and he made the choice to give in to that fear. But when faced with this powerful council who could have thrown him in jail or had him executed, Peter stands his ground. He declares the name of Jesus and the salvation of Jesus. "There's no other way!" he says boldly.

What made the difference? The Holy Spirit within. God's "incomparably great power for us who believe. That power is the same as the mighty strength he exerted when he raised Christ from the dead" (Ephesians 1:19–20).

Take time today to reflect on this: the power that raised a man from the dead is available in your life. The power that transformed Peter is at work in you, too. Be strong and courageous in this mighty power.

Almighty God, You know my thoughts. You are in touch with what's going on in my head and in my heart. Your Spirit lives in me, the same Holy Spirit that raised Jesus out of His borrowed tomb. Help me to live today like I really believe what I believe. Holy Spirit, prove to me today that You are living and working in me, for real. Amen.

DAY 6

So keep up your courage, men, for I have faith in God that it will happen just as he told me.

—Acts 27:25

OUR VERSE FOR TODAY IS TAKEN FROM THE ACCOUNT OF A SHIPWRECK, when the storm is at gale force, so severe that the crew has lost control of the ship and hasn't seen the sun or the stars for many days. All hope is lost. They are sure they are going to die. Paul is on board, and he calls the men together and tells them that "An angel from the God I serve and to whom I belong told me last night that I don't need to be afraid because God will be good and will save all our lives. And I believe it will happen just as he said! So keep up your courage" (Acts 27:23–25).

Paul, too, depends on what God says will happen. It's why he tells the men they do not need to be afraid. Shipwreck will come, but their lives will be saved. "God said it. I have faith in God that it will turn out exactly that way!"

My friend, I pray that you and I both can say that just as emphatically. Courage comes from knowing that "it will happen just as God said."

Father, forgive me for getting too wrapped up in the tough days that are part of my life, and not listening for Your voice to give me the promise that You're not going anywhere, and You're committed to get me through anything and everything. Give me the boldness to make the people around me aware of my trust in You. Whatever happens, I'm going on record: I trust You. Amen.

DAY 7

So be strong and courageous, all you who put your hope in the LORD!
—Psalm 31:24 (NLT)

MY COURAGE DOESN'T COME FROM MYSELF. I am convinced of Christ's presence within me and the dependability of His promises. That's what gives me courage. Can courage be developed? YES, it can. In 2 Chronicles 16:9, we read, "For the eyes of the LORD range throughout the earth to strengthen those whose hearts are fully committed to him." Committing our hearts fully to Him develops courage. Having faith in God means we put our hope in Him, not in ourselves. We make our decisions based on what He has said will happen and on what He has said he will do. We don't depend on our own strength and resources.

A sense of God's presence brings with it an awareness of His strength and resources. If we want to exhibit courageous living as a way of life, we spend more time with Him, we learn His promises, we keep our eyes on our mighty God, we recognize His power at work in us, and we make the choice to act, relying totally on His greatness, His goodness, and His promises. We put our hope in Him. That's how we'll be able to live strong and courageous.

God, please help me to guard my heart against deception. Please help me focus my attention on You and Your promises. Please, Holy Spirit, convict me when I doubt and encourage me when I agree. Let my faith get toned and strong as I exercise it in service to You, minute-by-minute, day-by-day, as I continue to live the life You always planned for me. For your glory, alone, is my prayer. Amen.

Notes and Prayers

DECISIVENESS

The more we practice being decisive, the better we get.

—Paul Weaver

DAY 1

Choose for yourselves this day whom you will serve. . . . as for me and my household, we will serve the LORD.

—Joshua 24:15

I LOVE JOSHUA'S CALL TO DECISIVENESS. He drew a line not in the sand but in concrete. He led the way by declaring his own decision so firmly. The people of Israel followed, repeating three times that their choice also was to follow the Lord. Unfortunately, there were many times they didn't follow through on that choice.

Think thoroughly. Salvation is a gift from God. Choosing to follow Jesus cannot be a glib verbal assent; we must follow through and bring every aspect of our lives under His control and lordship.

Think courageously. God is looking for those with fully committed hearts so that He can strengthen them and do amazing things in their lives (2 Chronicles 16:9).

This is the most important decision you'll ever make. It's also a decision for joy. In the hours before Jesus' arrest, He had many things He still wanted to say to His disciples. "I'm telling you all this," Jesus said, "so that you will be filled, even overflow, with my joy" (John 15:11). If you want joy in your heart, make the decision that Christ will have the throne in your life. Put Him in first place. Be as decisive as Joshua about following Jesus.

Father God, I choose You today in every circumstance before the day even starts! Remind me when I am tempted to waver that my first allegiance goes to You. Grant me the firmness to choose confidently each appropriate action and thus make good and godly decisions.

Prayers on DECISIVENESS by Barbara Borntrager.

Day 2

He humbled himself by becoming obedient to the point of death, even death on a cross.

—Philippians 2:8 (ESV)

WHEN WE CHOOSE TO FOLLOW JESUS, He is our example. "Have the same mindset as Christ Jesus" (Philippians 2:5). Read the accounts of the long night in the Garden of Gethsemane. Jesus agonized over this decision to submit to God's will. Finally, He came to the point of saying, "Not my will, but thine be done."

Think about the life of Jesus. Hebrews 5:8 tells us Jesus learned obedience by the things He suffered. Throughout His life, He had to make decisions about following God's will. In the wilderness, before He began His ministry, the devil tempted Him to take a shortcut. "Worship me," Satan said, "and I'll give you the world" (Matthew 4:9). Jesus had come to save the world. Here was a chance to gain the world in one easy step. But Jesus made His choice. He sounded a lot like Joshua. "I will worship and serve only God."

That first decisive choice, to follow Jesus, will be the groundwork for all other choices in your life. Other decisions will be difficult at times, but this decision builds the essential framework, your core values, to move through life making wise, life-giving, God-honoring choices, just as our champion did.

Thank You for going before us and modeling the life You ask us to live. Thank You for showing us Your struggle in Gethsemane. Jesus, you now understand our dilemmas and weaknesses. Thank You for never losing your focus but walking through Calvary to the bitter end in order to secure my eternal future at home in heaven with You. Amen.

Day 3

If you love me, keep my commands.

—John 14:15

WE'VE GOT TO ASK OURSELVES, "Do I love Jesus? Is it my heart's desire to please him?" If our answer to that question is as firm and decisive as Joshua's declaration, then this will also help us to be decisive in other decisions that face us. "The love of Christ constraineth us . . ." (2 Corinthians 5:14 KJV). The love of Christ controls and compels us. His love for us is a force that moves our hearts to act in certain ways, and our love for Him compels us to certain actions. Then His love *in* us, the agape love of Christ which the Holy Spirit grows within, guides us in our actions and attitudes toward others.

Our love for Him will keep us following close at the heels of His sandals.

To keep His commandments, we'll have to know them. We'll have to read His words as closely and attentively as His disciples listened as He taught. They didn't always understand what they heard. We don't always understand what we read. But Jesus promised the Holy Spirit will continue His teaching in us. And my experience has been that the better I get to know Him, the more passionately I love Him.

Our decision to follow Jesus builds a framework for making other decisions in life. Our love for Him strengthens that framework, pours it in concrete, as we resolve to read and obey and listen and obey.

Is it really my heart's desire to please You, Jesus? Do I know Your commandments to me in this day? As I read the Word, impress upon me exactly what You want from me today. Amen.

Day 4

Examine everything carefully; hold fast to that which is good.

—1 Thessalonians 5:21 (NASB)

I RELY ON SCRIPTURE TO GIVE ME A GOOD FOUNDATION for making godly decisions. 2 Timothy 3:16 assures us that these words are God-given for our benefit. Scripture will teach us, straighten us out when we head down the wrong path, and train us in right living. When we're faced with a difficult decision, those other paths sometimes look very alluring.

That is why we need to have Scripture "hidden" in our hearts—to keep us from sinning. We need to trust the Word, and obey it. In cases where Scripture does not specifically address your question, it is still God's active agent that teaches us, builds godly values, and shows us God's will for the way we live. Scriptures tune us into God's thoughts. We learn what pleases Him and what He hates. We see his big-picture plan and how we fit into it. All of those things help us make good, godly decisions. Even when we are hit with sudden, unexpected situations where we need to be decisive within a few brief moments, minds and hearts trained by Scripture will seek the godly path in the situation. Scripture is a weapon for sorting things out, testing all the spirits that attempt to speak into our lives.

Thanks for the divine arsenal provided in Your Word and its amazing ability to shoot down the enemy's lies. It's what I know by heart that my heart really knows! So today I resolve to memorize a verse as a bullet to kill a lie by the enemy, and then I'll keep it in my gun chamber!

DAY 5

You provide a broad path for my feet, so that my ankles do not give way.
—2 Samuel 22:37

YEARS AGO, SOMEONE SHARED FOUR PRINCIPLES WITH ME. I offer these as guidelines in the section on DISCERNMENT, but I want to review them here because they have been a great help to me in making good decisions.

1. *God will never ask you to do anything contrary to His Word.*

2. *Commit your questions and options to the Lord in prayer and seek His wisdom. He has promised to guide us in the ways that are best for us. He has assured us He will give wisdom if we ask. Then, you trust His promises.*

3. *Listen for His voice speaking to your heart. He will give you peace about the decision, or give you reservations.*

4. *Be open to God's use of circumstances to point the way. He opens or closes doors.*

To this list, I would like to add a fifth principle: *I take the decision to my "brotherhood,"* those people who know me best, who understand my heart, and will give me godly advice, which includes my wife Barb, my children, and my accountability group.

When these five things line up, I can move forward. This is the best way I've found to have confidence that my decision is in the center of God's will.

Lord God, I ask You for wisdom now in this decision I have to make: _____. Open and close doors for me. Let me hear clearly Your voice saying, "This is the way; walk in it" (Isaiah 30:21). Give me confidence to make a right decision.

Day 6

Trust in the LORD with all your heart and lean not on your own understanding; in all your ways submit to him, and he will make your paths straight.
—Proverbs 3:5–6

MAKING A DECISION involves taking a risk. Fear of making the wrong decision can hold us back. Sometimes we don't have much time to think about our decision, much less enough time to process it through the five checkpoints I suggested yesterday. This is when faith in God's promises will help us be decisive and keep us moving forward. He has given us repeated assurances that if we follow Him and trust Him in every aspect of our lives, He will direct our paths. When we are unsure, we can go forward *believing* that what God said is true. He will steer us in the right direction.

Plant His promises into your heart and mind. They will give you the courage to be decisive. Here are a few to get you started.

I will instruct you and teach you in the way you should go; I will counsel you with my loving eye on you.
—Psalm 32:8

I instruct you in the way of wisdom and lead you along straight paths.
—Proverbs 4:11

You guide me with your counsel.
—Psalm 73:24

But when he, the Spirit of truth, comes, he will guide you into all the truth.
—John 16:13

For God is working in you, giving you the desire and the power to do what pleases him.
—Philippians 2:13 (NLT)

Father, You promised to instruct me in the way I should go. You will counsel me with Your loving eye. I trust Your divine guidance to lead me in any modifications I will need to make.

Day 7

Now may the God of peace—who brought up from the dead our Lord Jesus, the great Shepherd of the sheep, and ratified an eternal covenant with his blood—may he equip you with all you need for doing his will. May he produce in you, through the power of Jesus Christ, every good thing that is pleasing to him. All glory to him forever and ever! Amen.

—Hebrews 13:20–21 (NLT)

HE WILL EQUIP US WITH ALL WE NEED FOR DOING HIS WILL. He has promised that. He equips us in armor that He has provided for us. The belt of truth and the sword of the Spirit prepare us for making tough decisions. The helmet of our salvation protects our minds, and the shield of faith will quench those fiery arrows of doubt as we make decisions. The armor enables us to stand firm in doing God's will.

Finally, through His power He will produce in us the good things that are pleasing to Him. He is working in us, even when we might feel unsteady and unsure. He is there, producing the character and works He has planned for us.

These are promises that anchor your faith to Him as you face decisions.

All the glory goes to Him, forever and ever. Amen.

Father, produce in me all that is pleasing to You. I wear the truth of the Holy Scriptures and carry those verses to crush the lies of the enemy. My mind is protected by a helmet of salvation through the blood of Jesus. My shield glistens with the blood of Jesus to quench Satan's fiery darts. Thank you for anchoring my faith in YOU. Amen.

Notes and Prayers

_____

_____

_____

_____

_____

_____

_____

_____

_____

_____

_____

_____

_____

_____

_____

_____

_____

_____

Steve Wingfield

DEPENDABILITY

*Dependability is necessary for achieving the trust and influence
that is the foundation of effective leadership.*

—Paul Weaver

DAY 1

*My eyes will be on the faithful in the land, that they may dwell with me; the one
whose walk is blameless will minister to me.*

—Psalm 101:6

DEPENDABILITY IS BEING RELIABLE AND WORTHY OF TRUST. Thoroughness,
which will be discussed later, and dependability are two traits that are interdependent. They can hardly be separated. A person who is thorough and pays
attention to details and accuracy is usually someone who is also dependable.
We can count on them to take care of details, and to do it right. Conversely,
the dependable person is also a thorough person. Dependability requires that
we are thorough in carrying out our duties, assignments, and promises.

By now, you've noticed how intertwined these character traits are. One
depends on another. One grows and sustains others. One is a necessity for
another. You can't be productive if you are not diligent. You won't have compassion if you cannot empathize. We want to put these traits under the lordship of Christ. He is the one we serve—not our boss, our board, our team,
or ourselves. We are servants of the Most High God. As such, we do serve
our boss, our board, our team, and even ourselves. But God holds the throne
in our lives.

*God, help me to be faithful and dependable to others in need. Lord, help my life
reflect You and may I be found blameless in Your sight. Forgive me, Lord, where
I have failed or not lived up to expectations that I conveyed to others. May I be
attentive to details and serve with a spirit of compassion. Amen.*

Prayers on DEPENDABILITY by Alan Greene.

DAY 2

Like clouds and wind without rain is one who boasts of gifts never given.

—Proverbs 25:14

MY DAD WOULD SAY, "Son, your word is your bond. If you say it, keep your word." I think it's a very important principle, and I've tried to live that out. If I tell somebody I'm going to be at a place at two o'clock, if I can't be there, I'm going to do my best to call and tell them I'm running late. I believe that if you say you're going to do something, you ought to do your best to keep your word. Otherwise, we're like skies in the middle of a drought when clouds gather and winds blow, but they never deliver the hoped-for rain. A promise never fulfilled.

Of course, you don't have to say YES to every request that comes down the pike, but when you do say yes, you want to do your very best to make sure it gets done.

I pray that when people see me, they will be reminded that I am a follower of Christ, so I want my actions to match my words. And if my actions are going to match my words, I have to be a man of my word. I have to be dependable. I hope that's your desire, too. Work at it. Let your word be your bond, and let your actions back up what you say.

Lord, forgive me for words spoken by me that have not been followed through on. May I be a person of my word and honor You with what I say to others. Let my yes be yes and my no be no, fulfilling my words as promises kept. Amen.

Steve Wingfield

Day 3

Put on your new nature, created to be like God—truly righteous and holy.
—Ephesians 4:24 (NLT)

As we grow older, many of us look in our mirrors and see our dad or our mom. We not only begin to look more like our parents, we sound like them, too, taking on some of their ways of speaking or picking up their sayings and gestures or their attitudes and ideas. In the same way, our new birth gave us a new life and new nature that is to grow up "looking" like our heavenly Father. He created this new life in us, and He intends that we exhibit the family traits.

My heavenly Father is the one person I know who is totally, utterly dependable in doing what He says he will do. I trust Him completely to keep His word. My relationship with Him depends on His faithfulness. Dependability really comes out of faithfulness, a commitment to something or someone. He is passionately committed to His people.

> *Great is thy faithfulness, O God my Father.*
> *There is no shadow of turning with Thee.*
> *Thou changest not, Thy compassions they fail not.*
> *As Thou hast been, Thou forever wilt be.*

His faithfulness will endure forever. I am banking on that. And in patterning my character after my Father's, I'm working on being faithful and dependable.

Dear God, when I put my trust in Jesus, You gave me a new nature and Your indwelling Holy Spirit. Please let me live reflecting the image and nature of You. I confess that sometimes I have lived like the old nature and I recommit my life to You. May I become more like You, my heavenly Daddy living and reflecting Your love for others. Amen.

Day 4

Do to others as you would have them do to you.
—Luke 6:31

At its simplest, dependability is following the Golden Rule. When you are reliable and consistent, other people can be sure you will come through for them. That's what you want, too, dependable relationships. You want to know that when something is promised, the other person will do everything they can to keep that promise.

"Putting confidence in an unreliable person in times of trouble is like chewing with a broken tooth or walking on a lame foot" (Proverbs 25:19 NLT). Relationships don't work well when one party is not dependable.

It is also a matter of respect for others, and putting their interest above our own plans, ambition, and wishes. We are to serve others as Christ did. He put His entire life on the altar for the good of others.

Lord Jesus, You teach us to serve, love, and treat others with honor and to do so in the way we would want to be treated. May we be dependable in our relationships with everyone. Lord, help us to think of the needs of others first and then follow through by reaching out to them with love and compassion. Amen.

DAY 5

But I will rejoice even if I lose my life, pouring it out like a liquid offering to God, just like your faithful service is an offering to God.

—Philippians 2:17 (NLT)

BEING DEPENDABLE IN OUR INTERACTIONS WITH OTHERS provides a solid base for relationships to grow and be productive. This line written from Paul to the Philippians tells us that it can also be an offering to God.

Faithfulness displays dependability. We must be faithful as we grow more and more like our Father. Our service is an offering, a gift to Him; and like the Israelites of old, we want our offerings to be pure and unblemished.

Romans 12 encourages us to present our bodies as a living sacrifice to him. That would encompass everything we do in these bodies. It includes whether or not we keep commitments, whether we use the hours of our day to serve others or serve ourselves, and whether we are trustworthy stewards of the time and resources He has given us.

Take time today to adjust your thinking. Change your view of dependability. Take it from being a requirement for interpersonal relationships to being an offering to the God who has rescued you and given you a new life.

Lord Jesus, my life is of no value unless it glorifies You and serves Your purpose to others. May my life be an offering to You, Oh God, use me as You will in service to others. Increase my faith to be a true living sacrifice to You. Amen.

Day 6

Many will say they are loyal friends, but who can find one who is truly reliable?
—Proverbs 20:6 (NLT)

THE GREAT PREACHER BILLY SUNDAY once said that "an excuse is a skin of a reason stuffed with a lie." I'm not sure that's always right. Excuses aren't always full of lies. But it does point out that an excuse is almost never a good response. Even Webster agrees. The dictionary says an excuse is an attempt to remove blame or to get a release from responsibility.

Scripture doesn't have commandments against making excuses. It does tell us other things that are related, though. One of the first that comes to mind is Jesus' warning to let our nay be nay and our yea be yea. He was talking about not swearing oaths, but we get the message that what we say need not be embellished. We are told to speak honestly and sincerely, and show respect, but when excuses tumble out of our mouths, their primary purpose is protection of our egos.

So many other Lodestar traits come into play when we are tempted to offer quick excuses. Courage and honesty demand the truth. Sincerity prompts us to ask forgiveness. Ownership means we'll acknowledge the lack. Empathy understands how our inaction has affected others. Transparency prompts an open conversation. You get the idea.

Lord, help me to be a reliable friend. I confess that I have fallen short at times and could be more reliable in my relationships. Keep me from self-serving excuses and let me offer true, self-less friendship to others in a way that is dependable, reliable, and faithful, reflecting You and Your nature. Amen.

Steve Wingfield

Day 7

Whatever happens, conduct yourselves in a manner worthy of the gospel of Christ.
—Philippians 1:27

I WANT TO BE DEPENDABLE IN MY COMMITMENT as a representative of Jesus Christ. I want to be reliable, so that He can count on me to stand firm in carrying His name and acting on His behalf. I want to be worthy of the trust He's shown in me, entrusting me with His Good News.

Our meditations keep coming back to this, and that is because this is the essence of our lives now—Christ lives in this world by living in us. We carry His message. He's given it to us to take care of and scatter to all the world through every opportunity we have. This is the purpose to which we've been called and the reason we are still here, walking on this earth.

My heart's desire is to be reliable and worthy of the trust He's given me. I'm not always there, and at times I need to go to Him and ask His forgiveness for not living out my commitment—but it's where I want to live. It's how I want to live. God bless you as you stand firm in Him.

Dear God, our heavenly Father, I know You have made me worthy of eternal life through the blood of your Son Jesus as it was shed for me on the cross. Let me now walk in a manner worthy of the gospel of Jesus. Lord, shine through me so that others may see You. I want to be so close to You that others will see Your love, compassion, and holiness. May I bring glory to You, Father, as You fill me with Your Spirit today. Amen.

Notes and Prayers

_____

_____

_____

_____

_____

_____

_____

_____

_____

_____

_____

_____

_____

_____

_____

_____

_____

_____

DETERMINATION

The key to a successful life of leadership is to resolve that you will never throw in the towel and give up.

—Paul Weaver

DAY 1

And let us run with endurance the race God has set before us. We do this by keeping our eyes on Jesus, the champion who initiates and perfects our faith. . . . Think of all the hostility he endured from sinful people, then you won't become weary and give up.

—Hebrews 12:1, 2, 3 (NLT)

DETERMINATION RISES IN ALL OF US when we are passionate about a goal or cause. Obstacles or setbacks become motivation to keep pushing ahead. We refuse to give up. We find a way to make things work. The enemy that rises up and delays us, sometimes temporarily and sometimes permanently, is discouragement. Discouragement assaults determination, even in the most passionate, committed person.

Jesus is your champion in every sense of the word. He's run the same race and fought all the same battles you will face. He faced critics, hostility, and ridicule. He was rejected, and His heart broke over those who would not accept what He knew to be true. Even His followers had trouble grasping His vision. Such circumstances would set the stage for discouragement and painful loneliness. But He refused to retreat. He fought for you. He went through all of the battles for you. He even died to rescue you. He is still working on your behalf and will not leave you defenseless and helpless.

Jesus, I pray that You would give me the courage to face my battle today. Thank You that You died on the cross for me and because of that I can have the strength to face whatever lies before me.

Prayers on DETERMINATION by Don Metzler.

Day 2

For everything that was written in the past was written to teach us, so that through the endurance taught in the Scriptures and the encouragement they provide we might have hope.

—Romans 15:4

I WILL ALWAYS POINT YOU TO JESUS AND TO THE SCRIPTURES. The Scriptures hold life and comfort, energy, and strength. And whether "running our race" means the race of faith or the race of one project you have worked on for years and are determined to complete, the Scriptures will encourage you when the enemy tries to discourage you.

One of my favorites is Philippians 4:13: "I can do all things through Christ who strengthens me." Another is Jeremiah 29:11, that tells me the Lord is determined to stick with me, so I need to be determined to stick with him. Romans 12, verses 1 and 2 push me to stay the course. Isaiah 41:10 tells me not to be discouraged; the Lord is right beside me to give me strength and help.

Jesus, too, desperately needed the comfort and encouragement of words from His Father. He spent long hours in prayer, often at night, the only time of the day when He could be alone with God. Then He went to His Father for strength, courage, and comfort. Jesus automatically went to the Lord to keep up His endurance. That's where we can go, too. That's where we *must* go. "But those who hope in the LORD will renew their strength. They will soar on wings like eagles; they will run and not grow weary, they will walk and not be faint" (Isaiah 40:31).

Father my soul is weary and discouraged. Strengthen me, as You have promised. Amen. (Inspired by Psalm 119:28)

DAY 3

And Saul's son Jonathan went to David at Horesh and helped him to find strength in God.
—1 Samuel 23:16

AT TIMES, LEADERS CAN FEEL VERY MUCH ALONE. When they are (like Jesus) under fire of criticism or resistance, or when they're finding it difficult to plant their vision in their team, or when obstacles or setbacks seem to say that another path must be ploughed, times like these unlock the door to discouragement. And at times like these, you need relationships with people who believe in you and encourage you. I'm talking about a small group of people who know your heart, who will stick with you through the good times and bad, and who share a positive, faith-filled outlook.

Proverbs 22:24–25 tell us that we "catch" the attitudes of our circle of friends. If anything, you want to catch the attitudes of those with minds God has transformed, those who see with eyes of faith and believe in the promises of God. Strong relationships with like-minded people can help you up when you stumble in the mud of discouragement on your path. They can encourage and help you out of the muck that wants to drag you down and trap you.

While others are encouraging you, God is also at work. In everything, He is molding you for the mission He has given you. So whatever comfort and support you get in your walk He will use to train you to comfort and support others whose determination is floundering (2 Corinthians 1:4). You will learn from your experiences, and you will grow.

Lord Jesus, open my eyes and heart today to anyone whose determination has stumbled and needs help getting up. Amen.

Day 4

One thing I do: Forgetting what is behind and straining toward what is ahead, I press on toward the goal to win the prize for which God has called me heavenward in Christ Jesus.

—Philippians 3:13–14

DETERMINATION SETS A VISION IN YOUR HEART OF HEARTS. For me, it is that desire to represent Jesus well. Determination holds up even when we're knocked back by our own failures. Setbacks like this can be disappointing, but they don't have to mean defeat. All of us have a past. But your past does not define who you are and who you can be. Even in the setbacks, God is molding you, working for your good. God has been teaching you, giving you building blocks you can use for future gain. Setbacks are sometimes a result of our sin, but the Lord is always working to make us the best we can be.

Determination keeps you straining toward your goal, toward that vision planted in your heart of hearts. As in all of our other traits, when the Holy Spirit energized a determination, that is the most powerful determination of all. That determination keeps looking forward, not backward. It does not look at the past, but looks toward the future, at all God says can and will be. With that determination, you keep working to get there. You refuse to be chained by feelings of failure from past disappointments, or guilt because you have messed up. "Forgetting what is behind," Paul said, "and straining toward what is ahead, I press on toward the goal . . ."

God, thank You that You forgive our past and we are new creations in You. Help me to grow from my past experiences and serve You with more determination today than ever. Amen.

Steve Wingfield

Day 5

But those who trust in the LORD will find new strength. They will soar high on wings like eagles. They will run and not grow weary. They will walk and not faint.

—Isaiah 40:31 (NLT)

"I CAN DO NOTHING ON MY OWN." Jesus was fully human when here on earth. He knew what it was to have to depend on His Father's power and strength. He knows what's going on with you right now. Tell Him you need Him, and He will help you in this area. He will give you strength to keep working toward your goals. His help will bolster your determination. That's a promise. You can take it to the bank, my friend.

After all, He's the one who started this work in you. He is so invested in you that He even gave His life for you. He is the great Shepherd who provides everything His sheep need, and He is never going to abandon you. Listen for your Shepherd's voice.

His glorious power strengthens those who walk with Him. That power will give you "all the endurance and patience you need" (Colossians 1:11). By His power, He'll do things you've never imagined. Galatians 2:20 can be the testimony for each one of us who place our trust in the Lord: "The life I now live in the body, I live by faith in the Son of God, who loved me and gave himself for me."

Jesus, thank You in advance for the strength You will give me today. May Your strength give me the courage and determination I need to face the challenges to which You have called me. Amen.

Day 6

Let us not become weary in doing good, for at the proper time we will reap a harvest if we do not give up.

—Galatians 6:9

GOD PROMISES A HARVEST IF WE DON'T GIVE UP. The very word *harvest* implies a planting time, a time of working and tending, and then, finally, a time of harvest. We see the process illustrated in every field of crops. The same process is required for most of our goals in life. "Success isn't overnight. It's when every day you get a little better than before. It adds up." Those words are from Dwayne Johnson, and they apply to every aspect of life, even the development of our character and our spiritual walk. For example, every time we make a decision to keep on keeping on, we are building and strengthening our determination. Every time we choose to do the honest thing in a small matter, we are fortifying our desire to be honest in all our living. Whatever goal we are pursuing, every step takes us closer to the harvest.

After all, we are building for an eternal future, a life that will not fade away. We may not always see the harvest here, but we can count on God's promise that there *will* be a harvest. Remember 1 Corinthians 15:58: nothing you do for the Lord is ever useless. Everything counts. Romans 5:4 tells us that struggles produce perseverance, perseverance develops character, and character produces hope. Our hope is certain. God promises a harvest if we don't give up.

God, help me to see the harvest You are bringing forth in my life. Please give me patience through the necessary working and tending in preparation for the harvest that is to come. Amen.

DAY 7

Everyone who competes in the games goes into strict training. They do it to get a crown that will not last, but we do it to get a crown that will last forever.

—1 Corinthians 9:25

AT THE END OF MY RACE, I want to hear Jesus say, "Well done, Steve." I'm determined to keep my eyes and my heart fixed on Jesus Christ, the author and finisher of my faith. I'm determined not to give up. I want to be able to say, "I've fought the good fight, I've finished the race, I've kept the faith."

Whatever it is that God has called you to do right now, don't give up. If He has called you to it, He'll provide everything you need to see it through. Ask the Spirit to give you the endurance and strength you need for each task He gives you—and to finish your race strong as you run toward the eternal prize. Pour that Spirit-energized, extraordinary determination into whatever you do.

Most of all, I pray that you'll keep your eyes on Jesus and your love for Him will fuel your determination to be His representative in all you say and do. Paul closed his letter to the Ephesians with this: "Grace to all who love our Lord Jesus Christ with an undying love" (Ephesians 6:24). An undying love for Christ. I pray that is the source of your determination.

Jesus, no matter what obstacles come along my path, please give me the strength, the courage and the determination to serve You with my whole being. Help me to honor You with my life as I press on for the prize You have waiting for me in eternity. Amen.

Notes and Prayers

_____

_____

_____

_____

_____

_____

_____

_____

_____

_____

_____

_____

_____

_____

_____

_____

_____

_____

Steve Wingfield

DEVELOPMENT

In order to develop ourselves or our team, we need to possess an accurate view of ourselves and where we need to work on our strengths first and then our weaknesses.

—Paul Weaver

DAY 1

For I have worked harder than any of the other apostles; yet it was not I but God who was working through me by his grace.

—1 Corinthians 15:10b (NLT)

DEVELOPMENT CAN BE DEFINED AS intentional and deliberate growth and advancement. We don't get locked in a box. We desire progress. We stretch ourselves instead of settling comfortably in one place. As Christians, we want to use all the tools at our disposal to be effective and productive in our leadership, never forgetting that whatever we are and whatever we achieve is God working through us. He equips us for our work. It is His power imbuing our growth and development.

God's purpose is to make us His masterpiece, growing into the person He has planned for us to become, fully equipped to do the work He has planned for us to do. It is nothing we can manufacture or create on our own, but we do have to say, "Yes, Lord," in submission to His leading.

As is true for all of the Lodestar principles, development in the Christian leader's life has spiritual dimensions. We are already living an eternal life here on this earth, and all we do has eternal effects. Who you are and what you become is all by the grace of God.

Lord, I surrender all of my desires, plans and will to You. Place me on the potter's wheel and mold me, make me, and shape me into the life You wish for me. Amen.

Prayers on DEVELOPMENT by Pastor Wayne Wingfield.

Day 2

The LORD will fulfill his purpose for me; your steadfast love, O LORD, endures forever. Do not forsake the work of your hands.

—Psalm 138:8 (ESV)

GOD WANTS US TO GROW. He wants us to keep developing as individuals. In the Scriptures we find startling statements about God's plans for us. If we were to claim these things on our own, we'd be called arrogant and maybe even crazy. But these are God's truths. And any dreams or goals people might have that are limited to the earthly realm fall far short of what God has in store for those who belong to Jesus. Let the world call me crazy. I am excited about everything God has planned for me.

Here are two of the amazing truths. Philippians 1:6 tells us God has begun a good work in us, and He is going to carry it on to completion until the day of Jesus Christ. Philippians 2:13 adds that God works in us to give us the desire and power to act according to His will and plan.

That doesn't mean we can be lazy and content with whatever comes along. We have plenty of verses that tell us to strive, to make every effort, and to work hard. But it is God who will supply the resources you need, even the desire that makes you want to grow.

He hasn't finished yet, so I want to keep growing as long as I live.

Lord, it's painful at times to surrender my will and way to You! Help me day by day to stay on the potter's wheel and to surrender to You my life and all of my team members. Amen.

Day 3

For we are God's masterpiece. He has created us anew in Christ Jesus, so we can do the good things he planned for us long ago.

—Ephesians 2:10 (NLT)

WHAT IS GOD'S PLAN FOR OUR DEVELOPMENT? Prepare yourself for more amazing truths from God's Word to us. God intends to develop a new you and a new me. He has given us a new life and a "new self, which is being renewed in knowledge in the image of its Creator" (Colossians 3:10). If we belong to Christ, we are new people, a new creation. Ephesians 4:24 tells us this new self is "created to be like God in righteousness and holiness." He will transform our minds and hearts. His Spirit changes us, molding us into new people in the image of Christ. That is spiritual development planned by God, my friend!

God wants us to develop and grow into our mission here on earth. Our purpose is to bring glory to Him and point people back to Him by proclaiming the gospel of Christ. My desire is to grow in usefulness to my Lord, to keep growing until my very last day here. 2 Peter 1:5–9 encourages us to strive to develop goodness, knowledge, self-control, perseverance, god-liness, kindness, and *agape* love. These qualities will increase our effectiveness and productivity as partners with Christ. God has good things planned for us, transforming us into new creations and developing our effectiveness for Him.

Lord, I am ever reminded that, "You do not make any trash." Help me as a leader of my team to always remember that we are all gifted differently and help me to see the potential in each of my team members. Amen.

Day 4

By his divine power, God has given us everything we need for living a godly life. We have received all this by coming to know him . . . he has given us great and precious promises . . . that enable you to share his divine nature and escape the world's corruption caused by human desires.

—2 Peter 1:3–4 (NLT)

PAUL WEAVER'S ADVICE AT THE BEGINNING OF THIS SECTION tells us that we need an accurate view of ourselves. Does your view of yourself as a child of God who has been given leadership responsibilities include the fact that you've been given all the resources you need to be an effective, godly leader? This is another amazing truth from God's Word. His power gives us everything we need. That is His promise to His children.

Ephesians 3:16 tells us God has glorious, unlimited resources to empower us through His spirit. I want to live that life to the fullest. I want to know all those glorious resources He has made available to us. I pray that this is your heart's desire, too.

Charles Spurgeon said, "A man's mind is rich very much in proportion to the truth he knows." I believe our lives are rich in proportion to the truths in His promises that we claim as children of God. Jesus came to bring us to God, to make us His children, and to open heaven's door to us. His promises give us an accurate view of who we are as His children—and who we can be.

Lord, thank You for making me unique. Help me not to compare myself to others, and help me to pray that my team members will see You dwelling in me! Amen.

Steve Wingfield

DAY 5

Therefore, if anyone is in Christ, the new creation has come: The old is gone, the new is here!

—2 Corinthians 5:17

SCRIPTURE ALSO TELLS US THAT WE'RE TO FORGET WHAT IS BEHIND and strain toward what is ahead. I read a quote the other day that said, "Don't look back, that's not the direction in which you're going." That's probably a version of what Henry David Thoreau first wrote: "Never look back unless you are planning on going that way." We want to be looking and going ahead, not back.

And that is what God intends for us in the new lives He's given us. He says the old is gone—don't look back, don't let the past chain you, don't get bogged down because of what is behind you. It is *gone.* Jesus gave you a new life. His Spirit began a new creation in you. Again, this is not logical to those who don't know or believe God. But it is God's plan: Do away with the old, create anew.

So, in this new life we don't look back. We strain toward what is ahead. That word *strain* means we can't be lazy or complacent or half-hearted. We go after what is ahead with everything we've got. Our focus is on the goal. We run the race to win. What is ahead? The prize. The eternal crown of life. We are running this race for a prize that will never fade away but will last forever. Eyes forward, my friend. Strain toward the goal.

Lord, help me to focus on the team goals, to keep a clear view of the finished product of each team member. Help me to see each member as a contributing part to the whole. Amen.

Day 6

Work hard to show the results of your salvation, obeying God with deep reverence and fear.

—Philippians 2:12 (NLT)

Pursuing development in any area does require a deliberate, intentional plan. 1 Peter 2:2 encourages us to grow up in our salvation. That's the development God wants us to pursue.

What does it mean to grow up in our salvation? It is maturing in our walk with Christ, learning to live by faith in God's promises, learning to live as a child of the King and as His ambassador until the time He returns. Our salvation brought us much more than an escape from hell; it made all the promises of God ours and gave us new purpose and identity.

So to grow up in this life, to develop into all the potential this new life holds, we do need to be intentional and work at it. What will your plan be?

Colossians 1:10 tells us that the more we get to know God, the more we'll grow. Plan definite times with Him. Talk with Him. Listen to Him. Prayer is a gift of his grace. You can enter boldly right into the presence of the Lord of the universe.

Read his Word; it reveals His will and truth. Scripture is God-breathed "so that the servant of God may be thoroughly equipped for every good work" (2 Timothy 3:17). The Bible will give you that accurate picture you need. It's also the sword the Spirit uses to protect and defend you.

Develop all that He has for you as a result of your salvation.

Lord, I know that I am saved by grace and through faith my responsibility is to obey. Empower me by Your Spirit to always trust and obey. Amen.

Day 7

May he equip you with all you need for doing his will. May he produce in you, through the power of Jesus Christ, every good thing that is pleasing to him. All glory to him forever and ever!

—Hebrews 13:21 (NLT)

Dr. Paul Rees, pastor of First Covenant Church in Minneapolis, was a guest speaker for a week of meetings at a church I was pastoring in Virginia. Dr. Rees was eighty-three at the time. He came to faith at the age of five and was called to the ministry at the age of seven. Over the many decades of his life, he never wavered from that call. During the time he was our guest, I just wanted to hang out and learn from this great man of God. I studied with him, prayed with him, and every night enjoyed a scoop of vanilla ice cream with him. At one point, I asked him, "Dr. Rees, at this phase of your life, what's your heart's greatest desire?" His answer: "I want to know more of God."

Dr. Rees wasn't content on a plateau. At eighty-three, he wanted to keep maturing. He was still hungering and thirsting after righteousness. That is the most important thing for us as followers of Christ: to say YES to our Lord.

His plan for us is a glorious destiny: a masterpiece, created anew in the image of Christ, joint heirs with Jesus. He has begun the work of His new creation in us, and He intends to finish His work. All glory to Him, forever and ever!

Lord, help to remember that You are directing my path and that my team members are watching. I pray that I will be an example and encourage everyone to do their best. Amen.

Notes and Prayers

_____

_____

_____

_____

_____

_____

_____

_____

_____

_____

_____

_____

_____

_____

_____

_____

_____

_____

Steve Wingfield

DILIGENCE

If we work with the end in mind, diligence will help us to finish well and without regrets.

—Paul Weaver

DAY 1

The soul of the sluggard craves and gets nothing, while the soul of the diligent is richly supplied.

—Proverbs 13:4 (ESV)

WHAT DOES DILIGENCE MEAN? Stick-to-it-iveness is a good start. Diligence means spending your time and effort in a steadfast, consistent manner to successfully accomplish your goals and to see the project through in its entirety. A diligent person sees something through to the end. He is steadfastly working toward a goal, without procrastinating, making excuses, or chasing distractions.

"Do you see someone diligent and skillful in his business? He will stand before kings. He will not stand before obscure men" (Proverbs 22:29 AMP). I want that to be a reality in your life, my friend. Another translation of our daily verse says that the soul of the diligent will be "made fat" (NASB).

Diligence attracts others to you. Doors open for diligent people, doors that are phenomenal because people see your attitude, they see your performance, and they know you're committed and won't abandon the job just because things get hard or uncomfortable.

Working with diligence produces personal satisfaction. Yes, diligence also means work, but I feel good when I know that I'm committed to a project and I won't be deterred from finishing the project or achieving the goal. If you will be diligent, God will honor your effort.

Lord, I want to be more diligent for Your glory. I want people to see that You are the inspiration and infusion of power that helps me be a stick-to-it person in my home, work, play and ministry roles.

Prayers on DILIGENCE by Brad Butcher.

Day 2

Be diligent in these matters; give yourself wholly to them.

—1 Timothy 4:15

THE IMPORTANCE OF DILIGENCE IS APPARENT IN EVERY ASPECT OF LIFE. When we make a commitment, we need to be diligent about sticking to that commitment. It might be as simple a thing as saying, "I'll be there by ten," and then showing up on time, or as big as taking on a complex project at work and seeing it through to the end.

My dad built diligence into me, teaching me to be tenacious. The Apostle Paul considered young Timothy "my true son in the faith," and he passed on much the same teaching.

> *Devote yourself to the public reading of Scripture, to preaching and to teaching. Do not neglect your gift, which was given you . . . Be diligent in these matters; give yourself wholly to them, so that everyone may see your progress. Watch your life and doctrine closely. Persevere in them . . .*
>
> —1 Timothy 4:13–16

These words are not applicable only to spiritual things. If we absorb and live by those words, they'll help us stick to it, get it done, and persevere in all areas of life. Choose the word or phrase that speaks to you and make it your declaration of diligence.

Lord, help me to follow the example of those who've demonstrated diligence in their daily lives, especially those who were diligent to serve you with their time, treasure, and talents. Abba Father, form in me _____ (your chosen word or phrase from above). Would you also remind me today that others are learning from me? As you do, I'll be sure to give You all the glory. Amen.

Steve Wingfield

Day 3

I press on toward the goal to win the prize for which God has called me heavenward in Christ Jesus.

—Philippians 3:14

THE HIGH SCHOOL I WENT TO HELD AN ANNUAL FIELD DAY. We participated in running and field events, and the person who accumulated the most points from wins or placings was given a medal and named "Field Day Champion." That award had never been won by a junior or an underclassman. When I was a sophomore, I was determined I was going to win that medal the next year. I had no assurance I would win, but I was going to give it my best shot. So almost every day for a year, I ran. I ran until I threw up. I was diligently going after that medal.

Field Day arrived, and I won four out of five events and came in second in the fifth. I was Field Day Champion! I still have the medal I won. It fits in the palm of my hand. A few years ago, God spoke to me. *You worked so hard for that win and a small, insignificant medal. How much more disciplined are you willing to be to run the race for the crown of life?*

Diligence is important in all areas of life. But it is our steadfastness in the race for the crown of life that will have the greatest impact on our lives, both now and into eternity. Run to win the prize!

Creator God, show me how foolish and unfulfilling it is to seek my own pleasure and glory in this life. Open my eyes anew to see Your eternal kingdom so I can live for the glory awaiting those who are diligent in living each day for You. Amen.

DAY 4

I have fought the good fight, I have finished the race, I have remained faithful. And now the prize awaits me—the crown of righteousness, which the Lord will give me . . . And the prize is not just for me but for all who eagerly look forward to his appearing.

—2 Timothy 4:7–8 (NLT)

DILIGENCE MEANS WORK. Besides just sticking to the job, we also have work to do in planning the way in which we are going to accomplish our goal. We want to be successful in our efforts. We don't just throw all our energy and time at a project willy-nilly; we are intentional about how we're going about it. Jesus' choices as He lived His earthly life were focused on completing the work God sent Him to do. He is our model.

Take some time today to consider how you can be more intentional in your faith. Ask the Spirit's guidance as you consider what you can do differently to be more diligent in pursuit of God's goals for you. Would it be planning definite times to be with Him, listening, talking, and reading? Would it be finding an accountability group who helps you in your walk? Would it be a dedication to knowing the Scriptures more thoroughly?

Make the choice to be diligent in your walk with Him. And look forward to the prize.

Lord, thank You for reminding me today that You have sent your Spirit to live within me so I can think and do as You. I receive Your power now to be diligent in setting aside time daily to meet with You and to regularly meet with another child of Yours to set some goals together. Amen.

Steve Wingfield

DAY 5

I am the vine; you are the branches. If you remain in me and I in you, you will bear much fruit; apart from me, you can do nothing.

—John 15:5

BELIEVE ME, OUR SPIRITUAL ENEMIES PRACTICE DILIGENCE. They steadfastly, consistently seek to accomplish their goal, that is, to destroy our walk with the Lord, our faith, and our soul. Just as distractions and procrastination are enemies of diligence in the workplace, they can also be enemies in our walk of faith. The spiritual forces against God's work will use our tendency to procrastinate, or the temptation to make excuses, or little daily distractions to get us off course.

When I spend time with the Lord, thoughts often pop into my head that distract me, thoughts that have nothing to do with my devotions or what I've been praying about. I have learned to keep a paper and pen handy, and if I jot down that thought, I can forget about it and concentrate on what the Lord is telling me at the time. Be diligent. Stay the course in following the Spirit's leading today. Don't let the enemy distract you.

How do we overcome these enemies? Jesus' Spirit in us is greater than any of those enemies (1 John 4:4). He promised if we hold tightly to Him, His life will flow through us, like life coming from the vine to the branches. And we will defeat the enemies of our diligent walk!

Savior, show me Your glory, so I see that all else is garbage compared to knowing You! Help me be diligent to talk with You about this until I have the breakthrough in my walk with You that You know I'm longing for. Amen.

DAY 6

But my life is worth nothing to me unless I use it for finishing the work assigned me by the Lord Jesus—the work of telling others the Good News about the wonderful grace of God.

—Acts 20:24 (NLT)

HOW COMFORTABLE IS YOUR LIFE TODAY? Comfort zones are danger zones for followers of Christ. The Spirit showed Paul that in every city, prison and hardship awaited him. How would you feel if the Spirit clearly showed you that in the year ahead, you would face cancer and loss of loved ones and legal action against you because of your faith?

A comfortable life certainly wasn't Paul's goal. And it can't be ours. Neither Jesus nor Paul could stay in their comfort zone. God's work called them to push on, into places that were hard and brought strong opposition. Their diligence in following God's call kept them going.

You and I are called by God, too. We are called to grow more and more like him. Growth itself means we move out of the known and comfortable and push out the boundaries of who we are now into who we will become. God's call also may be to situations where we are anything but comfortable—but it is where God calls us to be as His representative.

Don't let that old self convince you to stay in your comfort zone. You have a new life and Good News to share. Be diligent in both!

Lord Jesus, You've asked me to leverage everything in my life for the purpose of showing others who You are. For Your name's sake, help me to be diligent to walk daily in the power, love, and self-control of Your Spirit instead of walking in the empty comforts of self-focused living. Amen.

Day 7

By his divine power, God has given us everything we need for living a godly life. We have received all of this by coming to know him, the one who called us to himself by means of his marvelous glory and excellence.

—2 Peter 1:3 (NLT)

WE HAVE NO EXCUSES. Sometimes when the going gets hard or we meet obstacles that seem insurmountable, our diligence wanes. The Spirit of God lives in those who belong to Christ, and the Spirit brings a power to our lives that will fuel our diligence. God assures us He will provide everything we need in whatever task He's given us to do. A godly life doesn't mean a perfect life. It means a life devoted to being used by God, a life marked by his characteristics.

All of this—having a new life to live, Good News to share, and resources drawn from God's marvelous glory and excellence—brings joy to our diligence, doesn't it? Running this race is not drudgery or a chore, but joyful persistence, keeping our eyes on our Champion. Go back to the very first verse of this week: "The soul of the sluggard craves and gets nothing, while the soul of the diligent is richly supplied." Your soul will be richly supplied.

Everything! Lord, that's what You've promised us now that we know You. Please help me to keep my eyes trained on You and who You really are. Show me how to remind myself and my fellow "runners" that You are more than enough so we can keep on running with diligence the race You've put before us! Help me to endure until I hear You say, "Well done my good and diligent servant!" Amen.

Notes and Prayers

_____

_____

_____

_____

_____

_____

_____

_____

_____

_____

_____

_____

_____

_____

_____

_____

_____

_____

Steve Wingfield

DISCERNMENT

If we know the real truth, it will be a game changer.

—Paul Weaver.

DAY 1

Train yourself to be godly. For physical training is of some value, but godliness has value for all things, holding promise for both the present life and the life to come.

—1 Timothy 4:7–8

DISCERNMENT IS OFTEN LACKING IN THE WORLD TODAY. When a leader does not have it, there is deceit, bad decisions, cheating, and lying. The Scriptures say that when a country is rebellious it has many rulers, but a ruler with discernment and knowledge maintains order. You want to be a leader with discernment and knowledge, and a person with godly discernment is the best leader of all.

Godly discernment comes from the Holy Spirit. When we enter into a relationship with Jesus Christ, the Spirit endows us with gifts that are beyond human reasoning and intelligence. The gift of discernment helps us read people and situations around us. It gives us wisdom and guidance when making decisions and helps us to see what is wise and what is unwise.

God's plans are to prosper us and give us hope. He promises to guide those who humbly look to Him, and the gift of discernment is one of the ways He keeps that promise. For our part, we need to learn to listen to His voice and obey.

Dear Lord, send people into my life with this grace of discernment. Help me to guard my life from the frivolous and useless, and guide me into good decisions today. Amen.

Prayers on DISCERNMENT by Luke Weaver.

Day 2

All Scripture is inspired by God and is useful to teach us what is true and to make us realize what is wrong in our lives. It corrects us when we are wrong and teaches us to do what is right. God uses it to prepare and equip his people to do every good work.

—2 Timothy 3:16–17 (NLT)

GOD WILL NEVER LEAD YOU TO DO ANYTHING CONTRARY TO HIS WORD. *Know* the Word. It is God's kindness to us. He wants us to know Him, His thoughts, and His ways. The Bible holds the keys to life. It revives us when we need uplifting, gives us wisdom, reveals God's will. It shows us who we are and who we are to God. It tells us who God is and what He has promised His children. It lays out his plan for His creation. God's Word has the answers you need. Always weigh your decisions by the truth in the Word of God.

The Word is also a protection for us. When Paul described the armor God gives us, he called the Word of God "the sword of the Spirit." The Word is what the Spirit uses to demolish temptations, lies Satan whispers to you, strongholds in your mind that resist truth. The Spirit goes to battle for you with the Word of God in His hand. So be intentional about taking the time to go to the Word. Go with focus and hunger and thirst after his truth. It will help your discernment in all areas.

Dear Lord, today I grant You permission to shine the light of Your Word into my life. My wish is that You will discern my deepest thoughts and motives. Teach and prepare me for good works in this day. Amen.

Steve Wingfield

DAY 3

So let us come boldly to the throne of our gracious God. There we will receive his mercy, and we will find grace to help us when we need it most.

—Hebrews 4:16 (NLT)

YOU KNOW, THE WORLD AROUND US PRESSURES US TO ADOPT ITS WAYS, tries to sneak its values and standards into our thinking, and resorts to lies to lead us away from God's truth. Satan even works on us from within, manipulating that old sinful nature to resist what the Spirit would have us do and be. We're in a fierce battle, my friend, never question that. Life here is a war zone, and our enemies are spiritual forces.

We need help. We need a God of power and kindness and love to fight for us and to equip and strengthen us. And we have that God, a God like no other. Because our advocate is Jesus Christ, we have an open door to go straight to the Lord of the universe. Hebrews 10:22 says we can go right into his presence "with sincere hearts, fully trusting him." Jesus made that possible for us. And there, at His throne of grace, we will find help.

Pray. Build your relationship with the Lord of the universe who is also your Father. Be honest with Him. He knows you better than you know yourself. Ask for His help. Thank Him. Express your love for Him. Ask for the wisdom and discernment you need. Go boldly to the throne of your Father, and trust Him.

Dear Lord, I ask for the confidence that leads to boldness in Your presence knowing You will answer prayer. I know You will grant me a clean conscience leading to the fully trusting heart. Amen.

DAY 4

But when he, the Spirit of truth, comes, he will guide you into all truth.

—John 16:13

THE HOLY SPIRIT IS OUR GUIDE TO THE TRUTH. Lies and deception are Satan's strategies for worming his way into our thinking. But Jesus said His Spirit would lead us in the way of truth. His Spirit comes to live with us, *within* us. He comes to live intimately with us, even making His home here. Isn't it wonderful that Jesus didn't leave His disciples alone in this world to struggle through the darkness on their own strength and resources? We have been given a guide, the Guide who is in authority over everything.

Our Guide leads us to right living, molds our thinking, gives us right desires, produces fruit in our lives like nothing we can produce on our own, and changes us in every way to be more and more like the Lord we follow. In Romans 8:6, Paul wrote that listening to and following the Spirit's guidance will lead to life and peace. Letting our sinful natures control us leads to death. What a contrast! I want life and peace, don't you?

Ask for the Spirit's guidance to the truth every day. Then open your ears to Him. He will speak. He will increase your discernment. He is the one who sees and knows all people and situations perfectly. There is no doubt or question in His knowledge. Ask for His help. Then walk ahead in faith because He grants those prayers.

Dear Lord, today help me to be still and hear the voice of the Holy Spirit. Grant me that precious gift to hear Your voice and understand the meaning. I ask for the faith to adjust my life based on the truth I hear. Amen.

Day 5

In their hearts humans plan their course, but the LORD establishes their steps.
—Proverbs 16:9

DISCERNMENT CAN ALSO BE AIDED BY PAYING ATTENTION to open and closed doors. We can learn from Peter, praying on the housetop one day and feeling his stomach growl. In a vision, God presented him with all kinds of animals, reptiles, and birds to kill and eat. Peter was shocked. Those things were considered "unclean" and strictly forbidden to Jews. God was giving Peter a heads up that things had changed. Now the good news of the gospel was for everyone—both Jews and Gentiles, people the Jews had previously seen as "unclean." And just as God explained to Peter that He was sending him to a Gentile house, someone knocked at the door downstairs, saying they were sent to find a man named Peter.

God arranged those events with such precision that Peter couldn't miss the door God had opened. But we notice that God did have to repeat the vision three times. It was a major change in thinking for Peter, and maybe it took him a while to get the message. We need to pay attention, too. God will open surprising opportunities and we don't want to miss them. Or, He will close a door; godly discernment pays attention to that, too.

We should never base our decisions on open and closed doors only. We should, however, pray for the guidance He has promised us and then go forward in faith, trusting Him to keep His promise to order our steps.

Dear Lord, grant me the humility to accept Your plans especially when those plans differ from mine. I ask for grace to accept the closed door and look for the new window of God's opportunity. Amen.

Steve Wingfield

Day 6

And this is my prayer: that your love may abound more and more in knowledge and depth of insight, so that you may be able to discern what is best and may be pure and blameless for the day of Christ, filled with the fruit of righteousness that comes through Jesus Christ—to the glory and praise of God.

—Philippians 1:9–11

IN WHAT I CALL THE BROTHERHOOD, Christians develop *agape* love for each other. As their love grows, so does their knowledge and insight. This, in turn, increases their *discernment*. All together, they help each other live godly lives bearing much fruit and bringing glory to God until the day Christ returns.

One of the things you have received as part of your salvation is a bond of the Spirit with other Christians. Now we are all part of one body, and no one lives alone and separate. We are to encourage each other, build each other up, use our gifts to serve each other, and help each other weed out those things in our lives that need to go.

So, when I need discernment, the fifth checkpoint is those who know me best and to whom I am accountable. For you, that might be your spouse, an accountability group, or your closest friends. This checkpoint, again, cannot be taken as the sole voice to which discernment gives ear. All five points must be considered. If any one of them is waving a red flag at you, discernment demands that you pay attention.

Thank you, Lord, for placing people in my life who assist me in discovering better things You have for my life. Give me grace to seize the better and to express my love to You and others. Amen.

Steve Wingfield

Day 7

Be very careful, then, how you live—not as unwise but wise, making the most of every opportunity, because the days are evil. Therefore, do not be foolish, but understand what the Lord's will is.

—Ephesians 5:15–17

THESE ARE THE GUIDELINES THE SPIRIT HAS TAUGHT ME in growing the gift of discernment: *Ask what God's Word says. Pray about the situation. Listen for the Spirit's voice. Look for God's guidance through circumstance. Listen to input from those to whom I'm accountable.* If any of these five seem out of sync or throw up a red flag, then I need to look again at my decision, conclusion, or choice.

When I have failed to listen to the voice of discernment within me, I've gotten into trouble. Several times it has been on hiring decisions. Everyone else seemed gung ho about an applicant. I had a sense that this was the wrong choice, but I went along with everyone else, and later regretted it.

I have a sad memory of a breakfast conversation with a follower of Christ who had made a terrible choice. "Didn't you feel a check in your spirit?" I asked. "Didn't you feel the Spirit warning you?" The reply: "Yes, but I didn't want to listen." The deliberate decision not to obey brought upheaval and sorrow to many lives.

1 John 4 tells us not to believe every spirit, to test the spirits to see whether they are from God. The enemy will also tell us things contrary to the Spirit's wisdom, but one of the ways the Lord protects us is with His voice of discernment. We need to listen and obey.

Lord, give me a discerning heart. I desire to know and do Your will. Amen.

Notes and Prayers

_____

_____

_____

_____

_____

_____

_____

_____

_____

_____

_____

_____

_____

_____

_____

_____

_____

_____

_____

_____

Steve Wingfield

Discretion

Position, power, money, status, genetics, or last names do not make a leader.
It is soft skills that engender trust and give us influence.

—Paul Weaver

Day 1

Discretion will protect you, and understanding will guard you.
—Proverbs 2:11

"BUT THE THINGS THAT COME OUT OF THE MOUTH COME FROM THE HEART," Jesus said (Matthew 15:18). Our actions are the fruit of our thoughts and attitudes. Whether or not we show discretion in our words and actions is determined by what's going on in our hearts. Again, we remember wise King Solomon's urging to guard your heart because out of it flows everything you do.

As Christ's representatives, our goal is to live with godly discretion. That is, having a level of discretion that honors and pleases God and reflects His character growing in us. That's what the Spirit will develop in us if we follow His leading, just as He will develop and energize all the other traits we've been thinking about.

As we think about discretion, humbly submit to the Spirit's examination, showing you any areas of your life and leadership where discretion is lacking. Then follow His guidance in changing whatever needs to change so that you will have the protection and influence that discretion brings.

Lord, I am fixing my mind and heart on You right now! How revitalizing to remember all you went through to show Your love for me and provide my salvation! Today, Lord, empower me to live as You lived and to never give up! Amen.

Prayers on DISCRETION by Dr. Tim Robnet.

DAY 2

Let us therefore make every effort to do what leads to peace and to mutual edification.

—Romans 14:19

"LIKE A GOLD RING IN A PIG'S SNOUT is a beautiful woman who shows no discretion." Proverbs 11:22 is not only blunt, but also as relevant to men as to women. James was equally blunt. He wrote that your tongue—*yours,* take this personally because it's serious stuff—is a fire set ablaze by hell, a world of evil.

Why such strong language? We know that a lack of discretion can create cataclysmic pain and consequences that go far beyond the shock of a pig's snout. We should take James' warning personally. Our tongues can do great harm and slip into evil quickly if they are not guarded. Indiscretion of both word and action can offend others, embarrass them and ourselves, break trust, and deeply wound relationships.

But as Proverbs 18:21 tells us, the tongue also has the power of life, the power to bless, and the power to heal. Those who guard their tongues guard their lives (Proverbs 13:3), and the lives of others. You can promote peace in your life and others by what you say and do. You can build up yourself and others. Your words can be good and helpful, a comfort and encouragement to others (Ephesians 4:29). God's grace can flow through you to those around you (Colossians 4:6). Words and actions guarded by discretion have life-giving power—for you and for others.

Lord, in this day of pressure and struggle I look to You for strength and endurance. Help me remember "greater is the one in me than the one in the world." Lord, I am looking for You to show up in my journey today. Amen.

Steve Wingfield

Day 3

So let us put on the armor of light. Clothe yourselves with the Lord Jesus Christ.
—From Romans 13:12, 14

A BLAZING FIRE FROM HELL OR A GRACIOUSNESS THAT BESTOWS LIFE AND BLESSING? Our words and actions can be either of these. What determines which your words and actions will be? Discretion. Or lack of it.

The godly discretion we desire comes from the Spirit of Christ working within us. When we are baptized into Christ, we have "clothed" ourselves with Christ (Galatians 3:27). He lives through us. When our life as His branch is being drawn from His vine, it is His life we live in this world. That is why I am so passionate about representing Him well. I belong to Him. I wear His name. I want to exhibit His life with all the ability and energy He gives me.

> *Therefore, as God's chosen people, holy and dearly loved, clothe yourselves with compassion, kindness, humility, gentleness and patience. Bear with each other and forgive one another if any of you has a grievance against someone. Forgive as the Lord forgave you. And over all these virtues put on love, which binds them all together in perfect unity.*
>
> —Colossians 3:12–14

Take the time to carefully visualize yourself putting on each piece of this "clothing." Throughout the day, remember what you're wearing. And over it all, wrap yourself in the cloak of the same love that Christ shows to you.

Lord, I feel like a failure today. But I put my hope in Your promises that You will never leave me nor forsake me. Lord, in this day may I reach out to others who need a word of encouragement and a hand up to keep going. Amen.

Day 4

The hearts of the wise make their mouths prudent, and their lips promote instruction.

—Proverbs 16:23

WE FACE MANY DECISIONS EACH DAY, choices on whether or not to speak or act and decisions about how to speak and act. Many times, the choice is not as well defined as choosing whether to bless or to curse, whether to be a pig's snout or a channel of grace.

Proverbs 5:2 says wisdom preserves discretion. Somewhere I saw a quote that said, "A smart person knows what to say; a wise person knows whether to say it or not." Then exactly *how* do we speak in truth and integrity and loyalty and stewardship? The way in which we act or speak also has a great effect. We've all had the experience of speaking unwisely and lighting a spark that sets ablaze the fire of hell, although we never intended to do so. We don't want to stumble into such a situation again. How can we avoid it when the decisions are tough?

Every situation has its own specifics, but if you're facing volatile circumstances right now, the one thing I can tell you is that God honors the heartfelt prayer of James 1:5. If you lack wisdom, ask God, who gives so generously, "and it will be given to you."

God has promised to supply all we need as His people. Ask Him for His help to make wise judgments. Seek His wisdom in Scriptures. Knock on the door of His throne room and enter boldly to talk with your Father about what you need. Then walk in faith, trusting Him to keep His promise.

Lord, help me remember the joy I will know when I hear Your voice say, "Welcome home." Amen.

Day 5

The heart of the righteous weighs its answers, but the mouth of the wicked gushes evil.

—Proverbs 15:28

IN THE SCRIPTURES, *discretion* is often interchanged with *prudence* and *sound judgment*. All three qualities require a weighing of words and actions. We consider the facts and consequences of what we might say or do. If we're impulsive and shoot off the first words that jump to the tip of our tongue, we're headed for trouble. Proverbs 22:3 describes two outcomes: "The prudent see danger and take refuge, but the simple keep going and pay the penalty."

Paul Weaver recommends a five-second pause before letting those words escape. In those five seconds, consider not only whether you *should* say anything, but also *how* you should say it. If you see danger, take refuge. Take refuge in the Spirit's strength of restraint. Take refuge in His wisdom, asking for help in phrasing your words wisely and in having the right attitude as you say them. Take refuge in the Vine and ask for His life to flow through yours.

Patience, attitude, restraint, discernment, kindness, wisdom, humility, self-control—each of these attributes contribute to our discretion, our prudence, and our sound judgment. Which of those eight is most difficult for you? In your prayer today, ask the Spirit to teach you how to grow more like Him in that one characteristic. It will strengthen your discretion.

Lord, You are my Shepherd. I have everything I will need. Lord, You're the Chief Shepherd and You know exactly what's going on, no surprises for You. Lord, You are the Great Shepherd, no one nor nothing is bigger than You. So, I will rest in Your care. Life, bring it on. Amen.

Day 6

Therefore be imitators of God, as beloved children. And walk in love, as Christ loved us and gave himself up for us, a fragrant offering and sacrifice to God.
—Ephesians 5:1–2 (ESV)

WHY DOES GOD WANT US TO DEVELOP DISCRETION in our leadership and our living? Why is it so important for traits like honesty, transparency, and boldness to be tempered with discretion?

Ephesians 5 answers those questions. We're to live as God's dearly loved children, imitating Him as earthly children imitate their fathers. We are the family of God, and the chapter goes on to give a number of examples of behavior that are improper for God's people, not even a hint of these should occur in His family. Thoughtless, uncontrolled responses that come as knee-jerk reactions are not God's way of dealing with situations or people. His ways are purposeful, compassionate, and above all, loving.

Love will set a guard over our words and actions. Love will not allow our egos, our defensive reactions, anger, or selfishness to grab control of what we say and do. Love will filter and be cautious, because love considers how others are going to be affected. Love is patient and kind and is not boastful or rude. It does not dishonor others. It lives by truth, always hopes, protects, and perseveres (1 Corinthians 13).

Love binds discretion together with all other godly traits, and we not only carry the family name, we live it out as we deal with each other in love.

Lord, the harvest is not at the end of this day, but at the time of Your coming. Help me not to be short-sighted but to know that each moment counts for You and Your kingdom. When I am weary, Lord, remind me that I am honoring You. Amen.

Day 7

May the words of my mouth and the meditation of my heart be pleasing to you, O LORD, my rock and my redeemer.

—Psalm 19:14 (NLT)

The bottom line is that discretion is necessary for me in pursuing my goal: to do the best I can at representing Christ to the world around me. If I can't make wise decisions about when and how to speak or what action is appropriate, then I'm reflecting poorly on my Master. I belong to Him, and my purpose here on earth is to show others who He is. When discretion does not place that guard over me, I'm discrediting His name.

Paul wrote that we should make it our goal to do nothing to keep people from Jesus Christ and His gospel. "You will be my witnesses," Jesus said. His witnesses. We bear testimony to what Christ can do in a life, how He brings a new heart and transformed mind. I pray that my life will show that. I need a Spirit-directed discretion to post guards around my life so that I do not fail Him.

You may have learned Psalm 19:14 as a child. Now, the Spirit is speaking to you as an adult who knows the importance of the words of your mouth and the meditation of your heart. Pay attention to what He is saying. This is my heartfelt prayer, that both my words and my thoughts would be pleasing to the Lord, and I hope that's your prayer, too, and that you pursue it daily.

Lord, thank You that You reward us in this life and in the life to come. But beyond the rewards may we enjoy the journey living for You. Thanks for the everyday desire to worship You in obedience and praise. Amen.

Notes and Prayers

_____

_____

_____

_____

_____

_____

_____

_____

_____

_____

_____

_____

_____

_____

_____

_____

_____

_____

Steve Wingfield

> *Empathy is lubricant to the gears of leadership.*
> *Everything becomes easier, and the results will astound you.*
>
> —Paul Weaver

DAY 1

Be happy with those who are happy, and weep with those who weep. Live in harmony with each other. Don't be too proud to enjoy the company of ordinary people. And don't think you know it all!

—Romans 12:15–16 (NLT)

A SENSITIVE PERSON SEES THE WORLD THROUGH THE EYES OF LOVE. That is what empathy is all about. It's compassion and understanding in connecting with people. There are people who seem predisposed to understanding the feelings of others and listening with compassion. My wife would say that two of my brothers were given a double dose of the gift of empathy and it should have been spread around more over the family (meaning more to me, the youngest). And I know she's right. Empathy just doesn't come as easily to me as it did to those two brothers. I love people, but I sometimes struggle being empathetic. I have had to work at it.

This understanding and compassion is a trait of the Lord I represent. Empathy is not a weakness. It is a strength. Billy Graham said, "Tears shed for self are tears of weakness, but tears shed for others are a sign of strength." Empathy is an expression of the kind of love Christ wants us to show to everyone. It is a fruit of His Spirit working within me. So I ask Him to help me be more empathetic in my leadership and my personal life.

My eyes are cluttered with so many concerns. Help me, Lord, to see the needs and challenges of others through Your eyes. Amen.

Prayers on EMPATHY by Pastor Dr. Don Paxton.

Day 2

Finally, all of you, be like-minded, be sympathetic, love one another, be compassionate and humble.

—1 Peter 3:8

WE ARE TO BE REPRESENTATIVES OF CHRIST IN EVERY ASPECT OF OUR LIVES. So as leaders, we want to exhibit his compassion and care for others as we lead our teams, and one of the most productive efforts you can make as a leader is to model and build good relationships in your workplace. Empathy will help you build those relationships.

Empathetic listening nourishes relationships. It tells another person that you care, that you understand where she is and how she feels. It builds trust between people and cuts down on misunderstandings. This honest caring about others will do away with gossip and prejudice, two things you do not want in the workplace. Those things come as we listen to and seek to understand each other and build sincere and compassionate relationships.

Dietrich Bonhoeffer wrote, "We must learn to regard people less in the light of what they do or don't do, and more in light of what they suffer." Empathy silences a judgmental attitude and replaces it with a love that can see past actions to the battles and suffering in a person's life.

Empathy will also help you to see people not just for who they are but for who they can be. You'll be able to speak into their lives when you have that understanding relationship. Again, we see that this character trait works together with others like compassion, influence, sincerity, and generosity to make you a better leader.

Help me, Lord, to take time to listen to others' pains, fears, and needs. I am too quick to judge before obtaining the facts needed to respond rightly. Amen.

Steve Wingfield

Day 3

Be devoted to one another in love. Honor one another above yourselves.

—Romans 12:10

TODAY, FOCUS ON *HOW* YOU LISTEN TO OTHERS. Being able to correctly and compassionately understand the feelings of others requires that we be good listeners. We listen carefully, not to argue or debate, but to tune into how the other person feels. Empathy comes when we listen with a heart that wants to understand feelings.

Listening with empathy means we move our own feelings and ideas out of "first place" and we focus on the feelings and ideas of the other person. So often we "listen" more to our own feelings and thoughts even as someone else is talking, and then our own emotions drive our actions and reactions toward others. Empathy, though, moves our feelings out of the driver's seat.

Empathy paves the way for us to follow the rule of living that Jesus said is the second greatest commandment: Love your neighbor as yourself. Following this precept makes another person's feelings every bit as important as my own. My relationship with that person and my compassion is guided by my understanding of his feelings, so we had better learn to listen in order to understand each other. That "listening" includes paying attention to the feelings and thoughts behind the spoken words.

To live out Jesus' command to love others and treat them in the same way we want to be treated, we need to understand and truly care about them. We are going to move ourselves out of first place and focus on the other person.

Help me, Lord, to truly love my neighbors, putting them first by thinking more of them than my wants and wishes. Amen.

Day 4

Therefore be imitators of God, as beloved children. And walk in love, as Christ loved us and gave himself up for us, a fragrant offering and sacrifice to God.
—Ephesians 5:1–2 (ESV)

John wrote that real love is this: that God loved us and sent His Son as a sacrifice for us. Before we even knew Him, Jesus came to be with us and to carry the burden of punishment for our sins. That's what empathy is, being "with" another person wherever they are and sharing the burdens they carry. It is stepping out of our own shoes and walking in their shoes.

Jesus' instruction to His disciples, then, was that we are to love each other as He has loved us. So not only are we to be "with" each other in the sense of having compassion and sharing in each other's burdens, we are to take the initiative in empathy—just as our Lord took the initiative to reach out and build a relationship with us. He "gave himself up for us."

How can we show that same love to the world around us? We seek to understand them, even if they have rebuffed and rejected us. We seek to love them even if they have hurt us. We treat them with compassion and respect even when they are different from us.

Remember the Samaritan, coming to the aid of someone who saw him as an enemy? We give ourselves up to show God's love to others. God's love did that for the world, for you and me, and loving in that way makes us "true children" of our Father in heaven (Matthew 5:45).

Give me Your heart, Lord, to feel the hurts of others in order that I might weep with them. Amen.

Day 5

Our God is full of compassion.

—Psalm 116:5

TAKE TIME TODAY TO THINK ABOUT HOW WONDERFUL IT IS that God does understand *you*, the person you are, and your struggles, sadness, and joys. The Scriptures tell us He knows all our sorrows and understands our tears. He sees and understands everything we do. He knows the secrets of our hearts. Jesus understands those strong temptations. He's been through the same things we have. The words of an old song are always a comfort.

> *Does Jesus care when my heart is pained*
> *Too deeply for mirth or song*
> *As the burdens press,*
> *And the cares distress,*
> *And the way grows weary and long?*

> *Oh yes, He cares, I know He cares,*
> *His heart is touched with my grief;*
> *When the days are weary,*
> *The long night dreary,*
> *I know my Savior cares.*

I wish there were space here to quote all the verses of that song. Jesus cares when we walk in the darkness of fear, when we're grieving because we've failed to resist temptation, and when we lose those dearest to us. Our Savior has lived with us and been one of us. He knows and cares.

Lord, grant unto me peace when I am afraid. Do not allow my fears to keep me from focusing on Your promised power and presence. Amen.

DAY 6

Therefore, as God's chosen people, holy and dearly loved, clothe yourselves with compassion, kindness, humility, gentleness and patience.

—Colossians 3:12

WHETHER IN LEADERSHIP OR NOT, AS CHRISTIANS, we cannot ignore or intentionally push aside the importance of how we relate to other people. Jesus said that next to loving God with all we are and everything we have, the most important thing is that we love others. And the Scriptures are filled with practical instruction on how to do that.

Yes, we have instruction on "how to" love. Because love is not a feeling; it is what we do, the decisions we make about how we treat others. This is how we're to dress ourselves each day, putting on these qualities. All of them directly influence how we relate to others.

I can promise you that consciously putting on these clothes each morning will increase your empathy for others. The thing is, these are not clothes we would wear on our own. Our own tendencies are just the opposite of these qualities. These clothes are made by the Spirit of God—the God who is Love. So to put on these clothes, we need to ask the Spirit to dress us. That's the only way we'll live with compassion, kindness, humility, gentleness, and patience.

If you're a leader in any way, your example sets the tone for what happens in the workplace, or on the committee, at church, school, or the family. The quality of being able to understand others and be "with" them in their struggles will help you in all relationships. Ask the Spirit to help you grow your empathy. Get dressed for the day!

Remind me, Lord, how it hurt when I felt a lack of compassion, kindness, gentleness, or patience from others. Amen.

DAY 7

And all of you, dress yourselves in humility as you relate to one another, for "God opposes the proud but gives grace to the humble."
—1 Peter 5:5 (NLT)

WE CANNOT HAVE EMPATHY IF WE DO NOT POSSESS HUMILITY. When we talk about empathy, we must also think about humility. What is humility? Humility is having an accurate view of yourself.

Humility means we remember that we are all made of dust. I am not better than you. The prince and the pauper have the same value to God. He loves them equally. He works in every life, and humility sees that. Humility knows that our accomplishments come from the Lord. It is God's power at work in us, not ours. And just as God is still working on me, empathy remembers that He is still working on others, too.

Serving with humility means putting on the Spirit's clothing each day. Humility knows our own clothing won't do. Humility seeks to honor the other person. Humility allows us to step into their shoes and understand where they are without judging. Humility compels us to put aside our own ideas and emotions to truly listen to others and enter into their struggle. Humility helps us to encourage each other and sees God at work in each life.

Ask God to help you with any of the areas where you know humility is lacking. You will increase in empathy for others, one of the most important qualities for every son or daughter of God.

Lord, I can do nothing without You and all I attempt to do is unacceptable before You. Humble me, Lord, that others see more of You and less of me. Amen.

Notes and Prayers

_____

_____

_____

_____

_____

_____

_____

_____

_____

_____

_____

_____

_____

_____

_____

_____

_____

_____

Fairness is not treating everyone exactly the same.
It is all about treating every individual with dignity and respect
and giving people the benefit of the doubt.

—Paul Weaver

DAY 1

And walk in the way of love, just as Christ loved us and gave himself up for us as a fragrant offering and sacrifice to God.

—Ephesians 5:2

OUR LODESTAR DEFINITION SAYS THAT FAIRNESS IS FOLLOWING THE RULES honestly and reasonably, valuing equality, and treating everyone impartially and free of favoritism. What does Scripture say about following the rules? Whose rules are we striving to follow? The world's rules? Or God's rules? Because more often than not, the world's rules are contrary to God's rules. The world is dog-eat-dog. Get them before they get us. Take care of yourself first. You have rights. Use people for your own benefit. Get ahead whenever you can. Mow down opposition. The strongest rule the weakest.

But God's world operates on different principles. Love your neighbor as yourself. Serve others. Be kind to your enemies. Forgive. Give second, third, and fourth chances. Your life is not your own. You are not here to be rich and famous. You are not in this game for yourself but as representatives and partners of Christ, for the glory of God.

Dear Lord, help me do what is right when there is a decision to be made. Help me to love others as myself and to serve them in a way that brings glory to You. Lord, please help me to forgive others as You have forgiven me. Amen.

Prayers on FAIRNESS by Pastor Terry Lynn Wyant-Vargo.

Day 2

But the wisdom from above is first pure, then peaceable, gentle, open to reason, full of mercy and good fruits, impartial and sincere.

—James 3:17 (ESV)

Fairness treats people honestly and reasonably. This makes you approachable. People know the door is open for them to come and talk to you. That's vitally important in business, and it's vitally important in life. Here again, other Lodestar principles come into play: honesty, transparency, discernment, kindness, respect, sincerity, compassion and others. And the Scriptures, on which we build our lives, tell us this is the *right* way to deal with people—honestly and reasonably.

What does *reasonably* mean? The dictionary says it is being agreeable to reason, moderate, being level-headed and decent. Scripture pictures this as being sincere, compassionate, peaceable, gentle, and open to reason. Did you notice how many of these traits are part of the wisdom from above? (See our daily verse.) James 3:17 is a verse we will see often in these pages because so many of these traits are part of godly wisdom. Discernment is also necessary; being open to reason means you'll want to find the truth of a situation and the people involved.

Philippians 4:5 (ESV) says "Let your reasonableness be known to everyone. The Lord is at hand." Even in tough situations, in decisions where people are going to be unhappy with you or you know you'll be criticized, ask the Lord who is always beside you to give you a godly, discerning, reasonable fairness.

Father, in tough situations please help me to exercise godly discernment. Help me to deal with other people in a way that I would like to be treated. Lord, please help me to have wisdom from You to discern the truth for each situation. Amen.

DAY 3

For there is no difference between Jew and Gentile—the same Lord is Lord of all and richly blesses all who call on him.

—Romans 10:12

SCRIPTURE TELLS US THERE IS NO PARTIALITY WITH GOD. That's a wonderful gift, to know that God doesn't play favorites. Fairness values equality and treats everyone impartially. And if you noticed yesterday, the verse from James 3:17 says that godly wisdom is impartial. It does not show favoritism.

Favoritism might be the sneakiest enemy of fairness. We might strive to follow the rules, being honest and reasonable, but favoritism has a way of slipping in the back door when we aren't on our toes, and then it affects our thoughts and emotions and, ultimately, weakens our fairness. We don't like to call it *favoritism,* but let's be honest, some people are simply more likable than others, and other people know how to push all our buttons. And there can be that sly temptation to impress or please people who we think will help our career, our social status, or our personal goals. Our own desires can get in the way of fairness.

But God has made it very plain to us in His Word that there is no partiality with Him. With God, there is no Jew or Gentile, no slave or free, no male or female (Galatians 3:28). As his representative, I want to live that out in all my relationships as well, not only in business but in my personal life. Accountability relationships can help us detect this enemy of fairness.

If the Spirit is alerting you to any favoritism in your thoughts, ask His help in rooting it out.

Dear Jesus, I want to live a life that recognizes people as individuals. Help me to be alert to favoritism, and by the counsel of Your Holy Spirit, help me show no partiality to others in all areas of my life. Amen.

DAY 4

In everything, therefore, treat people the same way you want them to treat you, for this is the Law and the Prophets.

—Matthew 7:12 (NASB)

FAIRNESS IS ALL ABOUT HOW WE TREAT OTHERS. So much of the Scriptures address the ways in which we conduct ourselves in relationships. The simplest, most direct route to fairness is laid out by Jesus in what we've called the Golden Rule: Treat others in the way you want to be treated.

We want to be understood. We want to be heard. We want to be given consideration, grace, and respect. We want to be forgiven and given another chance. Jesus' guideline says that we are to give the same to others: understanding, hearing, consideration, grace, respect, and forgiveness.

Go back to the beginning of this section and read Paul Weaver's words on fairness. We are able to treat others with dignity and respect when we look deeper than the surface and see that we are all very much alike, underneath all the exterior barriers that might rise between us. Jesus did that. He looked right past labels like tax collector, fisherman, Roman, or adulteress, and saw people's hearts. He connected with their needs.

The world slaps all kinds of labels on people, and labels separate us. Jesus Christ sees one thing, hearts that He wants to call back to God or hearts that are already on their way home to God. I want to see others as Jesus sees and loves them, to treat them with dignity and respect and fairness.

Abba Father, You love all people and they are all precious in Your sight. Help me, Lord, to see other people through Your eyes. Help me, Holy Spirit, to treat them with dignity and respect at all times. Amen.

Day 5

But just as we have been approved by God to be entrusted with the gospel, so we speak, not to please man, but to please God who tests our hearts.

—1 Thessalonians 2:4 (ESV)

Our pursuit of fairness as leaders means there will be times we have to make tough decisions. People will sometimes be unhappy with us. What's that old saying? "You can please some of the people all of the time and you can please all of the people some of the time, but you can't please all of the people all of the time." That comes with the territory of being a leader.

Even with wisdom, discernment, and fairness, our decisions and choices won't always be popular. Sometimes, we'll even go against people who can have direct impact on our jobs or our businesses, like an unhappy customer or a frustrated superior.

In every decision, every day's thoughts and actions, whether small and generally unnoticed or huge, company-rattling decisions, we must always consider this: in the end, to whom am I accountable? Our ultimate loyalty cannot lie with any person on this earth. We serve Jesus Christ. We've been entrusted with His gospel, named His ambassadors to the world until He comes back to rule. Everything we do, we do as His representatives. That calling and purpose will guide us well in our leadership.

Jesus, You are the cornerstone of my life. Please help me to be Christ-like in all that I do, say, and think. Holy Spirit, through my life circumstances please help me represent You well. Amen.

DAY 6

His divine power has given us everything we need for a godly life . . . He has given us his very great and precious promises, so that through them you may participate in the divine nature, having escaped the corruption in the world caused by evil desires.

—2 Peter 1:3–4

YOU KNOW, FAIRNESS IS NOT ALWAYS GOING TO WORK IN YOUR FAVOR. At least, not in the world's eyes. Fairness is something we choose. We choose to put aside partiality and favoritism. We choose to give respect and understanding. We choose to treat them as we would want to be treated. But sometimes, that choice is difficult. Not only will the devil try to persuade us to act and think otherwise, but he may use people within our family or organization who actively resist fairness.

Treating others as Jesus did and loving as Jesus did doesn't always achieve the world's goals. Fairness, according to God's rules, doesn't always follow the "rules" of tough-minded, worldly business.

When you are staring at a tough situation, I encourage you to remember Peter's words: God has given us everything we need to live a godly life. His promises assure us of His help. Depend on His promises to help you, give you strength, guidance, wisdom, discernment, and everything else you need. Ask, Jesus said, and it will be given to you.

God has abundant resources for us that go beyond anything we can imagine. I encourage you to dive into those resources, my friend. He richly blesses all those who call on Him.

Son of God, You are my Way Maker. Be my portion of strength, guidance, wisdom, discernment, and everything that I need when I am facing a tough situation. Lord, please bless me so that I may be a blessing to others. Amen.

Steve Wingfield

DAY 7

For God wanted [his people] to know that the riches and glory of Christ are for you Gentiles, too. And this is the secret: Christ lives in you. This gives you assurance of sharing his glory.

—Colossians 1:27 (NLT)

As CHRIST'S FOLLOWERS, we have an advantage, not only in seeking fairness but in developing all these character traits. In Colossians 1, Paul calls this a "mystery" or a "secret" that God is now making known: Christ lives in us. "It is no longer I who live, but Christ lives in me" (Galatians 2:20). That is an amazing thing to claim, isn't it? But it's not only you or I claiming this. God's Word says this is so.

His Word also says that "we have the mind of Christ" (1 Corinthians 2:16). Now, this doesn't mean that we know everything that Jesus Christ knows. But it does mean that His Spirit guides us according to the mind of Christ. His spirit sets our sights on the realities of His kingdom and of heaven. He teaches us, reminds us of Jesus' words, opens our eyes to sin in our lives, and opens our ears to hear God's Word more clearly.

We are not operating solely on our own resources. We are thinking and acting and feeling by the power of the Spirit of Jesus Christ, and we have Him guiding our minds to be in alignment with His. God wants you to know the riches and glory of Christ's life in you.

Savior and Lord, fill my mind with Your thoughts. Help me to think and act in alignment with Your desires. You give me rest as I walk in obedience to You. Amen.

Notes and Prayers

_____

_____

_____

_____

_____

_____

_____

_____

_____

_____

_____

_____

_____

_____

_____

_____

_____

_____

_____

_____

_____

_____

Steve Wingfield

FLEXIBILITY

We should be the leaders we want our teams and families to emulate.

—Paul Weaver

DAY 1

Let us hold unswervingly to the hope we profess, for he who promised is faithful.
—Hebrews 10:23

FLEXIBILITY IS THE WILLINGNESS TO CHANGE OR COMPROMISE AS A SITUATION REQUIRES. Is this a desirable trait of representatives of Christ? Let us start out by thinking about the many Scriptures that tell us to stand firm, to hold onto our hope, to walk in the right path and never stray from it, to test each spirit, and to buckle the belt of truth around us like armor and let nothing move us. Does that sound inflexible to you?

To me, these words all tell me that we need to hold onto the truths of God's Word. Those are convictions. I have convictions I'm willing to die for. I pray that I would go to the death, even take a bullet, for my convictions, for those basic truths will never change, and we can never compromise on them. We need to hold unswervingly to these truths on which we've built all our hope.

Still, I believe a willingness to adapt, change, and compromise is a positive trait in leaders and representatives of Christ. While we hold steadfastly to the truth, let's also think about how and when and where God's Word also advises us to be flexible. I don't think that's a contradiction.

Give me, Lord, the same conviction You gave Your servant Jeremiah, so I will be able to endure reproach for Your sake and faith to say Your words were found and I ate them and Your words became for me a joy and the delight of my heart. Amen.

Prayers on FLEXIBILITY by Pete Lulusa.

Day 2

I have become all things to all people so that by all possible means I might save some. I do this all for the sake of the gospel, that I may share in its blessings.

—1 Corinthians 9:22–23

THE APOSTLE PAUL SAID HE BECAME ALL THINGS to all men so that by all possible means he could spread the message of the gospel, see people saved, and share in the blessings. It is urgent that we use every possible means to reach every possible person for Christ. This "becoming all things" is not license to descend into sinful behavior, but it is, as another translation (NLT) puts it, trying to find common ground to connect with others. We have got to connect first if we want people to open their ears to our message.

Paul also wrote that living peaceably and in harmony with each other will be part of our witness to the world. He created us all as unique individuals, physically, mentally, and spiritually. He designed us to be different. And as *different* parts work together, they create *one* healthy, functioning body. He designed us to be fluid as well as flexible. Whether it's in our evangelism to the world or living together in unity as the body of Christ, we'll often have to cut new channels in our thinking and our actions.

With humility I come before the throne of grave, and I ask that the power of your consuming fire to burn in me all that is sin. Fill me with love that I'll be able to love the lost for Your honor and glory. Amen.

Steve Wingfield

DAY 3

And Jesus said to them, "Follow me, and I will make you become fishers of men."
—Mark 1:17 (ESV)

IF YOU HAVEN'T ALREADY DISCOVERED THIS, following Jesus means you'll be going places you never imagined. I'm not saying that you'll be called to be a missionary in some remote country, but when we commit to following Jesus, we've got to be open to change. When Jesus called Simon Peter and Andrew one day as they were fishing, do you suppose they were expecting this or planned for it? Probably not. Still, "at once they left their nets and followed him." They certainly could not have known or even imagined the plans God had for them as fishers of men. That phrase probably puzzled them on the day Jesus extended His invitation, but they were decided on one thing: they were going to follow Jesus. And it changed their lives.

If you're going to be a follower of Christ, you'll have to develop flexibility, or fluidity. He may open doors you did not anticipate. He may lead you to serve in a way you never imagined. He has a plan and a purpose for you. Following Him will require you to cut some new channels.

We will have to be open to the unexpected and to change, but as we are, we can hold unswervingly to the truth of the promise that God will always lead us.

Lord Jesus, thank You for calling me to follow You. Thank You for this divine honor You, Lord, bestowed on those You call. You are not ashamed to call me Your brother and friend. Make me, Lord, a useful instrument for Your glory. Amen.

Day 4

And we all, with unveiled faces, beholding the glory of the Lord, are being trans-formed into the same image from one degree of glory to another. For this comes from the Lord who is the Spirit.

—2 Corinthians 3:18 (ESV)

An unwillingness to be flexible and to change may slow God's work in us. We have the promise in Philippians 1:6 that the good work He's begun in us He will carry on to completion. He is always working on us, changing us into His image. That is a promise we can hold onto. But we can be stubborn and resistant to His work within.

Scripture tells us God's plan is to change us. In Romans 12:2 we are told to let God transform us into new people. I want Him to bend me, shape me, in whatever way He wants to, so that I can be the person He wants me to be. Everything about the eternal life we've been given is about the *new* replacing the *old.* We live in a new kingdom, we have new hearts, new life, a new inheritance, new family, new power, new strength, new purpose, new minds, a new destiny. Everything about this life is new. Learning to live according to these new realities will require cutting new channels in our thinking, feeling, and acting.

We have got to be teachable, humble, and open to growth. God wants us to grow. It is His plan to move us "from one degree of glory to another." That is another promise we can hold onto, knowing He will keep His word.

Oh, sweet Jesus, I pray that I will always be looking for the blessed hope and the appearing of the glory of our great God and Savior Jesus Christ. Amen.

DAY 5

The LORD says, "I will guide you along the best pathway for your life. I will advise you and watch over you."

—Psalm 32:8 (NLT)

An unwillingness to be flexible can stop God's work through us. We have no better example than Simon Peter and God's command to him in Acts 10. Peter was a Jew and had lived according to the Jewish laws and traditions all of his life. He believed this was an essential way to live a godly life. As a matter of fact, he said to the Lord, "I have *never* eaten anything impure or unclean." But with a vision of many kinds of meats that He commanded Peter to eat, the Lord was teaching Peter that it was time to change some of his ideas. Notice the vision appeared to Peter *three times* before God felt Peter was ready to jump into His assignment to take the gospel to a Gentile household. Sometimes, it takes us awhile, too, but the Spirit is persistent.

Jesus was leading Peter somewhere Peter never expected to go. Fortunately, Peter got the message. He obeyed. His obedience opened the door to the gentiles, taking the gospel beyond the Jewish nation to the whole world.

God is always at work. Be prepared! Are you ready to obey when Jesus commands you to cut new channels?

O Lord, I came to ask You to forgive my hard and unwilling heart for not always trusting Your plans for my life. Put in me a steadfast obedience and fill me with Your Holy Spirit so I will have compassion for the lost and the needy. Amen.

Day 6

Blessed is everyone who fears the LORD, who walk in his ways!
—Psalm 128:1 (ESV)

WE'VE THOUGHT ABOUT HOLDING TIGHTLY AND STANDING FIRM. We've thought about letting go, changing, being flexible. How can we know which is appropriate in different situations? Psalm 119 opens with these words:

> *Blessed are those whose ways are blameless, who walk according to the law of the LORD. Blessed are those who keep his statutes and seek him with all their heart—they do no wrong but follow his ways. You have laid down precepts that are to be fully obeyed.*
> —Psalm 119:1–4.

I want my ways to be steadfast in obeying Him. I want to always walk in His ways. How can I be certain I'm doing that and still exhibit the flexibility necessary to reach out to the unsaved and to live in harmony with sisters and brothers in Christ? We need to ask for wisdom in knowing when to hold tight and when to release.

We have one key in those verses. We need to seek Him with all our heart. If we do, He will direct our steps. This is another promise to which we can hold firmly. A passage from Proverbs 8:33–34 tells me that God's wisdom is constantly increasing our good judgment, knowledge, and discernment. His wisdom will daily teach us.

Philippians 2:13 promises that God works in us "to will and to act in order to fulfill his good purpose." Stand firm in this truth. Ask for His wisdom, depend on the Spirit's teaching, and trust that He is working in you. When you ask wholeheartedly, He'll keep you on the right path.

Lord, I am trusting You. Show me where to walk, for I give myself to You.

(Inspired by Psalm 143:8 NLT)

Steve Wingfield

DAY 7

Let the message about Christ, in all its richness, fill your lives.

—Colossians 3:16 (NLT)

AS LEADERS WHO WANT TO REPRESENT CHRIST WELL, we want to be people of humility, welcoming input from others, open to growth and change, leaders who model the attitude, "Let's come together and make this happen." Scripture says, "Thanks be to God, who through us diffused the fragrance of his knowledge in every place" (2 Corinthians 2:14). This is the big picture, friends, our ultimate goal in whatever we are doing. This is our greatest purpose, to reflect the good news of Jesus Christ making us His people, changing us to be like Him, giving us new lives. The Apostle Paul wrote to the church at Thessalonica that "the word of the Lord is ringing out from you to people everywhere . . . for wherever we go we find people telling us about your faith in God" (1 Thessalonians 1:8).

Compare that to the words of God that Jeremiah delivered to Judah, a sad description of Judah's spiritual state: "But my people would not listen to me. They kept doing whatever they wanted, following the stubborn desires of their evil hearts. They went backward instead of forward" (Jeremiah 7:24). Stubbornness and refusal to live in Spirit-guided fluidity will result in the same—we'll go backward instead of forward—in our personal and spiritual lives and in our attempts to lead.

As a leader whose highest goal is to show Christ to the world, which of those descriptions do you want to describe your leadership?

I pray, Lord, that the beauty and the fragrance of Jesus Christ fill my heart to love You more every day. Give me, Lord, a soft and humble heart and stamp eternity on it. Amen.

Notes and Prayers

_____

_____

_____

_____

_____

_____

_____

_____

_____

_____

_____

_____

_____

_____

_____

_____

_____

_____

_____

_____

_____

_____

_____

FOCUS

Focus is the power to do great things with the available resources.
Think of your life not as a light that illuminates a small area with no impact,
but as a focused laser beam that has the energy to start fires.

—Paul Weaver

DAY 1

You will keep in perfect peace those whose minds are steadfast, because they trust in you.
—Isaiah 26:3

THE PASSION AND ZEAL TO BRING THE GOOD NEWS of Jesus Christ to all who will hear was nurtured in me by the mentorship of Dr. Elmer Towns. During a service at Liberty University, he encouraged students with these words:

> *See a vision, own a vision. See what God wants you to do, then own it.*
> *I do not want you to just have a dream. I want you to become the dream.*

Whatever the Lord commands you to do, that is your role in furthering the kingdom and leading people to Christ. This is focus: becoming the dream of what God wants you to do.

Focus is concentrated attention and energy. Focus is laser-intentional about what it wants to do. Those with focus echo the apostle Paul's words. He said, "This *one thing* I pursue," not "I dabble in forty things." There is the vision, the one thing above all else that directs choices, decisions about priorities, and allocation of resources.

For Christians, there is one all-embracing focus: the call of God on each one of our lives.

Lord, thank You for Your grace in my life. You have created me to make an impact in this world. May You give me the focus to not only do Your work, but to become Your work. Amen.

Prayers on FOCUS by Chris Johnson.

DAY 2

So we do not focus on what is seen, but on what is unseen. For what is seen is temporary, but what is unseen is eternal.

—2 Corinthians 4:18 (CSB)

THE BIBLE HAS A LOT TO SAY ABOUT FOCUS, and one of the first things we see is that we must train our focus on the correct realm. Colossians 3:3 tells us we have died and our lives are now hidden with Christ in God. Our earthly life has died with Christ. We've been raised to new life, a life in the eternal realm. So, "Set your minds on things above, not on earthly things" (Colossians 3:2).

This does not mean we don't pay attention to earthly things. We are carrying on Christ's mission, right here on earth, every hour of this day. But like focusing a camera or a telescope, we bring today into focus through the lens of the eternal. We make decisions and set priorities based on the values of Christ's kingdom. We strive to align our plans with the plans of the almighty Creator.

As we go about our daily lives, we seek first the kingdom of Christ. He promises that if His kingdom work is our priority, "all these things" will be provided for us.

We are already living our eternal lives as citizens of the unseen kingdom of heaven, and fifty billion years from now, that is where we will be living. Our work in that kingdom today will bring joy and fulfillment. Keep your focus there.

Lord, I repent for the times I got trapped in the temporal when You have called me to the eternal. Help me fix my eyes on You more than anything else this world has to offer. Amen.

DAY 3

But you, man of God, flee from all this, and pursue righteousness, godliness, faith, love, endurance and gentleness. Fight the good fight of faith. Take hold of the eternal life to which you were called.

—1 Timothy 6:11–12

SINCE OUR REAL LIVES ARE NO LONGER OF THIS WORLD, we are to get rid of the old nature: the evils of greed, selfishness, impurity, anger, and disobedience. We don't have to look very far to see that if our minds are set on the things of this world and operate as the world operates, we end up empty and in despair. Instead, we are to put on our new nature, born of the Holy Spirit, transforming us to be like Christ. Those who live according to the flesh set their focus on what the flesh desires; those who follow the Spirit have their focus on what the Spirit desires. Living according to the old nature is death. Living according to the Spirit is life and peace.

But we find, on a daily basis, that our focus wavers. We cannot depend on our good intentions alone to keep us on that path. The Spirit of God in us is our guide and our mentor. It is His power in us that makes the good fight possible and keeps our focus kingdom-sharp. Do not stifle His voice. Live in step with Him. He will keep your focus intense and clear.

Lord, help me to flee worldliness, to fight and focus on righteousness on a daily basis. As my focus attempts to waver, strengthen me to endure and fight the good fight. Amen.

Day 4

But as for you, continue in what you have learned and have become convinced of, because you know those from whom you learned it, and how from infancy you have known the Holy Scriptures which are able to make you wise for salvation through faith in Christ Jesus.

—2 Timothy 3:14–15

THE LETTERS TO TIMOTHY WERE WRITTEN TO A YOUNG MAN, words of wisdom offered by an older man reflecting back over his own life. Paul encourages the younger Timothy, who has most of his race still ahead of him, to continue in what he's been taught and have come to believe. Stay focused in your faith because you know those from whom you learned it.

Timothy learned from a faith-filled mother and a grandmother and from Paul himself (and doubtless others in the church). In our case, we can lean on other believers to help us keep our focus sharp. God has given His children a supernatural connection through the Spirit. It is a life-giving, life-guiding connection. Ephesians 4:12–14 tells us that we have been gifted to help each other grow up in our salvation and become more and more like Christ.

Continue, too, because you have the Holy Scriptures. In those Scriptures you will find what you need to live this eternal life. They contain wisdom for living out your salvation. Scripture will also be protection against the devil's lies, comfort and reassurance when you need it, and defense against discouragement. The Spirit uses the Scriptures and God's people to help us stay focused. Depend on both.

Father, I thank You for Your Word and Your Spirit that You have so graciously given to sustain and guide me in the way everlasting. Write Your word on my heart, and fill me with Your Spirit. Amen.

Steve Wingfield

Day 5

Therefore, holy brothers and sisters, who share in the heavenly calling, fix your thoughts on Jesus.

—Hebrews 3:1

WE MUST MAKE THE CHOICE TO LIVE IN CONSTANT RELATIONSHIP WITH OUR LORD AND KING. This will be the most important choice we make. Set your focus on Him. That focus then guides how you allocate your time, what values will guide your actions and words, and the goals you set for yourself.

It is powerful to say that I belong to the Lord and I want to grow and mature and be all that He wants me to be. But in order for it to happen, I have got to stay connected to Him, and stay focused on Him. The branch will wither and die if it is not connected to the Vine, drawing its life from the source of life.

This is the reason daily time alone with the Lord is so vital. Talking to Him constantly, praying about everything, telling Him what you need, and thanking Him for what He's done keeps you in touch and in peace. Reading His Word shapes your thinking, and the Spirit will use it to protect you in battles you will face each day. Keeping the vision of God's calling on your life in front of you, owning it, and then *becoming* it (as Dr. Towns said) keeps you holding tightly to the Vine for life.

Brothers and sisters, partners in Jesus' mission, called by God, keep your thoughts on Jesus. When your thoughts are focused on Him, your life will reflect His.

Lord Jesus, I surrender my heart, mind, and soul to You today. I ask that You transform me by renewing my mind, and reshaping my heart to desire You more. Amen.

DAY 6

No one can serve two masters. Either you will hate the one and love the other, or you will be devoted to one and despise the other.

—Matthew 6:24

THE DEVIL USES SO MANY THINGS TO DISTRACT US from our devotion to Christ and His mission. In Jesus' parable about the seed sown on different types of soil, He spoke of the thorny ground, where the Word is sown, but it is choked out by "the worries of this life, the deceitfulness of wealth and the desires for other things" (Mark 4:18–19). If we are not careful, our days become so busy, so full of the business of this world, that we lose our focus. Our focus is the business of our King and His kingdom! As we go about everything in our day, we are representing Him. That is our calling, the most important career we will ever have.

Stay alert. The enemy will lead us astray in any way he can. He'll tempt us to serve other masters. He'll distract us with things that take our focus off our calling and our devotion to our King. "The thief comes to steal and kill and destroy. I have come that they may have life, and have it to the full." (John 10:10). Seeking Christ's kingdom above all else, focusing on all of life through the eternal lens, will bring joy and fulfillment. Stay alert today!

Lord, help me to distinguish between Your voice and the voice of the enemy. I want to slow down long enough to focus on You. While the enemy seeks to steal, kill, and destroy, protect me and give me victory. Amen.

Steve Wingfield

Day 7

Let your eyes look straight ahead; fix your gaze directly before you. Give careful thought to the paths for your feet and be steadfast in all your ways. Do not turn to the right or the left; keep your foot from evil.

—Proverbs 4:25–27

THESE VERSES ARE A GOOD SUMMARY OF THE FOCUS WE WANT TO HAVE, MY FRIEND! Keep your eyes on the Lord, His calling on your life, and the vision of what He wants you to be. You are His representative in this world. You carry His name, are a citizen of His kingdom and a child of God. Keep your focus on His goals for you.

Give careful thought to the path you take. Be intentional about becoming the vision God has for you. Make choices that keep you connected to Him, that have eternal value, and that represent Him well. Don't go wandering off on other paths, no matter how strong the attraction. Don't look back, either. Eyes ahead. Eyes on the invisible.

And grow up. Pursue maturity in your discernment between good and evil. The enemy blurs those lines. Let the Spirit keep your vision sharp. Man or woman of God, pursue righteousness, godliness, faith, love, endurance, and gentleness. The more we mature in all of this, the more we will be showing Christ through our words and actions.

Fight the good fight of faith. Take hold of the eternal life to which you were called.

Lord Jesus, I am Your workmanship that You have destined to do good works. Help me to be faith-filled, faithful, and focused. Amen.

Notes and Prayers

_____

_____

_____

_____

_____

_____

_____

_____

_____

_____

_____

_____

_____

_____

_____

_____

_____

_____

_____

_____

FORGIVENESS

*The person who receives the biggest reward for forgiveness
is the person who does the forgiving.*

—Paul Weaver

DAY 1

*For if you forgive other people when they sin against you, your heavenly Father
will also forgive you.*

—Matthew 6:14

FORGIVENESS CLEARS THE RECORD OF WRONGS. That is what God has done
for us, and that is what we are to do for others. Just as God keeps on forgiving us when we stumble, we are to go on forgiving. Someone asked Jesus,
"How many times do I have to forgive him?" Have you asked that question,
too? The Jewish law required forgiving seven times. Even that might sound
excessive. "I forgave him once, but . . . six more times? Doesn't that make me
weak, a pushover?" That would be the world's response, wouldn't it? Jesus'
answer was emphatic, "No, not seven times. You forgive seventy times seven.
You just keep on forgiving." That makes forgiving a way of life.

One of the ways you might do this is by praying the Lord's Prayer every
day. I do. I pray it with my wife every day before I leave the house. Many
times I pray it in the morning before I get out of bed. Pray it reflectively,
carefully, thinking through the words you're saying.

Then live forgiveness. Make it a way of life.

*Lord, give me the strength to be like Jesus and forgive. And help me to remember
and take to heart that terrifying truth that if I do not forgive that person, neither
will You forgive me! Let me live in the freedom of forgiveness. Amen.*

Prayers on FORGIVENESS by John Schmid

Day 2

Blessed are the merciful, for they will be shown mercy.
—Matthew 5:7

FORGIVENESS, OR ITS OPPOSITE, holding a grudge and carrying bitterness and anger, will affect you even more than it does the person who has wronged you. Living in forgiveness will clear the road to healthier relationships, a healthier relationship with God, and a healthier *you*.

Those who don't forgive are the losers. Holding on to resentment, isolating oneself, and letting anger eat away at your life will destroy your peace. Forgive, let go of the wrongs in the past, and give people an opportunity to move forward. Forgiveness frees both you and the person who has offended you. Forgiveness frees us of all the destructive feelings surrounding the past: anger, tension, frustration, feelings of guilt and failure, and maybe even a desire for revenge. Those feelings on both sides of a situation can keep us in shackles. If we forgive, we make the decision to let go of those feelings. Forgiveness is a choice for freedom.

It's not just a one-time deal, because sometimes those feelings of loss and pain caused by someone else keep popping up. Forgiveness goes on and on, seventy times seven. We make the decision, again and again, to let go of the anger. And each time we make that decision, we strengthen the Spirit's influence in our lives—the Spirit's leading to live in forgiveness.

Lord, without Your mercy, I would be lost; condemned. Thank You for Your mercy. You and I both know that I don't deserve it. May I show that same mercy, not only for the other person, but so that I may be free of the bitterness that grows from festering unforgiveness and resentment. Lord, I want to be free. Amen.

Steve Wingfield

Day 3

Bear with each other and forgive one another if any of you has a grievance against someone. Forgive as the Lord forgave you.

—Colossians 3:13

C. S. Lewis wrote, "To be a Christian means to forgive the inexcusable, because God has forgiven the inexcusable in you." We all look at our lives and know that we do not have a clean record. We've said and done things we should never have said and done. We know that we haven't measured up to God's standard for living. We know that on any record of our lives, there would be plenty of black marks. Yet God's forgiveness cancels all records against us (Colossians 2:14). Christ took away that record and nailed it to the cross. He forgave all our sins. He no longer sees the inexcusable things we've said and done.

Have you come to Christ and asked Him to cancel the record against you? Have you realized the utter relief and joy and peace there is in knowing that you can go to God in confidence because He holds no record against you?

His forgiveness is complete, and once we know that we know this, we understand how forgiveness can transform a life and a relationship. We know because we have experienced it. We know what it means to be totally forgiven. The Lord canceled the record for us, so we must do it for others.

Thank You, Lord, that even though my sins and failures are many, my record in heaven is clear because of the precious blood of Christ and Your forgiveness. May I be one who "bears one another's burdens" and learn to live and get along with my neighbor, my brother, my family and with all of Your children. Amen.

DAY 4

And where the Spirit of the Lord is, there is freedom.

—2 Corinthians 3:17

FORGIVENESS IS HARD. It goes against everything in our sinful nature that is selfish, prideful, and wants revenge. The Holy Spirit guides us to forgive and let go of our record-keeping, but our sinful nature fights it. Maybe you are right in the middle of that struggle right now. You have been hurt, and you're still holding on to the pain, anger, or resentment. But Jesus has told us to keep on forgiving. And if He has told us to do it, then His Spirit living in us will also give us the strength and the will to do it. He will continue His work in us. If we keep our connection to the Vine strong, His life will flow into us.

An unforgiving spirit can hold us captive. It destroys relationships, shatters our peace, eats away at joy. But the Spirit of Jesus is stronger. In the struggle to forgive, the Spirit can free us from the chains of unforgiveness. When Jesus sets us free, we are truly free (John 8:36).

When we're in this hard battle, we can go to the Lord for help. We go in confidence because we're assured we will "find grace to help us in our time of need" (Hebrews 4:16).

Lord, I long for freedom. I am weary of the prison of unforgiveness. Give me the strength and the will to forgive the one who wronged me, not only to set him free, but to allow You to set me free. Remind me again, Lord, that if we are free in Christ (forgiven), we are free indeed! Amen.

Day 5

But I say, love your enemies! Pray for those who persecute you! In that way, you will be acting as true children of your Father in heaven.

—Matthew 5:44–45 (NLT)

WE'VE GIVEN THE WRONG TITLE to one of Jesus' most famous parables, the story of the Prodigal Son. We use that adjective *prodigal* to describe the son because of his wasteful, extravagant living. But the person in the story who was more importantly prodigal was the father.

The word *prodigal* also has a positive definition; it means profuse, lavish, yielding abundantly. That's what the father's forgiveness was, lavish and abundant. The son never expected to be welcomed back as a son. All he wanted was to live under his father's care as a servant. But his father opened his arms to his son, celebrated, and welcomed him back into his place as heir. That's prodigal forgiveness, my friend.

To the world, loving and forgiving abundantly as our Father does will look prodigal in the wasteful, foolish sense. Love our enemies? Pray for those who stand against us? Forgive those who have hurt us? The world would say, "Don't be a fool! You're insane and naïve to believe that!" Jesus says, "This is how true children of the Father will act."

Lord, like the prodigal son, I have wandered away from Your presence, from Your provision, Your protection, Your guidance. I wanted to run my own life and have my own way and now I see that I am headed for a life of living with pigs. I am no longer worthy to be called Your son. Father, I am coming home. I have wasted Your love. Thank You that Your forgiving arms are always open wide. Thank You that I have a place at Your abundant table. Amen.

DAY 6

And we all, who with unveiled faces contemplate the Lord's glory, are being transformed into his image with ever-increasing glory, which comes from the Lord, who is the Spirit.

—2 Corinthians 3:18

LIVING IN FORGIVENESS SHOWS OTHERS THE MERCY AND FORGIVENESS OF GOD. We are His children, and we are to imitate Him. For some, the only way that the forgiveness of God becomes real is when they see it imitated and repeated in human relationships.

After Moses had met with God on Mount Sinai, he came down from the mountain and his face glowed with God's glory so brightly that the people were afraid to look at him. "His face was radiant because he had spoken with the LORD" (Exodus 34:29). Do our faces, the lives put before the people we live with every day, reflect God's glory? Can they see that we've been with Jesus, that we've spoken with the Lord? Can they see a "family resemblance" between us and the heavenly Father?

Part of the Spirit's work in our lives is to accomplish a transformation, a fundamental change from *me* into *Him.* My forgiveness and mercy show others the character of my Father.

Leaders have a unique position from which to point people to the love and forgiveness of God when they practice the forgiveness that only the Spirit of Christ makes possible. We don't forgive to build up our own reputation and bring ourselves glory. We forgive to bring God the glory.

Lord, may my life shine in such a way that people will see how I live and glorify You in heaven. May I be such an example of "Christ-likeness" that people will be drawn to You. May I reflect Your glory. Amen.

Day 7

And whatever you do or say, do it as a representative of the Lord Jesus, giving thanks through him to God the Father.

—Colossians 3:17 (NLT)

WE WANT TO REPRESENT CHRIST WELL not only in what we say and do but also in who we are. The principles we will focus on throughout the Lodestar study are essential to leadership; and when God's Spirit empowers us through these traits, we are even more effective as His representative, carrying on His work and mission.

Many of these principles go hand-in-hand. For example, forgiveness requires compassion and humility. It is interesting that in the story of the Prodigal Son, the one thing we know of the father's character besides his extravagant forgiveness is that "he was filled with compassion" for his son (Luke 15:20). Compassion and forgiveness. It is hard to have one without the other.

All of these qualities are strengthened and taken to a new level when they are infused by the Holy Spirit's power. That is my prayer for us all as we go through this study, my friends, that He will be transforming us every day as we strive to become more and more of who He wants us to be.

Lord, transform me into the likeness of Christ. May I forgive and love and trust so much that I will reflect Your glory. Give me the power and freedom that comes from a life of forgiveness and compassion. May I love You and my fellow man with the love of Jesus. I praise you, Father! Amen.

Notes and Prayers

_____

_____

_____

_____

_____

_____

_____

_____

_____

_____

_____

_____

_____

_____

_____

_____

_____

_____

_____

_____

Steve Wingfield

GENEROSITY

Whatever we desire more of, we must give away.

—Paul Weaver

DAY 1

And I am praying that you will put into action the generosity that comes from your faith as you understand and experience all the good things we have in Christ.

—Philemon 1:6 (NLT)

GOD CREATED US TO GIVE. The sun gives light by day. The moon and stars give light by night. The Lord sends rain to water the earth and bring nourishment. Plants grow, then they decay and bring more nourishment to the earth, giving even in death. It's a cycle. Everything gives.

Billy Graham said that "God has given us two hands, one to receive with and the other to give with. We are not cisterns made for hoarding; we are channels made for sharing."

For those who are in Christ, though, that old is gone, the new creation has come. And in the new life He gives us, the Holy Spirit works at cleaning out that self-centeredness that keeps generosity from flowing freely. God's Spirit is at work, making us into what we were meant to be at the very beginning—God's children, from whom a river of love and kindness and goodness flows, as it does from God the Father who is so rich in love and kindness. Let the Spirit guide you into living generously.

As your river of generosity flows so freely to me to bring me a life of freedom and hope, Lord, let generosity flow through me and from me to others. The greatest gift You've given is the same one You've charged me to pass along, the Good News of life in Your Son, Jesus. Let love flow through me to others this day in Jesus' name. Amen!

Prayers on GENEROSITY by Andrew Palau.

Day 2

You will be enriched in every way so that you can be generous on every occasion, and through us your generosity will result in thanksgiving to God.

—2 Corinthians 9:11

WHATEVER RESOURCES GOD HAS GIVEN YOU He has given so that you can be generous in helping and serving others. It may be money and the ability to make money. I couldn't do what I do without friends whom God has blessed with this ability, and they are using that wealth to advance His kingdom. It may be giftedness in any area: administration, hospitality, artistic design, mechanical expertise, cooking, nurturing children, the gift of a green thumb, the ability to paint or capture a message in a photograph. Time is a gift, perhaps the most precious thing anyone can give—once given, it can never be replenished. In whatever way the Lord has made you rich, He's given you that resource to use generously to benefit others. Our Lord reminds us that it might even be just a bottle of cold water that you hand to someone else instead of drinking it yourself on a sweltering day.

Think about what the Lord has put into your hands, and ask the Spirit to show you ways you can be generous "on every occasion."

Lord, You have told me I am "fearfully and wonderfully made." You made me; You've given me gifts from which to give from. Help me understand how You have made me and the gifts special to me from which I can encourage and enrich others. One thing I know I can do is ask You to replace any cynical word and thought with a life-giving word to lift up spirits and encourage those around me. Use me today, God! Amen.

Day 3

Give, and you will receive. Your gift will return to you in full—pressed down, shaken together to make room for more, running over, and poured into your lap. The amount you give will determine the amount you get back.

—Luke 6:38 (NLT)

Jesus said, "It is more blessed to give than to receive" (Acts 20:35). Whether we're giving of our time, our talents, or our money, the joy that comes when we give is at times overwhelming. You might think you're blessing someone else (and you are) but, in fact, many times you will be the recipient of even greater blessing. I have found that to be absolutely true in my life. God's economy is different than our economy. It may not seem logical or make practical sense according to the world's thinking, but it makes spiritual sense. God says, *Give, and it will be given to you.*

We don't give to get, though. We are missing the point if that is why we give. That's motivated by selfishness. Generosity is a selfless way of living that gives out of a heart of love and gratitude. It is a way of life of stewarding what God has given us, letting everything flow through us to benefit others.

God's Word teaches us to be givers. The happiest people I know are givers. God's design for a full, free, joyful life includes living generously.

Heavenly Father, thank You! I am so grateful for Your wonderful provision. I can remember people You've sent into my life over the years who have helped me and given with no expectation of return. Bless them and make me more like them. Would You give me something this day that was specifically meant for me not to keep, but to pass along? Amen.

Day 4

And God will generously provide all you need. Then you will always have every-thing you need and plenty left over to share with others.

—2 Corinthians 9:8 (NLT)

IN HIS LETTER TO THE CORINTHIANS, Paul assures us that God will always provide, and generously. He'll give us plenty so that we can have the added joy of sharing with others.

My dad lived a generous life, and I saw it modeled early on. We were walking down Main Street one day. I was only four or five. It seemed every-one knew and greeted my dad. One man approached and asked Dad for money for a cup of coffee. My dad took out his wallet and looked in it; it was empty. He took out the change purse he carried and dumped out the contents, just two dimes and a wooden round tuit. We three walked into a hamburger joint, and Dad put those two dimes on the counter and said, "Give my buddy a cup of coffee." Then he turned to the man and addressed him by name. "You don't have to live this way. God's got a plan for your life, and he can help you get over this alcoholism."

I was thinking, "*Man, my dad's giving all our money away!*" But when we two were back outside, we had walked no more than ten steps before Dad bent over, reached down, and picked up a dollar bill lying on the sidewalk. No one else was around, so we had no way of knowing who it might belong to. Dad put it in his pocket and said, "Son, remember: you can never outgive God."

God will provide. Not only in dimes and dollars, but in all forms of gifts of grace. Be generous. You'll find He will always be outgiving you.

Lord, give me eyes to see the opportunities around me. Soften my heart and embolden my spirit to know what to do and do it. Fill my heart with understanding of Your provision and a gratitude for it, that I would be known for kind-hearted generosity. I want to have a reputation, especially in the eyes of my children and family, as one who trusts in You and acknowledges that every good gift is from You! Help me in this, Lord. Amen!

Steve Wingfield

DAY 5

"Sell your possessions and give to those in need. This will store up treasure for you in heaven! And the purses of heaven never get old or develop holes. Your treasure will be safe; no thief can steal it and no moth can destroy it."
—Luke 12:33 (NLT)

THE EARTHLY THINGS OF THIS WORLD ARE JUST THAT—OF THIS WORLD. They'll stay here when we move to heaven. The only thing we're going to take with us is someone else. You've heard this said before: You'll never see a U-Haul behind a hearse. We're going to leave it here. We can't take it with us.

The best investment we can make for our future—a future that goes on long after the few short years we may still have here—is investment in people, that they might get to heaven, too. I don't say that just because I'm an evangelist. This should be a way of life for all of us, the one thing we devote our lives to. It's our calling as followers of Christ. We share His mission.

Jesus said when we tend first to His kingdom's work, then all the necessary things we need for this earthly life will be given to us. Focus on the kingdom, He said, and let your heavenly Father take care of the rest.

I am not of this world. Heaven is my home! This life, You have told me, is like a vapor, then I'll have all of eternity in that place—no sorrow, tears, lacking, wanting, pain, or jealous striving. I want to live like that now, practicing for those days, today. Help me, Lord, to do it! Amen.

Day 6

They even did more than we had hoped, for their first action was to give themselves to the Lord and to us, just as God wanted them to do.

—2 Corinthians 8:5 (NLT)

WHAT GENEROSITY IS NOT: IT IS NOT RULES ABOUT "HOW MUCH." There is one law at work, and that is the law of sowing and reaping. Sowing sparingly will give a sparse harvest. Sowing generously will result in an abundant harvest.

C. S. Lewis, one of my favorite writers, wrote that "I am afraid the only safe rule is to give more than we can spare." If we think about what we "can spare," then our self-centeredness immediately steps in and begins its arguments for itself. But if we give beyond that, we defeat selfishness. Then we are giving not just our resources but all of ourselves and our lives into His hands.

The words of the old hymn "Take My Life and Let It Be" express this giving of ourselves to the Lord. We give Him everything we are and have, consecrated to Him. Our time, our hands, our feet, our voices, our minds, our wills, our hearts, and our money.

Take my love; my Lord, I pour
At Thy feet its treasure-store
Take myself, and I will be
Ever, only, all for Thee,
Ever, only, all for Thee.

When this becomes our prayer, generosity—pouring ourselves into others—is not just a trait. It is our life.

God, help me to put others before myself, to stretch myself to serve more than looking for service. Give me patience, a peaceful spirit, and kind words to deposit in others, like I'd put money in a bank, knowing it will be safe and productive in there, more than if squirreled away. Amen.

Steve Wingfield

Day 7

And we have received God's Spirit (not the world's spirit), so we can know the wonderful things God has freely given us.

—1 Corinthians 2:12 (NLT)

As we wrap up our time thinking about generosity, let's take a day to rejoice in the amazing generosity that God has shown toward us. Scripture tells us that as the world wandered further and further away from God, He regretted even creating humankind. It broke His heart to see the evil in the world. Now, it's hard to imagine that God had such regrets, knowing how much He loves us. But He did.

Instead of abandoning or destroying us, though, His kindness and love created a way to rebuild our relationship to Him. Nothing we could do could achieve that. But He provided a way, and with the way, He gave us life—the life He intended at the beginning.

God wants us to know Him. He doesn't leave us alone to somehow work our way through the tangles of this life. He walks with us, supplying what we need from His vast stores. He goes beyond our basic needs. He blesses abundantly with good gifts that add joy to our journeys.

Today, no matter what is going on in life around you, focus on the wonderful generosity God has shown to you. Thank Him for it. Rejoice in it. Continue to learn how to live generously, in gratitude to our heavenly Father, and with a desire to grow into His character.

Oh, God, thank You for offering me this free gift of life. Free to me, costing everything to You. I receive it with tears of gratitude. Gracious heavenly Father, thank You! Now use me to spread the word of that gift available to all who'd receive it. Amen!

Notes and Prayers

_____

_____

_____

_____

_____

_____

_____

_____

_____

_____

_____

_____

_____

_____

_____

_____

_____

Steve Wingfield

GRATEFULNESS

Gratitude changes the mundane things in life into something special.
—Paul Weaver

DAY 1

Gracious words are a honeycomb, sweet to the soul and healing to the body.
—Proverbs 16:24

LIVING WITH GRATEFULNESS CHANGES THE ATMOSPHERE. People who breathe this atmosphere look for the positive. They won't give in to defeat. They'll build each other up and encourage each other and tackle obstacles that come up. An atmosphere of gratefulness fosters productivity, growth, kindness, compassion, and a host of the other Lodestar traits in your team.

Expressing your appreciation also has an effect on you. Psychological studies of groups have shown that gratefulness is good for your mind and your body. It improves physical and psychological health and reduces stress. One study even concluded that you'll sleep better if you practice gratefulness. It also supports and enhances other desirable character traits. The words you speak reinforce whatever is growing within your mind and heart. Gratitude goes hand-in-hand with humility; it thrives on a positive attitude, and a positive attitude in turn is strengthened by gratitude; it makes us more generous; it encourages growth and kindness and empathy. It certainly makes us more likable. We all prefer to be around a positive person rather than one who wears a gloomy, negative shroud.

Express your gratitude. It doesn't always have to be a spoken word; it could be a written word. But our gratefulness needs to be expressed.

May I always remember that I am not a self-made individual, but rather I am the product of many lives who have joined me in my journey. I bless You, Lord, for each one of them today. In Jesus' name. Amen.

Prayers on GRATEFULNESS by Pastor Jim Harrison.

Day 2

It is good to give thanks to the LORD, to sing praises to your name, O Most High, to declare your steadfast love in the morning, and your faithfulness at night.

—Psalm 92:1–2 (ESV)

GRATEFULNESS NOT ONLY ENHANCES OUR LEADERSHIP and our interpersonal relationships, it strengthens our relationship with the Lord, the most essential relationship of all. David, writer of so many worship and praise songs, knew the power of expressing gratefulness to our Lord. Psalm 92 opens with the affirmation that it is simply good to be grateful and express your thanks. Then it goes on to tells us how to develop the habit of gratefulness; bookend the day with giving thanks.

In the morning, declare your trust in God's steadfast love. He is your shepherd, the Great Shepherd. He'll provide what you need, stand with you in every situation, guide your thinking, and keep you in His hands. Remember how much He loves you and the promises He's made to you. Then go forward into the day's journey.

In the evening, give Him thanks for His faithfulness to you through every step of the day. Recall how He has been faithful to His promises that day. Remember, and be grateful for the gifts of love He sent—those small things in your day that are gifts from His heart to yours, as Ann Voskamp calls the ordinary, wonderful gifts. Be specific in your thanks.

Lord, we thank You that this is the day that You have made, and we choose to rejoice and are glad because of it. May we be reminded this day of Your power and presence at work in us as we get out of our beds and sing from our hearts in the morning. When I rise, give me Jesus. Amen.

Day 3

Rejoice always, pray continually, give thanks in all circumstances; for this is God's will for you in Christ Jesus.
—1 Thessalonians 5:16–18

Today, memorize three Scripture verses. It won't take long. They're some of the shortest in the Bible. The first two verses are only two words each.

> *Rejoice always* (1 Thessalonians 5:16).
>
> *Pray continually* (1 Thessalonians 5:17).

Verse 18 is a little longer, but commit it to memory too: *Give thanks in all circumstances*. In all circumstances. Yeah, we'll have hard times and tough circumstances, but we are to live with grateful hearts. That doesn't leave any room for complaints, whining, excuses, envy, or playing the victim.

Rejoice. Pray. Give thanks.

Why? Because this is the will of God for us who are in Christ Jesus. This is how He wants us to think and feel and live (because gratefulness is a matter of thinking and feeling and living). Could He be any clearer than that? Sometimes people ask what God's will is; they think the Bible is ambiguous or vague about it. Not here, not in these verses. This is God's will that our lives are saturated with gratefulness. Talk about keeping our attitude in line, we're keeping it in line with God's will.

So, we've got those three verses memorized, right? Rejoice always, pray continually, give thanks in all circumstances, because this is God's will for us. Now, let's go live it.

Lord, in the circumstances of life, help me to realize that You are a sovereign God, that You can be trusted, and that You have invited me to call upon You. You are great and worthy to be praised. Amen.

Day 4

Whatever is good and perfect is a gift coming down to us from God, our Father.
—James 1:17 (NLT)

"A GRATEFUL HEART IS A MAGNET FOR MIRACLES." I read that quote some-where. And don't we all have times when a miracle would be just grand? But are we grateful for all the seemingly small things in every day of our lives? For example, clean water. All we need to do is open the tap or flip open a cap. We don't walk miles to fill water jugs. We can have a long, hot shower almost any time we want. Or sunshine on a day when you need an energy boost. Or that phone call from a friend you haven't talked with for years. Or a beautiful new snow. Or a word of appreciation from someone who didn't even know you were struggling with discouragement. A few minutes for a nap. Your favorite worship song on the radio as you drive to work. A whisper from the Spirit to remind you that God is right there with you.

Yes, sometimes a miracle dazzles us. But don't miss all the small gifts God gives you every day. Dietrich Bonhoeffer wrote, "We pray for the big things and forget to give thanks for the ordinary, small (and yet really not small) gifts. How can God entrust great things to one who will not thank-fully receive from him the little things?"

If a sparrow cannot fall to the ground and a cup of cold water does not go unnoticed, may I always remember, You love me and You are watching over me and You have promised never to leave me. Lord, I am grateful. Amen.

Day 5

Then we your people, the sheep of your pasture, will praise you forever; from generation to generation we will proclaim your praise.

—Psalm 79:13

LIVING IN GRATEFULNESS IS NOT A MATTER OF RECEIVING AN ABUNDANCE OF BLESSINGS. It is a matter of perspective and choice. Hearts and minds that have chosen to live with gratitude look at the goodness in their lives, not at lack or want or shortcomings.

There is so much I'm thankful for: God's goodness, His provision, His blessing. To know I've been forgiven, that my sins have been taken away, that He has gone to prepare a place for me and I'm going to live with Christ forever—what joy that brings, regardless of what's going on in my life. He loves me with an everlasting love and nothing can change that.

Read Psalm 23 slowly and thoughtfully and realize how that is true in your life. The Lord is your Shepherd. His eye is always on you, and His care is constant. Your Shepherd is humble and gentle, and He invited you to learn from Him and lean on Him. And He is sitting at the right hand of God, making intercession for you.

Living with a heart full of gratitude is a wonderful, joyful way to live. Don't let the devil steal that from you; he would like to destroy it and darken your life. But let us, the people who live in the care of the Great Shepherd, praise Him forever and live out the fullness of gratefulness that overflows from our hearts.

Lord Jesus, thank You for a prepared table and a cup that is overflowing. Help me to be content with the things that You provide and in the circumstances I find myself in. Give me a thankful heart. Amen.

Steve Wingfield   Guiding Principles 163

Day 6

And let them offer sacrifices of thanksgiving, and tell of his deeds in songs of joy!
—Psalm 107:22 (ESV)

PSALM 107 IS A WONDERFUL PSALM. It sings of the Lord's goodness, His faithful love, and His rescue of us all, from all kinds of dangers and stormy, desperate lives. When people call for help, the Lord answers them and saves them. "Has the Lord redeemed you?" the writer asks. "Then speak out and tell others!" Express your gratitude. Bring that sacrifice to Him, your Savior and King.

Those who are saved, who come to Jesus, become part of His spiritual temple here on earth, wrote Peter. The temple, where God dwells, is now His people. And we "offer spiritual sacrifices that please God" (1 Peter 2:5 NLT). The old system of sacrificing animals, birds, and grain on the altar of the tabernacle or temple is now a spiritual act of offering up our sacrifices to Him. One of those sacrifices is thanksgiving. "Through Jesus, therefore, let us continually offer to God a sacrifice of praise—the fruit of lips that openly profess his name" (Hebrews 13:15).

Our gratefulness is entry into worship. We enter His gates with thanksgiving and His courts with praise. Has He redeemed you? Then speak out in gratitude. Worship Him with the sacrifices of a grateful heart today.

Lord, thank You for the blood of the cross, the ground upon which we are saved. Thank You for redeeming me from my past and myself, may I ever praise and serve You. To the glory of Your name. Amen.

Steve Wingfield

Day 7

Do not be anxious about anything, but in everything, by prayer and petition, with thanksgiving, present your requests to God. And the peace of God, which transcends all understanding, will guard your hearts and your minds in Christ Jesus.

—Philippians 4:6–7

When we choose to focus on the goodness God showers on our lives, we know a joy and contentment that protects us from falling into pits of envy, comparison, jealousy, and self-pity. Instead, we are grateful because we know how blessed we are to be in His care. Gratefulness overflowing from our hearts pours out into the lives of others and changes their world, too. It also pours into our worship and our relationship with our Father. Gratefulness affects every aspect of our lives and the lives we touch.

In Philippians 4, we see one more result of living with a heart of gratefulness: peace of mind and heart. This peace comes when we depend entirely on God and go to Him with our requests and our gratefulness for what he has done, is doing, and will do. We'll see all our circumstances through that lens of gratitude.

If you're longing for peace of heart and mind, gratefulness is essential. Prayer well-seasoned with thankfulness brings a peace beyond worldly understanding. Then it is God's peace guarding our hearts and minds. The grateful heart and mind have a strong defense against worry and despair—the peace of God.

Out of gratitude for all that You have done for us, may we present our lives back to You as a living offering, a sacrifice that is holy and acceptable to You. Change us so that we might be like You, not like the world, but like You. In Jesus' name. Amen.

Notes and Prayers

_____

_____

_____

_____

_____

_____

_____

_____

_____

_____

_____

_____

_____

_____

_____

_____

_____

_____

_____

Steve Wingfield

HONESTY

Be courageous, and do the right thing. Remember that nine times out of ten,
the right thing will not be the popular thing to do. Do it anyway.

—Paul Weaver

DAY 1

That you may be blameless and innocent, children of God without blemish in
the midst of a crooked and twisted generation, among whom you shine as lights
in the world.

—Philippians 2:15 (ESV)

OUR HONESTY—OR OUR COMPROMISE OF HONESTY—tells the world about
the One we represent. We carry his name. It's a sad day when we hear,
"If that's the way a Christian lives, I want nothing to do with Christ or
Christianity."

No one can argue with the description in Philippians 2:15 of the world,
"a crooked and twisted generation." That was the world back in Paul's day,
and it is our world today. Many people would never call themselves "dishonest," but they will fudge a bit on the facts here and there, if it's to their
advantage. Or they will take advantage in a business deal, if an opportunity
presents itself. Or they present themselves as someone they are not, in order
to make a good impression or get what they want from another person.

As we think about living honestly, ask the Lord to show you any areas
in which you might not be as honest as possible and to give you the courage
to change.

Lord, give me the courage to always walk in truth by the power of Your Holy
Spirit and to shine as a light in this dark world. Forgive me when I have failed
to call on You, the giver of my strength, for You, Jesus, are the Way, the Truth and
the Light. Amen.

Prayers on HONESTY by Vicki Greene.

Day 2

LORD, who may dwell in your sacred tent? Who may live on your holy mountain? The one whose walk is blameless, who does what is righteous, who speaks the truth from their heart.

—Psalm 15:1–2

PEOPLE WHO LIVE WITH HONESTY ARE OFTEN SWIMMING UPSTREAM. It takes courage to live upright, truthful, and open lives. Courage, feeling the fear but doing the right thing anyway, no matter the cost or difficulty. It is our Great Shepherd who guides us into living upright, truthful, and open lives. Such living brings the freedom of truth, God's approval, respect and trust in relationships, a clear conscience, and peace.

One of the most precious benefits of honesty is that it protects your relationship with the Lord. Psalm 140:13 says "the upright will live in your presence." Psalm 11:7, "the upright will see his face." When we tolerate dishonesty in ourselves, it is difficult to live in His presence and see His face. We try to hide parts of our lives and hearts from Him. That's impossible, of course, but our sin cuts us off from the joy of His presence. That is something I cannot live without, the joy and peace of living in His presence. I want the life another psalm describes, planted in the Lord's own house and flourishing in the courts of our God (Psalm 92:13).

Lord Jesus, teach me to follow in Your ways, always seeking after Your approval, not that of man. May I be content to dwell in Your presence. You, oh Lord, are where my strength comes from. May I always be pleasing to You. Grow me in Your ways, oh Lord, as I seek after Your face, that I may live in the light of eternity not this temporal life. In Jesus' name. Amen.

Steve Wingfield

DAY 3

The integrity of the upright guides them, but the crookedness of the treacherous destroys them.

—Proverbs 11:3 (ESV)

LIVING IN HONESTY COVERS MORE THAN SPEAKING THE TRUTH. Our Lodestar definition includes "being upright" and "open in communication." *Upright* meant "straight and right." It is contrasted by someone who walks crookedly, deceitfully, and wrongly. Walking uprightly is walking in the right way, shunning evil, doing no wrong. It's living in such a way that we do not have to hide or cover up anything.

Speaking truthfully is a part of living uprightly. Job vowed that as long as he had breath his lips would speak no evil, and his tongue would speak no lies (Job 27:3–4).

The upright are guided by their integrity. They stay on the straight path, not darting off here and there on shadowy paths that lead away from the Lord and His will. Let integrity and honesty guide you. If you want to be built up and be everything you can be, let the Scripture and the power of the Holy Spirit be the directing, empowering force in your life, and He will direct you. "The way of the Lord is a refuge for those with integrity; they will never be uprooted" (Proverbs 10:29–30, paraphrased).

God, teach me to be an example of one who walks in integrity. May it be said of me "they knew God and walked with him." May no evil talk come off my lips. Give me discernment, and learn to shun any evil that would come my way, so that You may be glorified by my life. Forgive me, Lord, when I have failed and caused anyone to stumble because of my disobedience to You. Thank You Lord, for loving me and forgiving all my sin and wicked ways. Amen.

DAY 4

Therefore each of you must put off falsehood and speak truthfully to your neighbor, for we are all members of one body.

—Ephesians 4:25

GOD HATES LYING AND UNTRUTHS. He tells us that bluntly and repeatedly. One of the gifts of grace God has given us is the community of believers, but we miss out on the blessings of that community if we do not live openly and honestly with each other. Lying is part of the old man, and you're done with that.

All of humanity is broken. That is why 1 John 1:9 was written for us, so we can get back on the right track. It's also why God gave us that Spirit-connection with other believers so that we can help each other, encourage each other, and build each other up. We need to be honest about what's going on in our lives, otherwise, we've cut ourselves off from the benefits of the community of Christ.

There are those who speak the truth but say it in such a way that it's hurtful. My dad taught me you catch a lot more flies with honey than you do with vinegar. Learn to speak the truth in love. Be compassionate with your honesty. Be loving. Love does not harm; it does not tear down but builds up. To find the joy of belonging to the body of Christ, live honestly and openly.

Reveal to me Your truth, Lord, and convict me of my self-righteousness, so I may bring glory to You. May I be a beneficial part of the body of Christ by my words and deeds. Thank You, Lord Jesus, that I can be part of the body of Christ, serving one another in Your name. Amen.

Steve Wingfield

DAY 5

Lying lips are an abomination to the LORD, but those who act faithfully are his delight.

—Proverbs 12:22 (ESV)

C. S. LEWIS SAID THAT INTEGRITY IS DOING THE RIGHT THING even when no one is watching. Integrity *will* do the right thing, but we've got to remember that there is never a time when no one is watching. God sees everything, all the time, and He is the one who matters most. We are accountable to Him for everything we do.

Let me encourage you again to find an accountability group that will walk beside you in your walk with the Lord. You can't be close friends with everyone, but you need a group around you who will have your back, where you can be honest and say, "I'm struggling in this area." Meeting regularly, being honest and open with each other, and encouraging and building each other up will help you walk uprightly. Your accountability partners will help you be honest as you examine your motives and attitudes. They'll help you review your actions honestly.

Your best accountability partner is the Holy Spirit. Ask Him to examine you and see where you need to confess and be cleansed. Ask Him to show you how to walk straighter along the right paths. Be open in your communication with Him. Ask Him to show you what you've been hiding from yourself. It is my heart's desire that my Lord will be delighted with what He sees in my life. I hope that is your desire, too.

Lord, may I live with the awareness that You are always watching and always listening. At the end of my journey here on earth I want to hear You say to me, "Well done good and faithful servant." Amen.

DAY 6

Finally, brothers and sisters, whatever is true, whatever is noble, whatever is right, whatever is pure, whatever is lovely, whatever is admirable—if anything is excellent or praiseworthy, think about such things.

—Philippians 4:8

WHAT WE LET INTO OUR MINDS CAN QUICKLY TAKE ROOT, grow, and invade the heart like a weed—even when we do not want it to grow there. We need to guard our eyes and ears, the gates of our mind. This includes being wise about the company we keep. Proverbs 22:25 warns that we "may learn the ways" of our friends; they have an influence on our minds. Diligently guarding the mind guards the heart, and everything that flows out of the heart.

Read through the list of *whatevers* on which we should focus our thoughts. Each one has a relationship to honest and upright living.

As leaders, we lead the way in building the culture of our organization or team. Focusing on what is true, noble, right, pure, lovely, and admirable creates the kind of environment you want. A leader who lies, is secretive and manipulative, and will be dishonest to reach goals, will soon find that team members are distrustful and may adopt the same behaviors. One of our goals must be to guard the environment of those we lead.

Lord Jesus, help me to keep my eyes fixed on You, the perfecter of my faith. Let my eyes not wander from Your guidance. Keep my heart and mind focused on You and Your ways. Teach me daily to walk in Your path. You are the hand that guides me. May I trust in You and You alone. Amen.

Steve Wingfield

DAY 7

For the eyes of the Lord are on the righteous and his ears are attentive to their prayer, but the face of the Lord is against those who do evil.

—1 Peter 3:12

SCRIPTURES SAY GOD CANNOT LIE; IT IS NOT IN HIS CHARACTER. We are His children, created to be like Him. Dishonesty should have no place in our character, either. Jesus called Satan a liar and the father of lies. Our lineage is through our heavenly Father. We are part of His new creation, where lies will have no place.

For many, pursuing honest living may be the most difficult battle of all, as the old self attempts to live in the old way—using a bit of deceit when it's to your advantage, protecting your ego when you don't want others to know the truth, cheating "just a little" on your taxes, or presenting a false image of who you really are. That's what goes on in the world around us all the time. The temptations to live the same way are sly and strong and start small. We must make decisions every day to live uprightly in all the small ways. Otherwise, those "small" dishonesties eat away at our integrity, like tiny moths chewing holes in cloth and destroying it.

The eyes of the Lord are on the righteous; He hears their prayers. He is there to help you and give you strength in every battle against every temptation. God bless you as you stand firm in His power.

May only truth come from my lips and may no lies be found coming from my mouth. Hear my cry for forgiveness as I seek to walk uprightly before You, Jesus. Amen.

Notes and Prayers

HUMILITY

Pride is the enemy of all that is good.

—Paul Weaver

DAY 1

But Jesus called them together and said, "You know that rulers in this world lord it over their people, and officials flaunt their authority over those under them. But among you it will be different. Whoever wants to be a leader among you must be your servant."

—Matthew 20:25–26 (NLT)

JESUS AND ALL OF SCRIPTURE IS CLEAR—pride will only be damaging to us and to our lives. The Bible gives us strong warnings against pride and great promises for humility. Those who are in leadership positions are especially warned to live with humility and be on guard against pride.

Humility is not forcing yourself to do something because you must. Oh, you might grit your teeth and act in a way you think a humble person *should* act, but the real inner man always shows through. Humility is a mind-set and a condition of the heart. So is pride. As we look into the Scriptures this week, ask the Spirit to transform your heart and mind in whatever areas He finds pride and an absence of humility. He's all about changing us so that among us who are representatives of Christ, *it will be different.*

Oh Lord, make me a servant. Forgive me for the times I flaunted my position. For the times I used my authority to push people down instead of lifting people up. I am sorry for making it about me instead of about You. Help me to serve the needs of Your people and to reach out to Your people in this world. God, make me a servant. Bring me humility that only You can bring. Amen.

Prayers on HUMILITY by Bob Lantz.

DAY 2

No discipline seems pleasant at the time, but painful. Later on, however, it produces a harvest of righteousness and peace for those who have been trained by it.
—Hebrews 12:11

GOD OPPOSES THE PROUD. He keeps His distance from them. They will be humiliated and punished. And He knows how to humble them. As children, we all had to learn some things the hard way. Our parents taught us well, but we all had times when even the most obedient of us just had to do things our way. And we learned painful lessons.

We have examples in the Bible. One of the most amazing is the story of Nebuchadnezzar. Proud and powerful, the king looked over his kingdom and all he had accomplished and thought, "By my own mighty power I've done all this. Wow. I'm amazing." God took him in hand and taught him who was really in charge. He spent seven years mentally ill and living like a wild animal before he learned the lesson; and then God restored his health and kingdom. Nebuchadnezzar became a believer who proclaimed God's sovereignty and glory throughout his entire kingdom.

If you need to be taught humility, don't fear the Lord's discipline. Welcome it. Desire it. *Thank Him* for teaching you. He favors and supports the humble. Wouldn't it be wonderful to have the Lord say about you, "I trust her and speak to her face-to-face. She sees me as I am."

Father God, I need Your discipline. Help me to be willing to go to the foot of the cross and to let down my ego. I want to be a man after Your own heart. Help me to receive Your discipline so I can find true humility and make my life more about You. Amen.

Day 3

"Take my yoke upon you and learn from me, for I am gentle and humble in heart, and you will find rest for your souls."
—Matthew 11:29

WE MAY SOMETIMES THINK THAT SINCE HE WAS GOD, Jesus had life under control. But He said that, like us, He could do nothing on His own; He had to rely on His heavenly Father (John 5:30). The author and sustainer of all creation chose to step down, become like us, and live in the mess of our world. He did it to give His life in service even for people who rejected Him, to bring them hope, and then, to die, labeled a criminal.

We may never have to physically die for someone, but have we seen dreams die because of God's call to do something else? Have I given up my plan for this day because the Spirit moved me to give my time to someone else? Have I denied myself something I had a "right" to because I have someone else's good in mind? Have I quenched the loud demands of self and instead served others in any way? Have I swallowed my pride in a certain situation because I want to be Jesus' kind of different?

How do we get the mind of Christ? By walking closely with Him. When we're linked to Him, He will show us how humility acts and speaks. He will fashion our minds after His own.

Jesus, I want to be more like You. You had all the power in the world and yet You humbled yourself to the point of death, even death on the cross. Forgive me for my weariness to do good. Find the pride in me that causes weariness and remove it! Amen.

Day 4

God opposes the proud but shows favor to the humble.
—James 4:6

JUST AS THE WARNINGS TO THE PRIDEFUL ARE NUMEROUS AND GRIM, so the promises to the humble are numerous and wonderful. To set that contrast in our minds and to know how God sees the difference between the proud and the humble, here are some of the promises to those with a humble heart.

> *The Lord leads the humble and teaches them his way* (Psalm 25:9).
> *The humble will see their God at work and be glad and encouraged* (Psalm 69:32).
> *God cares for the humble* (Psalm 138:6).
> *He supports the humble* (Psalm 147:6).
> *The Lord crowns the humble with victory* (Psalm 149:4).
> *He is gracious to the humble* (Proverbs 3:34).
> *Humility brings wisdom and honor* (Proverbs 11:2 and Proverbs 29:23).
> *Those who humble themselves will be exalted* (Matthew 23:12).
> *The humble will be filled with fresh joy from the Lord* (Isaiah 29:19).
> *The Lord will bless those with humble hearts* (Isaiah 66:2).
> *The Lord will lift up the humble in honor* (James 4:10).

There is one more, the ultimate promise, from a prophecy in Zephaniah 3:11–12. God says that all proud and arrogant people will be removed from His holy mountain. "Those who are left will be the lowly and humble, for it is they who trust in the name of the LORD." The humble are the citizens of God's kingdom. The ground is level at the foot of the cross.

Father God, help me to trust Your promises. In Christ they are YES, and through You they are AMEN. Help me to humble myself before You. I want Your presence. I want true humility. I want to be who You've created me to be. No more. No less. Amen.

DAY 5

The humble will see their God at work and be glad. Let all who seek God's help be encouraged.

—Psalm 69:32 (NLT)

DR. ELMER TOWNS, MY FRIEND AND MENTOR, suggests that the leader who is discouraged needs to look three ways. First, look inward, to see if the root of the trouble is within, and ask the Lord's help in that examination and then in the correction of the problem. Second, look outward, and seek the help, counsel, or expertise of someone who may have the knowledge and wisdom you need at this point. Third, look up, and remember that the Lord has promised to be with you forever and supply all your needs. Your weakness allows His strength to work.

Humility can and will do all three things. Pride, though, will never look inward for the problem, will not ask for help from others, and does not see God as the answer. Humility before God will see Him at work in every encounter and every situation and gladly accept that He is in control and is working out His plans. Humility knows God is present. One who leads in humility will say as Christ did, "I can do nothing on my own."

Lord Jesus, I know that when I humble myself into Your marvelous presence, then I find joy, joy in Your presence, and then my heart is glad. Lord God, help me to trust the community of believers that You put in my life to see things in me that are holding me back. Help me to always look upward. I know You will meet all my needs. You are the Way Maker. In Jesus' name. Amen.

DAY 6

Remain in me, and I will remain in you. For a branch cannot produce fruit if it is severed from the vine, and you cannot be fruitful unless you remain in me.

—John 15:4 (NLT)

ANYTHING GOOD IN ME IS A RESULT OF WHAT THE LORD HAS DONE. Without Him, I am a useless, dead branch. Our culture wants to teach us to be proud of who we are and what we can accomplish. But the truth, the accurate picture, is that we are broken, sinful, and far from what God intended His creation to be. We wanted to do things our own way instead of God's way, and we messed it up pretty good. But God does offer us redemption, new life, and a new heart. He creates something new in us. It all depends on Him, not on what I can do myself. I'll only be alive in this way if His life flows through me.

Jesus also says that if we do stay vitally connected to Him, great things will happen! We will bear much fruit. The branch will be healthy and growing and productive. That, too, is an accurate view of ourselves. The world might label this arrogant or fanatic; it's neither. It is the truth. Our weakness makes way for His mighty power to work.

Dear Jesus, apart from You I can do nothing. God, forgive me for thinking it's my talents, my ability, or my strategy that bears fruit. Bring me to the end of myself. All I want is You. I trust what You have for me is enough. I come and humble myself at the foot of the cross. Amen.

Steve Wingfield

DAY 7

Be completely humble and gentle.

—Ephesians 4:2

IN EPHESIANS 4:2, Paul uses the same words to encourage us as Jesus used to describe Himself: humble and gentle. That's the attitude of mind and condition of heart we desire, having the same character that Jesus did.

Are we living in the humility God desires of those He has called to be His holy people? We've all heard jokes about people boasting of being humble, and we won't do that. But we can test ourselves against certain characteristics of humility. Has the Spirit been speaking to you about any of these?

Humility gives all the glory to God, bowing to only one God on the throne.
Humility knows all good flows from God. He sustains us. His plan will prevail.
Humility knows who we used to be and who we are now.
Humility knows that "weakness" is a place where God's mighty power can work.
Humility knows it is a branch, dependent on the Vine for all of life.
Humility welcomes correction.
Humility asks for God's discipline.
Humility quenches self in favor of others.
Humility asks for help.
Humility walks as close as it can get to Jesus.
Humility looks for its reward and honor from God alone.

Walk humbly before God, my friend, always keeping in mind His presence, who He is, and who you are. And He will delight in you.

Lord God, You have called us to be humble and to be gentle. Meekness is not weakness, but strength under control. I have no strength in myself. I trust in the name of the Lord God. Not by might, not by power, but by my Spirit, says the Lord. Amen.

Steve Wingfield

Notes and Prayers

_____

_____

_____

_____

_____

_____

_____

_____

_____

_____

_____

_____

_____

_____

_____

_____

_____

INFLUENCE

Influence is a magnet, drawing others toward it without demanding allegiance.

—Paul Weaver

DAY 1

One who is righteous is a guide to his neighbor, but the way of the wicked leads them astray.

—Proverbs 12:26 (ESV)

INFLUENCE: THE POWER TO PRODUCE CHANGE without forcing or demanding. Influence is a matter of character, not position or authority. No matter what position you're in at your job, in your home, at church, in social circles, or simply as a neighbor to those on your street, you can have influence.

You aren't born with influence, and influence doesn't just automatically come to you. You may gain a certain amount of influence because of your particular job or your position or an office you hold in the church, but true influence does not come from a title or a name on the door. You don't even have to have a title or office door to have influence.

Influence is earned by who we are and what we do. Like so many other character traits we'll be thinking about, it's built and sustained by many other qualities like humility, kindness, integrity, wisdom, sincerity, fairness, decisiveness—and more. And because it is the ability to produce change, it means that if these qualities are part of your leadership, then these characteristics also begin to spread throughout your entire organization and affect increasing networks of people.

God has a purpose in giving you whatever influence you do have.

Abba Father, make my life more than an influence lecture, let it be an influence laboratory. As I live my life may others know I am Yours by the fruit of Your Spirit growing from within me. In the name of Jesus. Amen.

Prayers on INFLUENCE by Kerry Willis.

DAY 2

As a result, you can show others the goodness of God, for he called you out of the darkness into his wonderful light.

—1 Peter 2:9 (NLT)

IT'S A MODERN WORD. *Influencers.* We don't hear Jesus using it in the Scriptures, but this was His mission, and He made it the mission of every one of His followers. Why was Jesus sent? To redeem the world. To save it and bring it back to God. After His death and resurrection, He told His disciples, "The Father sent me, and I'm sending you out to be my witnesses all over the earth."

We are to be influencers. Jesus said He was the light of the world. He also tells His disciples, "You are the light of the world. People don't light candles and then put them under a basket; they put them on a candlestick so everyone in the house has light." Jesus set His light aflame in us, and He has set us in the world to give the world light.

When you answered God's call to become one of His own, He gave you a new purpose in life: to show others His goodness, His mercy, His love. God is calling people to come back to Him, and you and I are part of His plan to reach out to the world in darkness. We are to be influencers, drawing people not to ourselves and our agenda but to God and His kingdom.

Loving Father God, I want to be a holy influence on everyone I encounter. Beyond mere words, let the way my life tenderly points others to You be proof that the goods my life displays are really an outflow of Your goodness. In the name of the one called Wonderful. Amen.

DAY 3

We continually ask God to fill you with the knowledge of his will through all the wisdom and understanding that the Spirit gives, so that you may live a life worthy of the Lord and please him in every way: bearing fruit in every good work, growing in the knowledge of God.

—Colossians 1:9–10

JOHN WESLEY, THE GREAT ENGLISH THEOLOGIAN AND EVANGELIST, reportedly declared that he had learned more about Christianity from his mother than from all the theologians in England. Whether or not you are in a position labeled as "leadership," you can be an influencer. This is God's purpose for you.

When Jesus told His disciples they would take His message to the ends of the earth, what do you suppose they were thinking? Remember, they were ordinary people who had lived ordinary lives before they met Jesus. Don't you suppose they wondered how they would accomplish such an ambitious undertaking?

If we have the same thoughts—*What can I, an ordinary person, accomplish?*—the secret is the same the disciples-turned-apostles found: the Spirit's power. The Spirit's power gives wisdom, understanding, and guidance. It is not we ourselves who take the message to the world. It is the powerful Spirit of Christ working in our everyday lives.

John Wesley also wrote, "Give me one hundred preachers who fear nothing but sin and desire nothing but God, and I care not a straw they be clergymen or laymen, such alone will shake the gates of hell and set up the kingdom of heaven upon earth."

Please help me to gain influence that benefits others as I give my full attention to Your holy wisdom. Remind me that my human wisdom is only ignorance when contrasted with Your pure mind. In the name of Jesus. Amen.

DAY 4

I make myself a slave to everyone, to win as many as possible.

—1 Corinthians 9:19 (BSB)

ONE OF THE MOST IMPORTANT ACTIONS YOU CAN TAKE to earn influence is to pour yourself into others and invest in the lives of the people around you. It is not just a cute little cliché to say that things are more caught than taught. People observe how you relate to them. They notice ways in which you invest in their lives. And when you do that, you are gaining what I like to call influential capital. Whether on the job, in church, or in social circles, influence gains you strong leadership and healthy relationships.

The more you invest in others, the greater your influence will be. That's a powerful statement, and I want you to own it.

The generosity that enables you to invest in others comes from a servant attitude, a mindset that follows Christ's example of humility and service. Let us not forget the reason we are pouring into others—not simply to change or control them but to serve them for their "progress and joy in the faith" (Philippians 1:25). Jesus, our example, laid down His equality with God and was born as a human for the purpose of going to the cross "to free us from every kind of sin, to cleanse us, and to make us his very own people" (Titus 2:14 NLT). As a servant, He gave His life for others.

We are His representatives, and whether we are leaders with influence or neighbors with influence, He has put His mission into our hands.

Jesus, You gave Your life so that I could be saved. Because of what You did for me, may I use every available means to reach every available person. Amen.

Steve Wingfield

Day 5

And let us consider how we may spur one another on toward love and good deeds, not giving up meeting together, as some are in the habit of doing, but encouraging one another—all the more as you see the Day approaching.

—Hebrews 10:24–25

THE INFLUENCE GOD HAS GIVEN US is not to be used only to shine light in the lives of unbelievers but also to encourage others who are walking the same path we are. All parts of your body are interdependent. Even your little toe is important—it enhances your balance, as do the tiny, unseen hairs in your inner ear. Every part of the body adds to the effective function of the whole. You, my friend, are part of the body of Christ. Our lives our intertwined, just as parts of our physical bodies depend on each other.

How can we influence the lives of other disciples? Praying for each other is one of the most important ways we build each other up. Paul wrote that we should be persistent in our prayers for all believers. He even asked for prayers for himself, that he might find the right words and the boldness to preach the gospel message to the gentiles (Ephesians 6:18–19). Love each other as Christ's representatives, and build real relationships. Be accountable to each other. Encourage each other. Be open to sharing your needs; let others help you. Keep reminding each other of the truths of God's Word and God's plan. Invest in each lives of others.

May it be said of me: "How beautiful are the feet of those who bring good news of good things" (Romans 10:15 AMP). *Good news is influence, indeed! In the name of Jesus. Amen.*

DAY 6

For we are God's handiwork, created in Christ Jesus to do good works, which God prepared in advance for us to do.
—Ephesians 2:10

THOSE WHO BELONG TO JESUS CHRIST HAVE THE SPIRIT OF CHRIST LIVING IN THEM, and it is the Spirit who gives us the greatest influence we may have. There is a powerful spirit at work in the children of God, and He equips us to have influence, each in his or her own network of business, church, social networks, and at home. We have each been given different gifts that the Spirit will use for His purposes.

God does have a purpose in giving us gifts—and that purpose is to give us influence in both the body of Christ and in the world in which we live daily. Jesus said to let our light shine so that others would praise God (Matthew 5:16). Peter wrote that we're to use our spiritual gifts to serve one another (1 Peter 4:10). Paul's advice to young Timothy was to keep himself pure so that he would be a clean vessel, fit for the Master to use for good works (2 Timothy 2:21). The gifts of influence we've been given are not for our personal use or gain; they are given for the Master's work.

Influence is a magnet, a force that prompts change. It is to be used to turn everyone's eyes not to us, but to our heavenly Father.

Dearest Almighty, personal loving God, let it be true that the blood of Jesus has purified my motives through and through. Then and only then will You be glorified, magnified, and satisfied through my life's influence, which is really "Christ in me, the hope of glory." Amen and amen. (Colossians 1:27b)

Steve Wingfield

DAY 7

But you, man of God, flee from all this, and pursue righteousness, godliness, faith, love, endurance and gentleness.

—1 Timothy 6:11

OUR SCRIPTURE TODAY PUTS THE SPOTLIGHT ON WHAT WE WANT TO PURSUE and how we want to build our character. It's from Paul's letter to a young protégé, Timothy, and it is wise counsel for us. Preceding this verse is Paul's discussion about traits that are *not* to be a part of who we are as Christ's representatives: arrogance, greed, and pride, all products of self-focus and moral compromise. These things will ruin our influence for the kingdom.

I encourage you to take time to ask the Spirit to show you what things in your character might be limiting your influence. Ask Him for wisdom about this. Use David's prayer in Psalm 119:29, "Keep me from deceitful ways, from lying to others and myself."

As the Spirit gives you insight and understanding, pray the next verse in Psalm 119, "I choose the way of faithfulness and truth" (119:30 paraphrased). Then, as people of God and *influencers* for God, flee from those things limiting your influence for the kingdom, and pursue righteousness, godliness, faith, love, endurance, and gentleness.

Abba Father, if I know my heart, I am above all things a seeker of Your righteousness. Yes, I want to be in right relationship with You above all else. I have no agenda of my own, only an allegiance to You. Let me impart to others a sacred desire to live faithful and true as a servant leader. Lord, make me like You. You were a loyal servant. Please make me one, too. In the name of my King, Jesus. Amen.

Notes and Prayers

_____

_____

_____

_____

_____

_____

_____

_____

_____

_____

_____

_____

_____

_____

_____

_____

_____

_____

_____

Initiative

People with initiative and character will rise to the top, and they will take companies, departments, and their own personal lives from good to great.

—Paul Weaver

Day 1

Do not withhold good from those to whom it is due, when it is in your power to act.

—Proverbs 3:27

OUR SCRIPTURE TODAY IS A PROVERB written by the wise King Solomon. This principle is not limited to business, social networks, or any one area of life. It's a principle of sound, upright living at work, at home, in your neighborhood. People are watching, and they'll notice you as someone who recognizes what needs to be done and does it. You're not somebody who tries to do the least amount necessary to get by. You're looking for ways to make things better or to solve a problem, and you take action. Even if it's something as simple as emptying an overflowing wastebasket, your actions are motivated by the necessity for solutions, not by the requirements of a job description.

When you recognize what needs to be done, and you have the ability to do something about it, do it. Look beyond your job description. Don't make excuses that it's someone else's responsibility. It is *your* responsibility.

Lord, make me an instrument of Thy peace and love. Give me, Lord, a soft and generous heart and open my eyes that I may see and know the needs of others around me. Your Word says he who is gracious to the poor lends to the Lord. Help me, I pray, to be that servant with thanksgiving. Amen.

Prayers on INITIATIVE by Dr. Erwin Lutzer

Day 2

For once you were full of darkness, but now you have light from the Lord. So live as people of light! For this light within you produces only what is good and right and true. Carefully determine what pleases the Lord.

—Ephesians 5:8–10 (NLT)

SHOWING INITIATIVE IN BIG AND LITTLE THINGS WILL ADVANCE YOUR CAREER. But our most important career is being a representative of Christ. In that calling, we have a wonderful book of wisdom and instruction, the Scriptures. I've been a follower of Christ for over forty years, and I love Scripture. It addresses all the character principles we teach at Lodestar, and more. And it applies to all of life, not only business and leadership.

Concerning initiative, James wrote a sobering truth: "If anyone, then, knows the good they ought to do and doesn't do it, it is sin for them" (James 4:17). Choosing to ignore what we know is the right thing to do has spiritual implications. In this week's devotionals, we'll look at more Scriptures that address our motivations and initiative and the impact on all aspects of life.

Be on the lookout for things that need to be done and take the initiative to get them done. What happens on the outside is an indication of what's going on inside. Ask God to put an armed guard around your heart, "And the peace of God, which surpasses all understanding, will guard your hearts and your minds in Christ Jesus" (Philippians 4:7 ESV).

My Lord, I confess that my light is not very bright. Please forgive my sin and restore in me that light that shines in the darkness, for I know that I should be a son of light, not of darkness. Be merciful to me, O Lord. Amen.

DAY 3

Remain in me, as I also remain in you. No branch can bear fruit by itself; it must remain in the vine. Neither can you bear fruit unless you remain in me.

—John 15:4

INITIATIVE—THE ABILITY TO SEE WHAT NEEDS TO BE DONE AND ACTING ON IT—is a product of spiritual health, and spiritual health depends on our staying connected to the source of life. Jesus' words in the verse above stress the life-giving connection of the branch to the vine. A few verses later, we have an image of a branch that is separated from the line of the vine: dried up and withered.

You know, this is really key to all of the character traits in the Lodestar program. Our connection to the Vine is what grows and gives potency to the desirable qualities that we need as leaders and as representatives of Christ. The bottom line is that our relationship to Jesus Christ is the foundation that affects every area of our lives.

Take some time today to assess your relationship with Christ. Is His life and power flowing into you? Or are you feeling dried up and withered? If you aren't feeling connected to Him, what can you do to change that? James, the brother of Jesus, wrote a letter to believers filled with great practical truths, and he gives us this simple fact: "Come close to God, and God will come close to you" (James 4:8 NLT).

Oh God, help me, please, to work out what You work in my heart. I pray, Lord, that You will enlarge my vision and my faith will be gratified in You, that I might be a fruit-bearing Christian, pleasing to You. In the matchless name of Jesus, amen.

Day 4

But I say, love your enemies! Pray for those who persecute you! In that way, you will be acting as true children of your Father in heaven.

—Matthew 5:44–45 (NLT)

THE SUPREME EXAMPLE OF INITIATIVE IS SHOWN TO US BY OUR CREATOR. He saw what needed to be done. The world was sick with sin and enslaved by death. The world needed to be rescued. And He did it. Without being asked or coerced. As a matter of fact, the world didn't even care about Him, but He took the initiative to rescue us. Someone has said that *grace* is giving someone what they don't deserve, and *mercy* is not giving them what they do deserve. Jesus said that if we show acts of kindness to our enemies and pray for them, we are acting as true children of our Father in heaven.

Now, those words are easy to say. *Love your enemies. Do good to them.* Think about someone who has been unkind to you, betrayed your trust, tried to sabotage your influence at work, or slandered you. Can you be kind to them? Pray for them? Do something good for them? Some might say that's impossible. Yes, it is impossible without God in the picture. But I promise you, when you sincerely want to follow the Spirit's leading on this, He will take action to help you do it.

Our heavenly Father's character showed the greatest initiative possible. When we take this initiative of grace, we show His character, too.

My dear Lord, I ask for mercy and forgiveness, for I am weak in loving my enemies. Please send a revival to my heart so I could embrace the whole world and kiss it. With thanksgiving. Amen.

Steve Wingfield

Day 5

Whatever you do, work at it with all your heart, as working for the Lord, not for human masters, since you know that you will receive an inheritance from the Lord as a reward. It is the Lord Christ you are serving.

—Colossians 3:23–24

THE APOSTLE PAUL WROTE LETTERS to encourage the new Christians of His day. Christ's good news had spread to many countries and transformed lives at all levels of society. The verses for today are from a short passage in which Paul addresses people who were slaves. Hopefully, that is not your situation, but the truth Paul emphasizes is true for all of us today, no matter where we live in the social or business web of our world.

This is how we're to proceed when there's a job to be done: work wholeheartedly, with sincerity of heart and reverence for the Lord. Remember, you're working for Him, and your rewards will come from Him.

Whether we're the boss or we are actually slaves, taking initiative means we'll be doing what needs to be done, not because we're forced or ordered to do it, but just because it's the right thing to do. The truth is, when we are children of God, no matter our position, whatever we do we are working for the Lord, and so initiative becomes a way of life because we know that is the way He wants us to live.

Help me, Lord Jesus, not to work for time but for eternity. Help me to invest my time and all I have in people, the only eternal thing in the world. Teach me, Lord, to love in humility all people. In Christ's name I pray, amen.

DAY 6

But we have this treasure in jars of clay to show that this all-surpassing power is from God and not from us.

—2 Corinthians 4:7

WHEN HURRICANE KATRINA HIT OUR COUNTRY'S SOUTHERN COAST, a few of us were gathered around the television in my office, watching scenes of destruction. One of my co-workers said, "We need to do something." But what can a small group of people do about such devastation?

As clear as if the Lord was standing there with us, I heard Him say, "Adopt a city to help." So we did.

New Orleans was getting most of the attention. We found another city that had been at the epicenter of the storm and was desperately in need. I met with other interested people in our area, business leaders, political leaders, and religious leaders, and we talked about what we could do to make a difference. We connected with the leaders in that city, and we started praying and acting. Over two years' time we sent help, food, and other necessities. We raised well over three million dollars. God did amazing things for that city through our initiative. We saw miracle after miracle.

My friend, if you hear the Spirit prompting you, take the initiative to act on it. You'll see God's amazing power.

Oh God, I am like a glass half full trying desperately to spill over. Fill me, Lord, with Your sweet Holy Spirit that I may know the joy of Your salvation, and please give me a soft heart where You find pleasure. In His name, amen.

Steve Wingfield

Day 7

So we keep on praying for you, asking our God to enable you to live a life worthy of his call. May he give you the power to accomplish all the good things your faith prompts you to do. Then the name of our Lord Jesus will be honored because of the way you live, and you will be honored along with him.

—2 Thessalonians 1:11–12 (NLT)

How often do we feel the Spirit prompting us to take action but we do nothing? What holds us back? Sometimes it's fear. Sometimes it's uncertainty. We can often talk ourselves out of taking initiative. We procrastinate. And could it be that we're just plain lazy or careless?

In his devotional, *My Utmost for His Highest*, Oswald Chambers said that, "Carelessness is an insult to the Holy Spirit. We should have no carelessness about us either in the way we worship God, or even in the way we eat and drink."

The Holy Spirit's resources available to us can deal with our fear, uncertainty, and carelessness. We may sometimes feel those emotions, but we don't have to live them out. My prayer for us all is that we'll live a life worthy of Christ's call, and He'll give us the power to do all the good things the Spirit leads us to do. Then, as His representatives, we'll be honoring Him.

Oh, my Lord, it's hard to crucify the old self. I know, Lord, that I am needy and empty, for there is nothing too difficult or impossible for You. I know, Lord, that I have a sin-stained heart, lips, and hands. Lord, I am not praying for crutches. I want You, if it be pleasing to You, in mercy, to give me wings. In Christ Jesus, amen.

Notes and Prayers

_____

_____

_____

_____

_____

_____

_____

_____

_____

_____

_____

_____

_____

_____

_____

_____

_____

_____

INNOVATION

Problem solving and innovation are the tools for tomorrow's success.
When we look at problems as opportunities, we flip the switch on
our attitude, from disgust to innovation.

—Paul Weaver

DAY 1

See, I am doing a new thing! Now it springs up; do you not perceive it?
—Isaiah 43:19

GOD IS THE GREATEST INNOVATOR OF THEM ALL. All you have to do is read Genesis 1. In the beginning, God created. I would say he's got a lock on true innovation. Isaiah 43:19 might be the theme of the Bible stated in one verse: God, creating, redeeming what He has created, and doing new things to accomplish His purposes. Throughout Scripture we find this "newness." Jesus brought an announcement of a new way to live. He became the new way to get right with God and a new covenant with God. Newness is God's plan of redemption, right up through Revelation, where we learn of plans for a new heaven and new earth and "He who was seated on the throne said, 'I am making everything new!'" (Revelation 21:5). *Everything*.

If you belong to Jesus Christ, your new nature was created to be like God's nature. That's an amazing declaration, isn't it? We aren't being arrogant or fanatic by claiming this; it's right there in God's Word to us (Ephesians 4:24). He wants us to know this, to know that part of His plan for newness is that we are created anew and in His likeness.

Help me, Lord, to diligently seek after Your plan and purpose for my life, and to have the courage to step out in faith to live in the creativity and innovation that leads me into the abundant life You've provided for me.

Prayers on INNOVATION by Vernon Zook.

DAY 2

We were buried therefore with him by baptism into death, in order that, just as Christ was raised from the dead by the glory of the Father, we too might walk in newness of life.

—Romans 6:4 (ESV)

WHERE CAN I GO FROM HERE? It is important for us to ask ourselves that question in all of life. It applies to our spiritual walk as well, because if we have a new life in Christ, then our spiritual walk *is* "all of life." Walking with Jesus is about newness of heart, constant growth, and a complete change in the way we think and see life.

The gospel message is all about newness of life. God didn't leave us stuck in our sin. He provided a way for everyone who wants it to come back to Him and have the heavenly, eternal life that He first intended for humans to have. He didn't leave us stuck with the same old nature, or stuck with carrying the old burdens of guilt, or stuck with "empty lives," as Peter put it in 1 Peter 1:18. He changed all of that.

Our new birth into a new life brought a new heart, new citizenship, new purpose, new family, new status as God's child, new freedom, new power, new transformation—everything is new. The old is gone. We can walk in the newness! Belonging to Christ's kingdom is belonging to a kingdom where exciting things happen. God offers this life to us and we can claim it.

Lord, You loved me and saved me just the way I was. But now You've called me toward an amazing life of joy, peace, love, and fulfillment. By Your grace may I grow into that person You've called me to be. Amen.

Steve Wingfield

Day 3

Each of you should use whatever gift you have received to serve others, as faithful stewards of God's grace in its various forms.

—1 Peter 4:10

DEVELOPING AN INNOVATIVE MIND AND SPIRIT IS A MATTER OF STEWARDSHIP. We've all been given unique talents and skills, gifted beyond the ordinary in a certain area. In his first letter, Peter tells us we are to use these gifts well, stewarding them wisely in the service of others. They weren't bestowed on us merely so that we could rise above the crowd and gain fame and adulation. These gifts were given "so that in all things God may be praised."

Using these gifts well means we will always be looking for ways to *better* use them. We'll be looking for inventive ways to let God's grace flow through those gifts. Peter gives hospitality as an example. Those with the gift of hospitality who are thinking innovatively are on the alert for fresh ways that they can reach out and let the grace of God flow through them to others. They are looking for ways to engage people and relate to them in the love of Christ. That's a Spirit-filled hospitality.

This is our goal, that through whatever gift God has given us, we will be His instruments in our world. He's entrusted a gift to you, to be used for His purposes. Will you use it well to further His kingdom? If you do, you can expect and attempt great things.

Lord, help me today, to make the most of who You've created me to be, and what You've given me. I surrender all I am and all I can do to Your plan and purpose for my life. Use me to be an encouragement to someone today. Amen.

Day 4

He said to them, "Go into all the world and preach the gospel to all creation."
—Mark 16:15

BILLY SUNDAY ONCE SAID, "Let's quit fiddling with religion and do something to bring the world to Christ." That's blunt. It's also mild language for Billy Sunday. As a baseball-player-turned-evangelist, he used language and a speaking style that often shocked more conservative Christians. But he connected to people. He delivered God's message of love, grace, and forgiveness to thousands of men and women in the language of the streets they could understand.

I am convinced God wants us to use innovative methods to shine His light into each generation. God never changes. His gospel never changes. But the world changes and culture changes, and we need to adapt and find ways to enter people's lives and be contagious enough that they want what we have. A simple, and obvious, example is the use of technology. You might have the gift of songwriting, but putting music out into the world on 8-track tapes will no longer reach an audience.

Billy Sunday preached the gospel over one hundred years ago, in a different time, to a different world. Yet the message of Jesus Christ and the love of Jesus that reaches out to people are still the same. People still need Christ's salvation. They still need the new life the Spirit can give. They still need forgiveness. They still need a free and open relationship with their Creator. We need to use every available means to reach every available person.

Lord help me to have a, "Do whatever it takes" kind of attitude as I share the love of Jesus with the people You bring into my life. Amen.

Day 5

Trust in the LORD with all your heart and lean not on your own understanding; in all your ways submit to him, and he will make your paths straight.

—Proverbs 3:5–6

INNOVATION, seeing new ways to solve problems or create greater efficiency, is key in business leadership. Steve Jobs said, "Innovation distinguishes between a leader and a follower." People who can think "outside the box" and come up with fresh ideas and unique approaches will have doors open for them, they'll have opportunities for advancement, and they will be influential and energizing team members. Innovation is essential.

But being innovative, whether in business or in presenting Christ to the world, also means we're taking a risk. We're taking a chance on something new. It may not work as we hoped. We might encounter unexpected pitfalls. Fear of failure or unexpected consequences can hold us back from utilizing our capacity for innovation.

I'm convinced that a capacity for innovation is a God-given ability. So how do we overcome the caution or fear that might hold us back? 1 John tells us there is no fear in love. I know God guides our plans when we commit our work to Him. I know I'm in His hands. I know His Spirit is leading me, and He cares about every detail of my life. I know God loves me and His plans for me are good. I *believe* Him, and so I can rest in all of those promises as I pursue innovative ideas. My confidence in His promises frees me.

Lord, may the fear of failure and what others may think of me be overcome by my commitment to step out in faith and do what no one else is doing, to reach those no one else is reaching. Amen.

Day 6

Whatever you do, work at it with all your heart, as working for the Lord, not for human masters… It is the Lord Christ you are serving.

—Colossians 3:23–24

THIS LIFE WE'RE LIVING NOW IS A GIFT of the Creator who is making all things new for us. We've been given this new life for a purpose, according to His plan. So *whatever* we do, remember we are doing it as His servants.

We bear His name. We are His representatives. If we preach a sermon tomorrow, we are doing it for Him. If we lend our lawn mower to a neighbor, we are acting in service to Christ. If we paint a house, our work is for Him. When we look at our days in this light, there is no question—in everything we do, we'll work hard to do the very best we can. We want to honor Him and represent Him well.

Approaching life with an innovative spirit is a natural outcome of our desire to do our best for the Lord. We not only strive to do our best, we look for ways to improve. We want to work with excellence. And excellence is usually a push beyond the status quo. We do not want to simply slide along and settle for whatever happens. We want to be creative, growing, learning, resourceful—pushing forward, pushing beyond better to best.

Because we're doing it for our Lord.

Everything I do today God, I do to honor and glorify You and to bless and encourage those around me. You have provided unlimited opportunities for me through my work, my family, my neighborhood, and my community to make a difference for You. I want to make the most of all You've given me for all of You. Amen.

DAY 7

Like newborn babies, crave pure spiritual milk, so that by it you may grow up in your salvation.

—1 Peter 2:2

BARB AND I HAVE BEEN BLESSED WITH ARMFULS OF GRANDCHILDREN. It's been a joy to watch them grow, developing their own special interests and gifts, becoming the unique people God created them to be. That is the natural growth and progression God has also begun in our eternal lives. Salvation is more than being saved from hell. It means we have a brand-new life and a new identity. And we are to "grow up" in that new life.

In Ephesians 4:11–16, Paul wrote about the gifts that Christ gives the church. The purpose of these gifts is to help us grow up in our salvation, "that we will be mature in the Lord, measuring up to the full and complete standard of Christ" (v. 13). Maturing is an expected thing in the Christian walk, but the goal is amazing—the full and complete standard of Christ! It's where this work that God has begun in us is headed, what God is already working on.

Thus, innovative thinking becomes one more trait empowered by the Holy Spirit. We don't innovate just for the sake of change. We innovate to do something better, more efficiently and effectively. As we become more and more like Christ in everything we do, we will naturally be thinking of ways to do life better—*all things* in life.

God takes joy in seeing us grow up.

Lord, help me to grow up every day and in every way to become more like Jesus Christ. Help me today, to do things better than I did yesterday, to love You more, and to know You better. Amen.

Notes and Prayers

_____

_____

_____

_____

_____

_____

_____

_____

_____

_____

_____

_____

_____

_____

_____

_____

_____

_____

_____

Integrity of an organization's leader is so important that the whole establishment can be brought down with one bad decision.

—Paul Weaver

DAY 1

Create in me a pure heart, O God, and renew a steadfast spirit within me.
—Psalm 51:10

INTEGRITY ISN'T A MATTER OF THE REPUTATION we've created for ourselves; it is a matter of who we are at the very core of our character. God knows us intimately. He knows our thoughts. He understands what goes on in our hearts. Proverbs says, "guard your heart, for everything you do flows from it" (Proverbs 4:23).

When Satan rebelled against God and set out to ruin the creation where everything was good, he attacked that very core of our humanity. It's an ongoing war, and he plants seeds of deceit, moral weakness, hypocrisy, and selfishness in the human heart.

The God who created us in the beginning and thus knows everything about how we operate can cleanse our hearts of those things. He can create new hearts in us, hearts of integrity and purity, devoted to Him—hearts that look more like what He created us to be.

So, as we think about integrity and its importance in our lives, if the Spirit speaks to you about things growing in your heart that crack and splinter your integrity, ask the Lord to create a pure heart in you. Jesus has already defeated all those powers intent on keeping you from living with integrity. He can create your heart anew.

Lord, show me the sins of my heart, remind me of Your steadfast love and the power that You and You alone have to cleanse me and make me new. Amen.

Prayers on INTEGRITY by Chris Kelty.

Day 2

I know, my God, that you test the heart and are pleased with integrity...

—1 Chronicles 29:17

IT HAS OFTEN BEEN SAID THAT INTEGRITY IS TESTED AND PROVED by what we do when nobody's looking. A person of integrity will do the right thing when no one else is witness to what they're doing. But I want to remind you that someone is always watching. Someone knows who we are under all the layers of image and reputation we've built up.

God created us to have a relationship with Him, and regardless of whether a person knows Him or not, one day all of us are going to have to give an account to the living God. He is the one who sees all that we do. He goes to the core, and sees it all.

I don't say that to put you in bondage. Instead, this gives great freedom. God created us to bring glory to Him. When we come to Jesus as Lord, He creates a new life and heart within us; the old is gone, the new is here. When I understand that I was created to bring glory to Him, it helps me live out the fact that I want to be a person of integrity.

The bottom line is that I want to be a person of integrity because I know that I answer to God. My purpose here on earth is to represent Him well. And only a life lived with integrity will do that.

Lord, open my eyes to the fact that I was made to bring Your glory. Help my life, in word and deed, be a reflection of that truth, and ultimately a reflection of You and Your goodness. Amen.

Steve Wingfield

Day 3

If we claim to have fellowship with him and yet walk in the darkness, we lie and do not live out the truth.

—1 John 1:6

WHAT IS INTEGRITY? Our definition in the Lodestar program is this: an uncompromising, consistent commitment to what is right. You know what a compromise is; each side gives a bit, and two viewpoints or agendas yield enough so that they can work together toward one goal. Compromise is often very necessary in life. One of the most important areas is marriage. All of you who are married know that you've got to learn to compromise to make a home run smoothly and happily. And everyone, married or not, has learned that compromise is a way to work and live together.

But when we are talking about *right* and *wrong* and your choices as a leader (in other words, we're talking about your integrity) then compromise is impossible.

I'm not saying you never compromise. In all sorts of projects and planning, you'll have to be flexible in your personal preferences. But you cannot compromise on your integrity. You cannot give in when it comes to a decision of right or wrong.

We can't compromise with the darkness. Righteousness can't give a little here and a little there and let darkness creep in. Integrity must be uncompromising. We must stand firm, stand our ground, when it comes to those things that are wrong.

"Resist the devil," James says, "and he will flee from you" (James 4:7). For the sake of your integrity, absolutely necessary in a leader, stand firm. Resist the darkness.

Lord Jesus, You came full of grace and truth. Help me to do the same, to walk in the light, and to be light in a world filled with darkness. Amen.

Day 4

But the Advocate, the Holy Spirit, whom the Father will send in my name, will teach you all things and will remind you of everything I have said to you.

—John 14:26

I WANT TO DO WHAT'S RIGHT, PERIOD. We read in Proverbs 11:3 that "the integrity of the upright guides them." That's being *consistent*, making our faith a way of life. Day in and day out, we are committed to living according to God's truth.

How do we stay consistent, firmly on the path of truth and righteousness? We stay in step with the Spirit. He keeps us on the right path. When Jesus told His disciples about the Spirit who would come to dwell in them, He said the Spirit would remind them of everything He'd taught and convict of sin. That's the same Spirit living now in all who belong to Jesus. He works to change us, to make us into people who reflect the Lord's glory.

Integrity is built through hundreds of little choices every day. We think one small decision in the course of our day may not matter, may be insignificant. But every choice we make does matter. Every little temptation we refuse, every time we stand firm and deny selfishness or hypocrisy in our choices or actions, every time we reject compromise of what is right, the Spirit is at work strengthening our integrity.

Our integrity guides our choices. And the Spirit is the guide of integrity. Follow the Spirit. He will bring consistency to living out your integrity.

Lord, You have promised Your Spirit, and yet I often try to rely on myself. Help me to trust in You and the power of Your Spirit, and not lean on my own understanding, knowing that You will make my paths straight. Amen.

Steve Wingfield

DAY 5

Above all, you must live as citizens of heaven, conducting yourselves in a manner worthy of the Good News about Christ.

—Philippians 1:27 (NLT)

WHEN INTEGRITY DICTATES WHAT YOU AND I DO AND SAY, we can't be bought. Temptations won't sway us. We will make the right choices. We will stand firm. Our integrity will see to that because integrity is committed to what is right. We have got to be committed. I don't know who said it first, but there's much truth in the statement, "You've got to stand for something or you'll fall for anything."

To what are you committed? We all have many commitments, but what is your one supreme commitment? I'm committed to representing Jesus and representing Him well. That's a guiding principle in my life. And I have that purpose because I'm now a part of His kingdom. That's where my ultimate loyalty lies—with my King.

God has moved you, my friend, from the kingdom of darkness to the kingdom of Jesus Christ. We are citizens of His kingdom. As citizens of that kingdom, we live according to what He says is true, according to His laws, and with all His resources available to us. Our past, present, and future are in His hands. We are accountable to Him. Even more, we live in gratitude and praise of our King. Take time today to talk with your King and renew your vows of loyalty to Him.

Lord, You are a wise and gracious King. You do not need me to be powerful or impressive, You simply want me to be faithful and obedient. Make it my ultimate prayer that Your will, not my will be done. Amen.

Day 6

All your words are true; all your righteous laws are eternal.

—Psalm 119:160

NOW WE COME TO THE LAST PHRASE OF OUR DEFINITION OF INTEGRITY: *what is right.* These days, values, morals, even religious beliefs seem to be arbitrary and transient. Clarity on what is right and what is wrong has become fuzzy, indistinct, and even, for some, non-existent. The lines between right and wrong seem to move, always changing.

How do we keep a consistent, uncompromising commitment to what is right when "what is right" is a moving target?

The target is not moving. It is constant, unchanging, and will stay that way into eternity.

Our target is not the world's truth but God's truth. The Word of our God stands forever, long after you and I are gone from this world, even after this world is gone. Psalm 111:8 says that God's precepts "are forever true, to be obeyed faithfully and with integrity" (NLT). Forever.

Jesus said He was the Truth and His Spirit would lead us to God's eternal, unchangeable truth. Get to know Jesus. Spend time in God's Word. Ask the Spirit's guidance. His Word and His Spirit are our guides to follow His truth faithfully and with integrity.

Lord, Your Word is true and everlasting. In a world full of ever-changing circumstances, allow my heart to abide in that which never changes—Your truth, Your love and grace, and Your Word. Amen.

Day 7

We pleaded with you, encouraged you, and urged you to live your lives in a way that God would consider worthy. For he called you to share in his Kingdom and glory.
—1 Thessalonians 2:12 (NLT)

What if there are things in your past that have not been the actions of a person of integrity? What if "that thing" back there behind you was a compromise with darkness? The first thing to do is settle the matter with the Lord. Ask His forgiveness and rejoice in His mercy. The next step is to follow the model of Paul: forgetting what is behind and straining forward toward everything God has for you up ahead.

Are you thinking that you can't forget what is behind? God forgets! He has canceled that record (Colossians 2:14). He says the old is gone, the new is here. That thing "back there" behind you is gone in God's eyes.

So, strain forward, looking ahead to everything He has planned for you. As our verse for today says, God has "called you to share in His Kingdom and glory." All week, we've been thinking about living as part of his kingdom. We're going to share in His glory, too. The Spirit is changing us, growing us into the image and glory of Christ. He's going to finish the job and bring it to completion. Paul says this perfection is the reason Christ first possessed us (Philippians 3:12). And ahead of us, the inheritance and the prize are waiting.

Lord, You have made me new, and You've promised that the good work You have begun will be brought to completion in Your perfect timing. Remind me of this beautiful truth, and the inheritance I have through You alone. Praise God! Amen.

Notes and Prayers

_____

_____

_____

_____

_____

_____

_____

_____

_____

_____

_____

_____

_____

_____

_____

_____

_____

_____

_____

Steve Wingfield

Joyfulness

*Joy is a condition of the heart and soul.
Adding joyful leadership to your business plan costs nothing, and money is a
poor substitute for joyfulness.*

—Paul Weaver

Day 1

*You have put more joy in my heart than they have when their grain and wine
abound.*

—Psalm 4:7 (ESV)

"THE JOY OF THE LORD IS MY STRENGTH." The joy that is a gift from God, a fruit of the Spirit, will be strength that carries you through every mile of your journey, no matter how difficult or easy. It will be a refuge for you, a refreshment, a protection. It energizes and heals and calms.

Just as Jesus said He gives peace that the world can never give, so He gives joy that the world can never give. You won't be able to manufacture it on your own. It's not something you can train yourself to do or a goal you can achieve. True joyfulness comes from one source—the God of all hope and joy and peace.

"May the God of hope fill you with all joy and peace as you trust in him, so that you may overflow with hope by the power of the Holy Spirit." Life doesn't get any better than that!

Father, You want my joy tank to be full. It has become the defining characteristic, the strength in my life. Too often I settle for less. Too often I allow the pressures of the day to weigh heavy on me. Too often I don't choose joy. Help me, Lord, to see the wonders that You've placed in my life, the protection You've surrounded me with, the future that You've given me. Lord, help me concentrate on You and know that true joy comes only from You. Amen.

Prayers on JOYFULNESS by Drew Price.

Day 2

Then my soul will rejoice in the LORD and delight in his salvation.

—Psalm 35:9

GOD HAS BROUGHT YOU FROM THE KINGDOM OF DARKNESS TO THE KINGDOM OF CHRIST. He has set you free from slavery to sin and the fear of death. He's adopted you as His child, giving you full rights to an inheritance as a son or daughter. He's canceled the record of your old life and given you a new life, one that will last forever. You are still in the world, but you're already living this eternal life, and He is at work changing you into the person you were created to be to bring Him praise and honor. He loves you dearly and is dwelling with you. He's given you His Word to let you know who He is, what He is planning, and what He promises to do. You belong to the King who will be victorious in the end and rule forever.

Try, if you can, to imagine life without this gift. Without hope. Without God. Without freedom. Life with guilt. With death. With sorrow. If we try to imagine life without God's salvation, we start to realize how this great gift has changed everything about our lives. Gratitude floods our souls. We rejoice that He has rescued us and given us this life and brought us to this place of great privilege, where we can live joyfully and confidently (Romans 5:2).

Dear Lord, it's in Your salvation that I shout with joy! My enemies, my problems, my fears, they fade away when I consider your eternal salvation. In You, I have victory! In You, I have strength! In You, my future is secure. Oh, the joy I have because of You. How blessed I am to be your child! Amen.

Steve Wingfield

Day 3

"I am the good shepherd; I know my sheep, and my sheep know me."
—John 10:14

THIS IS OUR GREATEST JOY: KNOWING AND BEING KNOWN BY CHRIST. The joy of those who are cared for by the Great Shepherd is not dependent on circumstances. No, it is not even dependent on all those things our Shepherd provides, as in Psalm 23. Our joy is in our relationship with Him, a relationship He made possible through a suffering, sacrificial life because He loved us and *wanted* us to know Him.

You've experienced this on an earthly level. You know what it is to take joy in a relationship when you know each other intimately. Even though circumstances may be difficult or situations are not at all happy, there is a comfort and a *belonging* in such a relationship. That person understands you. You know him or her, and they know you. There is joy in having that relationship.

He knows everything about me: my struggles, my stumbles, my triumphs, my likes and dislikes, my sadness, my disappointments, my history, my hopes—everything. He knows and He cares about it all, and He has opened the door for me to know Him. The Creator of the universe. The one who keeps the stars and tides in place. Almighty God. The one who died so that I could have the life He created me to have.

Joy to the world—because the Lord has come to us.

Dear Jesus, thank You for Your personal touch in my life. It's so great to know that You're not just the God of the universe, the stars, the sky, and the deep sea. You know me intimately. You care about me personally. You provide for me generously. It's this that makes my joy full. Amen.

Day 4

You make known to me the path of life; in your presence is fullness of joy; at your right hand are pleasures forevermore.

—Psalm 16:11 (ESV)

WHAT JESUS TAUGHT WAS HARD. It required a change of heart and a total commitment. Those who had once been enthusiastic seekers were starting to turn away. Jesus asked the disciples, "How about you? Do you want to leave, too?" Peter blurted out, "Where would we go? You're the only one who has the words of life" (John 6:68, paraphrased).

He makes known to us the path of life. Jesus is very explicit, very clear on how He wants us to live. Putting our hope and trust in Him will lead to life. Peter later wrote in one of His letters, "You don't see him, but in joy you love and trust him, and that will be the saving of your soul."

On this path, He walks with us. Always. We experience the joy of knowing Him and trusting Him with our lives. Dr. Elmer Towns said, "Joy comes not from what happens along the way—the way is often hard—but from his presence with us."

The reward and the joy of leadership do not always come, in this life, to those who share its discipline, its pain, and its anguish. A leader may labor unappreciated, unassisted, fighting almost single-handed, pushing forward the frontiers to make it easier for someone else who is coming. The glorious gleam is that Christ is the comrade. He travels the path, too.

I praise You, Lord, for Your sacrifice. And I ask You to remind me of it when I am faced with difficulty. Teach me to lay down my desires and replace them with Your heart. Amen.

Day 5

Be joyful in hope, patient in affliction, faithful in prayer.
—Romans 12:12

THE MOST ENJOYABLE PEOPLE TO BE AROUND are people who are filled with joy. They enter a room and change the atmosphere. The most difficult people to be around are grumps and people who are down on life. They change the atmosphere in a room, too!

All of us have difficulties in life. Frustrations and disappointments can come up on a daily basis. What makes the difference between people who are joyful in hope and those who seem unable to find joy or hope in any circumstance?

I want to live according to Romans 12:12, to be joyful in hope, patient in trouble, always praying. That first phrase, "joyful in hope," is key to joy. We don't know what God has planned for us, but I continue to trust Him because I know that His plan never fails. I know I can depend on Him to keep His promises. I know that His timing is perfect. I build my life on that hope, and that gives me joy.

Billy Graham said, "Joy does not depend on circumstances, but triumphs over circumstances." Joy is not a result of circumstances; it is part of our armor as we walk through circumstances. We are joyful in knowing God is present and faithful to His Word. Our joy depends not on external situations, but on the faithfulness of our God. Living this way produces a joy that cannot be defeated or stolen by anything the devil and his demons throw at you.

Heavenly Father, help me rely on the power of Your Holy Spirit to live a life of joy that changes not only me, but those around me. Amen.

Steve Wingfield

Day 6

Further, my brothers and sisters, rejoice in the Lord! It is no trouble to me to write the same things to you again, and it is a safeguard for you.

—Philippians 3:1

Paul wrote to the Philippians, "Rejoice in the Lord always. I will say it again: Rejoice!" (Philippians 4:4), and to the Thessalonians, "Rejoice always" (1 Thess. 5:16). Always? Yes, He repeated several times, always!

If this is a command, it tells us we have a part in rejoicing. Joy is a gift of the Spirit, but we play a part in keeping joy alive in our lives. We know there are factors that can drain us and let our joy seep away. Unforgiveness, jealousy, envy, stress, and our habits of thought are enemies of joyfulness. Billy Sunday said if we have no joy, "there's a leak in your Christianity somewhere." Be on guard against leaks!

The greatest threat to our joy is taking our focus off of Jesus. Like Peter, trying to walk on water, our joy lives when we're focused on our Lord. And when our eyes are constantly on Him, we cannot help but thank and praise Him for who He is and what He has done. That gratefulness changes our lives.

Our joy is in and of the Lord, so keep your eyes on Him, keep close to Him on the path, and keep on always talking with Him—and joy will define your life.

Dear Lord, thank You for Your repetition. Thank You for Your repetition. Thank You for Your repetition. The words You say over and over again make truth sink into my heart. Rejoice! Again, I say rejoice! Remind me daily to fix my eyes on You. Joyful, joyful, I adore Thee. Amen.

DAY 7

For our present troubles are small and won't last very long. Yet they produce for us a glory that vastly outweighs them and will last forever!

—2 Corinthians 4:17 (NLT)

WHEN I WAS IN COLLEGE, I visited a very successful businessman who was dying of cancer. I asked him, "How are you today?" His answer spoke into my life and has never left me. He said, "I've never been sicker, but my heart is filled with joy." What a testimony!

Even death loses its power when we are joyful in our hope. I believe Christians die well. We don't have to fear death. Jesus set us free from that fear and broke its power. I'm enjoying living, but I really believe that when my time comes, God will give me great joy. I don't have to fear it. I trust Him.

Proverbs 17:22 says a joyful heart is good medicine. Joy in and of the Lord is good medicine for all of life.

Heavenly Father, while the world focuses on death, You give life. While the world worries about the future, You control the outcome. While the world frets about today, You are the same yesterday, today, and forever. I'm eternally grateful that I can depend on You, Lord, and not the world. I'm humbled by Your grace and forgiveness when I'm deceived by the world. I praise You that You have overcome the world. Your victory is my joy. Your mercy is my joy. Your goodness is my joy. Your justice is my joy. Your holiness is my joy. Your faithfulness is my joy. Your lovingkindness is my joy. Amen.

Notes and Prayers

_____

_____

_____

_____

_____

_____

_____

_____

_____

_____

_____

_____

_____

_____

_____

_____

_____

_____

_____

Steve Wingfield

KINDNESS

People thrive under kind leadership, and they draw away from unkind leaders.

—Paul Weaver

DAY 1

He is so rich in kindness and grace that he purchased our freedom with the blood of his Son and forgave our sins.

—Ephesians 1:7 (NLT)

"I HAVE LOVED YOU WITH AN EVERLASTING LOVE; I have drawn you with unfailing kindness" (Jeremiah 31:3). This passage captivates me because that is how much God loves us. There is nothing I can do that is going to keep God from loving me. His kindness, compassion, and patience with me are amazing. Kindness opens doors into people's hearts and minds, in all languages and all cultures. Kindness is a language which goes straight through all barriers.

The greatest barrier was the one of sin between me and God. God's kindness reached right through that and destroyed it. I can't think of any act more kind than Jesus taking my load of sin and bearing it Himself and then disposing of it.

I am the recipient of many daily kindnesses from God. So are you, my friend. God's mercies and kindness are new every morning and will follow us all the days of our lives. I pray you and I can show His kindness, compassion, and patience to others as He has shown them to us.

Heavenly Father, thank You for the ultimate act of kindness You displayed by giving Your Son Jesus Christ to die on the cross for my sins. I ask that You open my heart and mind to help me truly comprehend how great Your kindness is, that I may, in turn, display it to those around me. Help me to be an ambassador of kindness to all I meet. In Jesus' name, amen.

Prayers on KINDNESS by Jessica Taylor.

DAY 2

But the fruit of the Spirit is love, joy, peace, forbearance, kindness, goodness, faithfulness . . .
—Galatians 5:22

WE'VE ALREADY LOOKED AT COLOSSIANS 3:12 several times in previous weeks. That's the verse that tells us the "clothes" we are to put on to be properly dressed as God's chosen people. Along with compassion, patience, and empathy, we're also to put on kindness and gentleness. Only God can dress us in those clothes. Only His Spirit working in us can produce the same kindness and gentleness toward others that God has shown us.

Colossians 3:10 also talks about us putting on our new nature, created to be in God's image. Our old nature is much more apt to be kind only to those who are kind to us. Or kind to those we think might benefit us in some way. Or to attempt kindness because we think we might be rewarded. The old nature looks at some people as insignificant and is indifferent to needs or is cynical or critical and judgmental.

True kindness can only flow from us as a fruit of the Spirit. The Spirit creates a new nature within us, bringing its fruit to our hearts and minds. The Spirit of Christ transforms us by renewing our minds. His Spirit makes His life our life. That is the miraculous power of the Spirit living within us.

Dear Lord, prevent me from leaning to my own form of kindness, which brings selfishness and cynicism. Open my heart so that I may be receptive to Your transforming power. Through Your Spirit, work in my life so that the kindness I produce is godly and glorifying to You. In Jesus' name, amen.

Steve Wingfield

DAY 3

Therefore, dear brothers and sisters, you have no obligation to do what your sinful nature urges you to do.

—Romans 8:12 (NLT)

IT'S A BROKEN WORLD—selfish, self-centered, hard-hearted, and hard-headed. And let's face it, that's a description of our old natures, too. Being focused on ourselves and our own needs and desires is the greatest enemy of kindness toward others. We are pretty much all about self until the Spirit moves in and makes His home with us.

Even then, Galatians tells us, the old nature will still rise up and fight what the Spirit is doing to transform us. But as we hand over control to the Spirit of Christ, He breaks the power of the old. Besides producing godly fruit in our lives, He breaks the chains of our old selfish nature. We are no longer "obligated" to obey those old desires. We are free to let Christ's love and patience and mercy and kindness flow through us to others.

Where do you find the old nature rising up and stifling kindness to others? Are there attitudes lurking within you that you know are not Christlike but you've just shrugged your shoulders and said, "That's just human nature"? Christ can break the power of that attitude or habit. Ask Him to do away with the chains of the old and to then bring His kindness into your heart.

Lord, illuminate my mind to the sinful things I may not be aware of. Work in me today to break the chains, and even the tempting thoughts, of my sinful bondage. Create in me a desire to be more like You, and help me to keep my eyes and thoughts on all that is godly. In Your name, amen.

DAY 4

Be kind and compassionate to one another . . .
—Ephesians 4:32

KINDNESS IS A HEART THING. Kindness is reaching out to help and build each other up. It might be something as extensive as mentoring someone, or it might be as simple as a cup of cold water. We have dozens of ways to show kindness each day. Think about how a cup of cold water on a hot day can revive you. What cups of water do we have to offer? A smile on a hectic day? A word or two of encouragement? Simply noticing that someone is struggling with the copier, and helping them out? Those small things are not so small—they can change a person's day. A word or two can have a huge impact; Scripture says the tongue has the power of life and death, and it may be the hardest part of us to train in kindness.

Big or small, every act or word of kindness tells someone they are valuable and cared about. As leaders, our responsibility is to create the climate of our organization, and we want to model kindness that reaches out to help each person become more of who God created them to be. Whether we are in leadership or not, our goal is to act as representatives of Christ, sincerely helping and encouraging because we care about people.

Precious Father, use me today! Through Your Spirit, guide me to those who need an act of kindness, both big and small. Remind me that kindness to others isn't about recognition for myself, but an opportunity to represent You well. In Jesus' name, amen.

Steve Wingfield

Day 5

Make sure that nobody pays back wrong for wrong, but always strive to do what is good for each other and for everyone else.

—1 Thessalonians 5:15

KINDNESS IS A HEART THING, BUT IT'S ALSO A HEAD THING. Every day, in many ways, we are faced with the choice: Do we act in self-interest or in the interest of others? One day I was on my way home from the office and when I came to the point where the highway goes from two lanes down to one, I checked my rearview mirror. There was a car a good way back, so I moved over into the one lane. Before I knew it, that car was on my bumper, and the driver was blowing the horn and gesturing in an angry, obscene way.

At a traffic light, he pulled up beside me. I put my window down; he did, too. I said, "Sir, I'm sorry. I'm not sure what I did, but will you forgive me?" That took the wind out of his anger. My attitude toward him was so unexpected, he didn't know how to respond.

I had a choice that day. I could have given back to him what he'd given me. But I believe as followers of Christ, we don't have an option. Our choice must be always kindness.

Lord, instill kindness in me, both in my heart and mind. Help me make the right decision when faced with choosing between my old sinful self and new godly self. And when I fail, help me to be quick to ask forgiveness, both to those I have transgressed and to You. In Jesus' name, amen.

Day 6

Those who are kind benefit themselves, but the cruel bring ruin on themselves.
—Proverbs 11:17

YOU KNOW, THE BOOK OF PROVERBS IS FULL OF PRACTICAL ADVICE FOR LIV-
ING. We need to visit those pages often. The verse today from Proverbs tells
me that being kind will do good for my own soul (the King James wording).
God wants His people to be clothed with kindness toward others, but He's
also designed us so that being kind is good for *us*—mentally, emotionally,
spiritually, and even physically. We know bitterness and anger do damage to
us physically. Those emotions hold us in bondage. The man who was upset
with me in traffic could have spent his evening fuming, with anger eating
away at him. I hope I defused that. But his anger did not control me.

More often than not, when I do an act of kindness, I'm the one who
gets blessed. Yes, I may have chosen to bless someone else with kindness, but
I also benefit. You've probably experienced the same thing. It does my soul
good to be kind, and my body even experiences biochemical changes that,
well, just feel good.

I think this is the Lord looking out for us. As the Spirit molds us and we
practice kindness, we find that it does *us* good in every way.

*Father, thank You for wanting Your best for me. Create in me a heart that exudes
kindness to those around me, regardless of their behavior or attitude toward me.
Remind me that those around me are watching my life and following my example
as I profess to belong to Christ. In Jesus' name, amen.*

Steve Wingfield

Day 7

Do not repay evil for evil or insult for insult. On the contrary, repay evil with blessing, because to this you were called so that you may inherit a blessing.

—1 Peter 3:9

JESUS WAS VERY EXPLICIT IN HIS INSTRUCTIONS FOR US. He said that when we show love, even to our enemies, and pray for those who do us harm, we act as true children of our heavenly Father, because He sends good things, even to *His* enemies (Matthew 5:44–45). The Golden Rule does *not* say "Do to others as they do unto you." No, we are not to *repay* evil. We're to be the initiators of kindness. God was. His kindness reached through to us before we even wanted a relationship with Him. That sounds like action to me. That person you've been thinking about all week? What kind act or word could you possibly give them? I challenge you to think of something you can do to be kind to them the next time you meet. We're to actively bless those difficult people in some way. Christ *died* for people who hated and rejected Him. Can we, His disciples, pray for and be kind to someone who has treated us wrongly? This is what He calls us to do. We will be blessed for it.

God, while I know this is a difficult command to follow, I pray that by Your Spirit I would be able to bless those who have hurt me. Help me to release the feelings of anger and bitterness I have, and replace them with kind intentions and prayerful thoughts for their good. I want to be more like Christ, as He blessed those who persecuted Him. Amen.

Notes and Prayers

_____

_____

_____

_____

_____

_____

_____

_____

_____

_____

_____

_____

_____

_____

_____

_____

_____

_____

LIKABILITY

Write your eulogy today, and then live your life to match it.
Laugh often, have fun, do not take yourself so seriously.

—Paul Weaver

DAY 1

Those who say they live in God should live their lives as Jesus did.

—1 John 2:6 (NLT)

PASSION IS WHAT MAKES OUR JOURNEY ENJOYABLE. Having a compelling emotion and commitment to something is what brings excitement to life. The Gospels don't tell us much about Jesus as a boy or a young man. But one thing we are told is that He grew up in "favor with God and man." As an adult, He was a great storyteller and brought a message of hope to people who had waited a long time for their Messiah, and I think His personal likability added to the attraction that drew the crowds. As the old adage says, we attract more flies with honey than with vinegar.

We are here to represent Christ well. I want to study what He has modeled and show Him through my life. The writer of Hebrews encourages us to run our race keeping our eyes on Jesus, the One who authors and perfects our faith, our "champion," as one translation puts it. So this week, as we think about our relationships with other people and this trait of likability, let's keep our eyes on our Champion and ask Him to teach us from His example.

Dear Lord, I want to be likable. Please give me a passion to know You more. I want to model my life after Christ's life. Help me live my life like Jesus did and use my life for Your glory. In Jesus' name, amen.

Prayers on LIKABILITY by Reid Sanders.

Day 2

You can show others the goodness of God, for he called you out of the darkness into his wonderful light.

—1 Peter 2:9 (NLT)

ONE OF THE FIRST THINGS WE MUST ASK OURSELVES is why we desire the trait of likability. From the world, we hear things like, "Being likable will get you further in your career," or "It pays to know the right people," or "Network. Network. Network." The world tracks social media "likes" and "followers" and "friends."

If our only desire is for popularity, we're on dangerous ground. Worldly approval is fickle and fleeting. Even more serious, James wrote that if we want to be friends with the world, we are setting ourselves up as enemies of God. We cannot serve the applause of men and the Lord Jesus Christ, but likability in a disciple of Christ can be a tool God uses.

Jesus reached out and drew people in, but He wasn't depending on popularity to get His message delivered. He touched hearts so that they would receive the good news of God's grace and the kingdom of heaven. He has made us partners in His work and purpose. I want to have an attractiveness, an approachability, a "contagious something" that people notice. I want them to see that Jesus' gospel message makes a difference in my life. If I'm a likable guy, folks are much more likely to hear what I have to say when I take every opportunity to direct their eyes to God and His grace.

Dear Lord, I want to partner with You for Your work and purpose. Help my life be attractive and contagious for You. I want people to see You in me. In Jesus' name, amen.

Day 3

For God called you to do good, even if it means suffering, just as Christ suffered for you. He is your example, and you must follow in his steps.

—1 Peter 2:21 (NLT)

JESUS LOVED PEOPLE. His love for others endured through being wrongly accused, beaten, and nailed to a cross. Even then, as He gasped for breath through His pain, His prayer was for those who were responsible for the cruelty. Christ's love put others first. Christ's love *suffered*.

Our culture today is all about taking care of *me* first. But we no longer are part of this world, and now our example is Christ. Following Him means we will think of others first. It often will not require suffering to the extent that Christ did, but it will require that we give up our own agenda or step out of our comfort zone or ask the Spirit's help in sorting out our feelings so that we can be patient, kind, not irritable, forgiving, and all those other hallmarks of agape love. Our Lord has shown us how to do it. His Spirit lives in us and is a spirit of love. May we keep in step with Him and keep on learning to love as He did.

Dear Lord, help me put others first. Help me to walk in step with You and teach me how to love like You did. In Jesus' name, amen.

Day 4

The LORD does not look at the things people look at. People look at the outward appearance, but the LORD looks at the heart.

—1 Samuel 16:7

Over the years, I've met many wonderful people. Some of them were very powerful, some, just ordinary people like you and me. I've learned that no matter who they are, likable people have the ability to make me feel as though I'm the most important person they've ever met.

Imagine you are Zacchaeus. You're a short man who usually gets shoved around in a crowd. So, one day you climb a tree to get a better view of everything that's going on. How do you feel when suddenly Jesus, whom everyone is hoping to have a few moments with, stops, sees you, and invites Himself to your place for dinner?

Or imagine you are a child, mostly ignored by the adults, but noticed by Jesus and taken up by His strong arms and placed on His lap for a few sweet moments of fun? Can you put yourself in the shoes of Nicodemus? Nervous about being caught talking to this man who is rocking the established religious community, you go in the dark of night and, possibly, get Him out of bed to talk with you.

Jesus drew crowds, but in His one-on-one encounters, I'm certain He made each person feel as though they were the most important person in the world. He looked past all the outward and saw each heart's struggles, needs, and dreams.

Dear Lord, give me Your eyes to see the hearts of others. In the busyness of life, help me to make time for others just like You did. In Jesus' name, amen.

DAY 5

Let no corrupting talk come out of your mouths, but only such as is good for building up, as fits the occasion, that it may give grace to those who hear.

—Ephesians 4:29 (ESV)

WHETHER OR NOT PEOPLE SEE YOU AS BEING LIKABLE has much to do with how they can or cannot connect with you. One very important way we connect with others is through our speech. Let's be aware of what's coming out of our mouths. A judgmental, critical attitude quickly diminishes a person's likability. People who are positive, optimistic, hopeful, encouraging, and gracious are much more attractive, and approachable.

Jesus was not influenced by status or power. He did not show favoritism. Instead of judging, He saw people for what they could be. When He called His first disciples and declared they would be fishers of men, they could not have imagined what He meant. He told the woman caught in adultery to go and sin no more. His words did not condemn her but told her there was still hope for her life. He invited Matthew, one of those despised tax collectors, to come and be one of His inner circle.

Jesus offered people hope. He met people with empathy, compassion, and optimism. He had a message of good news.

We are not to judge others. Judgment belongs to Christ alone when He comes back to earth. Our Lord has given us eternal encouragement and good hope. We are to let it flow through us to others as we speak forgiveness, compassion, and hope into the lives of others.

Lord Jesus, guard my tongue. May what comes out of my mouth build others up, not tear them down. I want to speak life, forgiveness, compassion, and hope into people's lives. In Jesus' name, amen.

DAY 6

My son, do not let wisdom and understanding out of your sight, preserve sound judgment and discretion; they will be life for you, an ornament to grace your neck.
—Proverbs 3:21–22

THE KINDNESS OF JESUS came hand-in-hand with a pursuit of righteousness, a devotion to truth and rightness. Likability is not only showing kindness to other people's needs. It is also being honest and truthful. I want to be known for kindness and truth. I want those ornaments gracing my neck, too. Even when I have to say a hard thing because it is truth, I want to be able to say it in a way that touches a heart.

Paul wrote to the young pastor, Timothy, that "a servant of the Lord must not quarrel but must be kind to everyone, be able to teach, and be patient with difficult people. Gently instruct those who oppose the truth. Perhaps God will change those people's hearts, and they will learn the truth" (2 Timothy 2:24–25 NLT).

Our model, Jesus, had harsh words for the Pharisees. They simply would not hear. But to those who were seeking truth, He was kind, even when the truth He spoke was hard. He was gracious to Nicodemus, but He was firm about the truth. "Unless you are born again, you cannot see the Kingdom of God" (John 3:3 NLT).

Ask the Spirit to teach you how to wear both truth and love.

Heavenly Father, I want to be known for kindness and truth. Help me to speak the truth in love for Your glory. Teach me how to wear both truth and love. I love You, Jesus. In Your name I pray, amen.

Steve Wingfield

Day 7

For the Kingdom of God is not a matter of what we eat or drink, but of living a life of goodness and peace and joy in the Holy Spirit. If you serve Christ with this attitude, you will please God, and others will approve of you, too.

—Romans 14:17–18 (NLT)

THE BIBLE HAS MANY INSTRUCTIONS FOR US ON RELATING TO OTHER PEOPLE, both believers and those who do not share our faith. Christ's Spirit teaches and molds us daily as we strive to follow the examples he's given us. Let's review briefly.

Our highest calling is to direct people's eyes to Christ, but if people don't like what they see in His representatives, how will they desire to know more of Him? Paul wrote to the Philippians that Christ's disciples should shine like bright lights in a dark, crooked world.

We want to model our lives after Jesus' example. In His interactions with people, we see Him living, and dying, for others. He looked deeper than the surface and connected with people's hearts. He spoke hope, encouragement, and grace rather than being critical and judgmental. He spoke truth.

Did you notice that the traits that make us likable are fruit of the Spirit? If we live by drawing our life from the Vine, living in and by His presence, that fruit will grow in our character. Then we will shine like bright lights in a dark world and we will be representing Him well.

Loving Father, help me to be likable so that others might be drawn to You. I want my life to be a mirror that reflects Your love, grace, forgiveness, and hope to others. Lord, help me model my life after Jesus' example by living out the fruit of the Spirit. In Jesus' name, amen.

Notes and Prayers

_____

_____

_____

_____

_____

_____

_____

_____

_____

_____

_____

_____

_____

_____

_____

_____

_____

_____

_____

Steve Wingfield

We cannot expect to receive loyalty from people we lead if we are not loyal to them.

—Paul Weaver

DAY 1

Never let loyalty and kindness leave you! Tie them around your neck as a reminder. Write them deep within your heart. Then you will find favor with both God and people, and you will earn a good reputation.

—Proverbs 3:3–4 (NLT)

ONE OF THE THINGS I WANT AT MY FUNERAL is twelve friends who will sit through my memorial service without looking at their watches, friends who I know will surround me with faithful support while I'm still living, committed to me, who invest in me, who tell me the truth, and who stick with me even when I mess up. That's loyalty.

I want loyal people in my life. But in order for that to happen, I have to put money in the friendship bank. We've got to be loyal ourselves. To have a friend, you have to be a friend. It is a badge of honor. I'm committed to my friends. I'm loyal to the people around me, and I want them to know that. I try to live out that loyalty in every way I can. We can't just claim to be loyal, we need to demonstrate our loyalty.

Invest in the friendship bank. Live out loyalty as a way of life.

Lord, Your Word says that in order to have friends, I must be a friend (Proverbs 18:24). *Help me to support those whom You have placed in my life. May I be blessed with life-long friendships. Amen.*

Prayers on LOYALTY by Tim McAvoy

Day 2

Your unfailing love will last forever. Your faithfulness is as enduring as the heavens.

—Psalm 89:2 (NLT)

Jesus said he'd be with me until the very end—and then the book of Revelation promises that my Shepherd will continue to guide me *forever*. I'm living on that promise of His constancy. Every morning I get up and know that His mercies have begun to flow, even before I walk out my door. His love endures forever. That captivates my heart, knowing He's on my side and He's going to stick with me even when I mess up. That's the faithful God He is. He is committed to showing us the truth about ourselves and our lives, committed to working for our good, committed to blessing us abundantly, committed to our growth and maturity. He is committed to strengthening us, guarding us from the evil one, and keeping us safe in the care of the Shepherd. Those are all promises He had made to us. We can rely on Him and His promises because our God is dependable and faithful. It's what gives us hope.

Several places in Old Testament prophecies we find these words: "The passionate commitment of the Lord of Heaven's armies will make this happen!" The Lord is passionately committed to His people. There's no truer model of loyalty. As His children who are to exhibit His character, let's ask Him to strengthen our own loyalty.

Oh God, when we are faithless, You remain faithful (2 Timothy 2:13). When I feel discouraged, please help me to remember all the times that You have been there for me. May I never forget Your mercies which are new every day. Amen.

Steve Wingfield

Day 3

A friend loves at all times, and a brother is born for a time of adversity.
—Proverbs 17:17

A CLOSE FRIEND OF MINE, A PASTOR, took the wrong path. He lost his credentials and his ordination was pulled. I couldn't ignore or condone the sin in his life, but I wanted him to know I loved him and was praying for him and was still there for him. When I called to tell him that, he said, "You know, you're the only person who's called."

Too often, friends jump ship when people go through tough times in their lives. People distance themselves when relationships get difficult. I want to be a dependable friend. I want to show up. As a follower of Christ, I don't have an option. I can't abandon someone who's floundering. Love "always protects, always trusts, always perseveres" (1 Corinthians 13:7). That's faithfulness. That's loyalty.

Our loyalty means we are *committed.* That's the "consistently" part of our definition of loyalty. Loyal people are there in good times and bad times. We desperately need this kind of commitment today, especially in a world where people are moving often, not only their residences but also in their jobs and their social circles. Our society's increased mobility and communication capabilities present us with so many options that we need to make wise choices. It may seem easiest to move on when things aren't going smoothly, but loyal relationships, whether interpersonal or in a business context, need commitment, a consistent "being there" at all times.

Lord of all, today I commit myself to serve You more fully and I commit myself to support my friends, even when they fail. May I be consistent and true, though I don't feel like it or the circumstances are not favorable. Amen.

Steve Wingfield

Day 4

The pleasantness of a friend springs from their heartfelt advice.
—Proverbs 27:9

Loyal people are not only present, they are actively demonstrating their support. This is the kind of friend I want; this is the kind of friend I want to be. As leaders, loyalty to the people we lead means that we are actively involved in their lives. True loyalty to a team or an organization is not simply proclaiming commitment to the whole; it is consistently demonstrating positive support for the individuals who make up that team.

God's Word tells us again and again how important it is to build each other up, to encourage each other, to "spur each other on." We tell the truth in love and hold each other accountable. This is true not only for personal friendships but also for leaders who are loyal to their teams.

Loyalty invests in the lives of others. It takes our time and energy and often our material resources. As leaders, our loyalty to those we lead means we pour into their lives, too. So we need to check our attitudes: *How do I handle the situation when someone messes up? Do I keep my promises? Does my team know that I always have their backs? Do I look for ways to support, encourage, and strengthen each individual? Do I delight in expressing appreciation and respect and gratitude to the team, both as individuals and as a group? As a friend or a leader, am I exhibiting traits of my Father in heaven?*

Faithful and true God, may I be one who is known for my loyalty. May those on my team know that they have my trust and support. Help me to see each one individually and find ways to encourage each and every one. Amen.

Steve Wingfield

Day 5

Whoever pursues righteousness and unfailing love will find life, righteousness, and honor.

—Proverbs 21:21 (NLT)

Agape love, the highest, purest love there is, originates from God only. Only the Spirit can transform us so that we are able to express traits like sincerity, kindness, diligence, patience, restraint, discernment, and loyalty (as examples) to the highest, most godly level.

Pursue this unfailing agape love and righteousness. Pursue the relationship with Christ that will bring these characteristics to full bloom in your life. Proverbs says that making this your goal and one focus will bring you life, righteousness, and honor. Another verse (Proverbs 14:22) tells us that those who *plan* what is good will find love and loyalty. Be intentional in your pursuit. Plan what is good.

One place where this will set us apart from the rest of the world is in the vicious political atmosphere in our country. As followers of Christ, we're commanded to submit to those in authority "for the Lord's sake" (1 Peter 2:13), unless their demands are contrary to conscience and our God. We may not agree with policies, but we need to be loyal to our country. I know some people will disagree, but I believe that when we intentionally stand apart from the disparagement and tearing down of authority that is so widespread today, then we are planning good. When we pray for our government instead of ranting, we are planning good. We want to pursue righteousness and unfailing love. That is our goal as representatives of Christ.

God of all creation, may love, a love beyond my capacity to comprehend, guard my heart and guide my actions. May the attributes of sincerity, kindness, diligence, patience, and loyalty be lived out in the context of Your love. Amen.

Day 6

If we are unfaithful, he remains faithful, for he cannot deny who he is.
—2 Timothy 2:13 (NLT)

I HAVE BEEN HURT BY DISLOYALTY. I have been disappointed when friends "disappeared" because we had disagreements or hit a rough patch in our friendship. What shall we do if someone we have been loyal to betrays us in some way? Is the "loyalty contract" off when one party abandons the other?

The old sinful nature wants revenge, for me to cut them off. They've abandoned me, so I'll "unfriend" them. I won't trust them again. They don't need to expect a second chance to take advantage of me. But where would the Spirit of Christ lead us?

The Spirit does not seek revenge. He seeks to make us like Christ, and Christ has modeled exactly this situation for us. We have no better example than the situation of Peter's betrayal of his dear friend. This is one of the most heartbreaking stories in the Scriptures. How did Jesus respond? He opened the door to rebuild the relationship.

Our God is a god of second chances, and we are to be His representative of grace in this world. Will you be loyal, even though your friend has not been? Will you forgive and stick with them? Will you continue to build them up and support them? Will you pray?

"Forgive as the Lord forgave you" (Colossians 3:13). I have not always been faithful, but He has! The Spirit is transforming me into His image.

Lord Jesus, You demonstrated the ability to forgive after You had been betrayed. Grant me that same ability to not seek vengeance, but to respond in forgiveness and love. Help me to restore broken relationships in a spirit of humility. Amen.

Steve Wingfield

Day 7

Create in me a clean heart, O God. Renew a loyal spirit within me.

—Psalm 51:10 (NLT)

AND WHAT IF THE DISLOYALTY HAS BEEN OURS? In Peter's case, the realization of what he had done in abandoning Jesus was devastating. If we've been disloyal, what can we do? If the Spirit is speaking to us about a particular situation, what's the next step?

Scripture tells us that the morning Peter saw Jesus on the beach, he jumped into the water and headed to the shore. He was so thrilled to see Jesus. But surely there were a few accusing doubts in Peter's mind. Would Jesus have stern words for him? Or maybe we can conclude from Peter's enthusiasm that he *knew* Jesus' character so well that he was confident of Jesus' committed love for him.

We've not always been loyal to Jesus, either. But we can renew our loyalty to God and be confident of his forgiveness and his faithfulness to us. *Nothing* can separate us from his love.

Likewise, in our earthly relationships, divided loyalties will result in instability. Sometimes, the problem is that loyalty to others is compromised by our own selfish interests. If we've been disloyal to others, we need to own the responsibility of what we've done and ask forgiveness, then do whatever we can to make up for the wrong. And if we ask God to give us a new spirit of loyalty, He will answer those prayers.

Jesus, faithful and true, my greatest disloyalty has been to You. Forgive me for the ways in which I've not acknowledged my utter dependence on You and sought to live life on my terms. May today mark a change in how I allow You to guide my life. Amen.

Notes and Prayers

_____

_____

_____

_____

_____

_____

_____

_____

_____

_____

_____

_____

_____

_____

_____

_____

_____

_____

_____

MOTIVATION

Motivation always starts with the leader. There are no motivated teams led by unmotivated people.

—Paul Weaver

DAY 1

Whatever you do, work heartily, as for the Lord and not for men, knowing that from the Lord you will receive the inheritance as your reward. You are serving the Lord Christ.
—Colossians 3:23–24 (ESV)

MOTIVATION: THAT INNER POWER PUSHING TOWARD ACTION, driven by desire, passion, and ambition. What motivates you? What pushes you? Proverbs talks about sluggards who have an appetite that is never filled. The sluggard's problem is that "his hands refuse to work" (Proverbs 21:25). He has no motivation. He is not pushed toward action and has no desire, passion, or ambition. "But the desires of the diligent are fully satisfied" (Proverbs 13:4). Motivation keeps us diligent as we work toward our goals. It pushes us and helps us get things done. It creates energy.

Motivation and diligence are not only important in what we do on the job but also in how we run the race of faith on this earth. As children of God and citizens of the kingdom of heaven, everything we do is for God and His glory. This is our greatest motivation. We work not for the eyes of our boss, our board, or the people to whom we report, but we work for the glory of God. We are serving Christ in all we do. We are His representatives. Realizing that fact will push us to action and drive our desires, passions, and ambition. I want to hear these words, "Well done."

Lord, guide my path, as my heart's desire is to be Your ambassador. Reveal yourself in me, so that I may continue to chase You with great intensity and endurance. Amen.

Prayers on MOTIVATION by Jeff Wilhelm.

Day 2

For God is working in you, giving you the desire and the power to do what pleases him.

—Philippians 2:13 (NLT)

Friends, as we follow the Spirit of Christ, we're swimming upstream against heavy traffic. Have you felt that? One of the big differences between Christ's followers and the rest of the world is that we're motivated in an entirely different way than those who are not led by the Spirit.

For those who have been born again into a new life, it is now the Spirit of God who provides that inner power and drive to action. In Ezekiel chapter 36, we have the Lord's promise to Israel, who had fallen away from Him. He was going to draw Israel back, to cleanse them of their filth, their stubbornness, and their idolatry. He would put His Spirit in them to "move you to follow my decrees and be careful to keep my laws" (Ezekiel 36:27). That wasn't a one-time promise for one situation and one people. This is God's promise to everyone who believes. The Spirit comes to live in us and gives us the motivation and energy to do God's will.

We are living in a world motivated by what's comfortable, convenient, popular, powerful, and successful in the world's eyes. Those things are always fleeting, changing, and unsatisfying. But we have to be motivated by the Spirit of God's leading. God works in us. His Spirit gives us a new heart that desires God's approval above all else. That is what moves and energizes us.

Allow Your Holy Spirit to fall upon me, God. May You motivate my heart to be in obedience to what moves Your heart. Amen.

Steve Wingfield

Day 3

But encourage one another daily… so that none of you may be hardened by sin's deceitfulness.

—Hebrews 3:13

IN BOTH HIGH SCHOOL AND COLLEGE, I played football and ran track, and several of my coaches were great motivators. They pulled stuff out of me that I didn't even know I had in me. Like my coaches, we can help other disciples of Jesus to be more of who God created them to be.

The Spirit of Christ draws us together and gives us a unity of purpose. We are meant to support, encourage, build up, strengthen, and minister to each other in our walk. All of the letters to the early Christian churches frequently emphasized how important it is to "spur each other on" in the living out of our mission.

In the eighteenth century, John Wesley formed small groups within the larger church, believing strongly that these smaller groups could best help people live their faith in practical, day-to-day ways. One of the goals Wesley put forward was that Christians should "do all the good you can, by all the means you can, in all the ways you can, in all the places you can, at all the times you can, to all the people you can, as long as ever you can." We can help each other do that when we have those honest, open connections with a small group of people to whom we're accountable.

Keep yourself connected to those who can speak into your life and help you become more of who God created you to be. Be a channel of the Spirit's encouragement.

Father, allow me to be a spark plug, energizing others when they cannot go on. Also, send people into my life whom I can lean on when I am low. Amen.

Day 4

Therefore, my dear brothers and sisters, stand firm. Let nothing move you. Always give yourselves fully to the work of the Lord, because you know that your labor in the Lord is not in vain.

—1 Corinthians 15:58

YOU MIGHT BE TIRED RIGHT NOW. Discouraged. Unable to hold onto any optimism. Your ambition has drained away; your desire is only a low ember; and your passion has wilted. If you aren't there now, have you known times like that? What keeps us going through difficult times or when we face obstacles that seem immovable?

Sometimes, our efforts seem to have been in vain. But we know they are not! Paul assures us that nothing we do for the Lord is useless. Nothing. Let's put that in a positive statement. Everything you do for the Lord matters. It makes a difference. He uses and works in everything we do for Him.

That promise makes a world of difference for us. We might not see results, we may never get feedback, but the Lord has promised that *everything* we do for Him really does matter. And that's what revives our motivation, our desire, our ambition. Because we trust our God to tell us the truth. We trust what He has promised us. We can live with great hope.

When we need a revival of motivation, the best place to go is to the wellspring of life—the God of all hope, the Spirit of power, the Jesus we love and serve. We have more than simple optimism—we have God's promises. His promises revive and sustain our hope and passion.

Lord, remind me that EVERYTHING I do is for Your glory. There is nothing insignificant when it involves Your calling! Your promises are true and everlasting. Amen.

Steve Wingfield

DAY 5

Once you had no identity as a people; now you are God's people.
—1 Peter 2:10 (NLT)

INSECURITY IS AN ENEMY OF MOTIVATION. Insecure people are uncertain, afraid to step out, to move forward, to take action. Any passion or ambition that tries to rise in them is paralyzed by their insecurity. To keep insecurity and fear from destroying your motivation, you need a clear idea of (1) who you are, (2) your goal, and (3) the resources available to you. We want to stand firm and have the courage to move ahead with passion and determination.

Who are we? Peter wrote that before we knew Christ we were people with no identity, but now we are God's people. God is the One who created you and the One who has given you this new life in Christ. He is the One who defines who you are, and the place to find His definition of you is in His Word. We don't look to job descriptions, self-assessment, or evaluation from the world. We look to our Creator to know who we are.

We are God's people. He paid an extreme ransom to rescue us from an empty life, a rescue planned before time began. He made us His sons and daughters and invited us to be part of his plan for His creation, partners with Christ in His mission, protected and kept safe by our Great Shepherd. Don't lose sight of who you are and waver in your motivation. You are a child of God.

Place my feet upon a firm foundation, Lord. Help me take my rightful place as a child of the Most High. May I never forget that a price was paid for me, I belong to You and You have a plan specifically for my life. Amen.

DAY 6

But my life is worth nothing to me unless I use it for finishing the work assigned me by the Lord Jesus.

—Acts 20:24 (NLT)

ONE THING NECESSARY TO MOTIVATION is that we have to have a clear view of our goal. We aren't just drifting through our days, waiting for heaven someday. In this new life in Christ, we have a purpose in each day.

You have probably discerned by now that the principle guiding my life is to represent Christ well. That is my deepest desire. It is what every Christian is called to do. I hope that is your heart's desire, too. You may word it differently. The Spirit may point to a Scripture and say, "*There, make that the framework for your life.*" Here are several other ways Scripture presents our one goal in life.

Declare his fame and praises (Psalm 102:21)
Show others the goodness of God (1 Peter 2:9)
A life filled with the richness of the message of Christ (Colossians 3:16)
Not living for self, but for him (2 Corinthians 5:15)
That the life of Jesus might be seen in me (2 Corinthians 4:10)
Doing everything as unto the Lord (Colossians 3:23)

In God's Word, you'll find more ways to state our great mission. As the Spirit leads, take one as your own guiding principle for all you say and do. Make it the banner that flies over your life.

Father, grant me the privilege of Your worldview, so I can set my sight on Your vision for my life. Burn that vision upon my heart, so I may reflect Your greatness in all that I say and do. Amen.

Steve Wingfield

DAY 7

I can do all things through him who strengthens me.

—Philippians 4:13 (ESV)

GOD IS FOR US. He is so much "for" us that He has come to live with us, intimately, and with great commitment. He is not going to leave us if we mess up or are not quite perfect. He is here, and His plans for us are for our good and for our success in living the life He intended for us. His resources are available to us, His power is working in us, and He is going to finish the work He's started.

The apostle Paul wrote that his confidence came from great trust in God. It was not his own resources and capabilities but God who enabled him to be an apostle (see 2 Corinthians 3:4–6). That is where our confidence must lie, too. We can trust God's promises that He will supply everything we need to live this life we're called to. All our hope rests in Him, and He is able and willing to carry us through. My life now is Jesus' life being lived out in me, and I live it by trusting Him. It is the only way I can live it (see Galatians 2:20).

The great evangelist Billy Sunday once said that "the only way to keep a broken vessel full is to keep it always under the tap." Keep yourself always under the tap of Christ's Spirit and power flowing through you. He will provide resources for you beyond anything you can imagine.

Lord, pour Your Spirit out on me today! Please remind me daily that You have called me by name and You walk with me daily. Your plans for me are far greater than anything I could dream of doing on my own. Amen.

Notes and Prayers

_____

_____

_____

_____

_____

_____

_____

_____

_____

_____

_____

_____

_____

_____

_____

_____

_____

_____

Steve Wingfield

Motives

We have a motive for almost everything we do; some motives are good, others are only self-serving, and others can be downright evil. Take inventory of these because long-term, our motives will be exposed.

—Paul Weaver

Day 1

For it is God who works in you to will and to act in order to fulfill his good purpose.
—Philippians 2:13

DIG DEEP. Ask God to show you truth about yourself. God has a higher purpose for us. God wants to work through us and through the gifts He's given us. As Christ's representatives, we are to live godly lives, dedicated to His use, refusing evil, pursuing a relationship with the Holy Creator.

Everything we do grows out of our motives, those inner desires that move us to action. So, if we are going to live godly lives, our motives also need to be godly. In Proverbs 21:2 we read that a person's ways might seem right to him, but God weighs the heart. Our motives are laid bare before Him, even desires that we will not admit to or do not recognize ourselves. So, we want to examine our motives with His guidance, and humbly ask Him to show us where we are acting out of motives that are not godly.

If you enter into this examination humbly and sincerely, you can expect a battle will be waged. Our old nature always fights against what the Spirit is doing within. But our Lord's power is greater! Ask for His light, His cleansing, and His power to work in you.

Lord, may I examine my heart daily so that I fulfill Your purpose for my life. Prepare me for battle as I seek You, Father. Let my actions reflect Your love and desires. Amen.

Prayers on MOTIVES by Jason Crabb.

DAY 2

We are not trying to please men but God, who tests our hearts.

—1 Thessalonians 2:4

IT IS POSSIBLE TO DESIRE TO LIVE A GODLY LIFE, but with the wrong motives. Jesus warned about doing "your righteousness in front of others to be seen by them" (Matthew 6:1). There will be no reward for those actions, Jesus said. Are we trying to please people and look "good" in their eyes? Our only goal should be to please God. And God doesn't look at the outward. He looks deep inside, at what is motivating us. He looks at the heart.

In 1 Corinthians 4:5 we read that God will bring to light and expose all the motives of our hearts when He comes back to earth to judge. "At that time each will receive their praise from God." Our greatest goal is to hear those words from our Lord, "Well done, thou good and faithful servant." The most important words any of us will ever hear.

We run our race with that goal in mind, that Jesus will meet us at the finish line and say, "Well done!" We can hear His praise and encouragement already now, each day, as we let God work in us, bringing our motives to light and cleaning out those dark corners where the old selfish nature is still trying to hide its secret motives. Let God do that today, so that tomorrow and the next tomorrow and all the tomorrows of your race can be run with this pure motive, to please Him.

Father, let my life be a reflection of You. I don't want to live my life as a man-pleaser, but as a God-pleaser. Let my words and actions be a light for others. Amen.

Steve Wingfield

Day 3

What causes fights and quarrels among you? Don't they come from your desires that battle within you?

—James 4:1

A HARBOR IS A PLACE OF SHELTER AND PROTECTION. To harbor something or someone usually means to give it a home, often secretly. James used this word when he warned not to *harbor* selfish ambition and envy (James 3:14).

That's what drives the world today—ambition, for one's own good and advancement, and envy, wanting something one doesn't have. The results of these motives? Fights, quarrels, disorder, killing, and evil practices. We don't have to look far to see the results in modern terms: power struggles, slander, "killing" of reputations, disregard for others in the race to the top of the ladder, broken relationships, cheating, lying, cruelty; the list could go on and on. Those selfish desires are the motives behind all of that. And those motives are of the devil.

A heart that harbors godly motives are pure, peace-loving, considerate, submissive, full of mercy and good fruit, impartial, and sincere. This wisdom and frame of mind is from heaven. Motives lead to actions which have consequences that shape our lives. Romans 2:6–8 tells us God "will repay each person according to what they have done. To those who by persistence in doing good seek glory, honor and immortality, he will give eternal life. But for those who are self-seeking and who reject the truth and follow evil, there will be wrath and anger."

Lord, today, perhaps like no other day I've seen in my lifetime, worldly ambition, greed, and power have become an open display of evil. My prayer is that You change people's hearts like only You can. Let them see that in Your life is better and there is an eternity to gain. Amen.

Day 4

But when the kindness and love of God our Savior appeared, he saved us, not because of righteous things we had done, but because of his mercy. He saved us through the washing of rebirth and renewal by the Holy Spirit, whom he poured out on us generously through Jesus Christ our Savior.

—Titus 3:4–6

WE ONCE LIVED UNDER THE POWER OF OUR OLD NATURE. Titus 3:3 phrases it as "deceived and enslaved by all kinds of passions and pleasures." Christ broke those powers. We are no longer slaves to them.

Long before Christ appeared on earth, God was already promising, "I will give you a new heart." We can claim that promise, brothers and sisters. When we come to Christ, He gives us rebirth and renewal. He gives us the Holy Spirit and begins that work of changing us to become like Christ. Our hearts and the motives that live there can be cleansed and purified. Remember, He has promised to give us all we need for living godly lives, and that certainly includes right motives.

We can say "NO" to those old selfish motives. Galatians 5:24 says that "those who belong to Christ Jesus have crucified the flesh with its passions and desires." The problem is, we can't do that ourselves. But Jesus' power can. Every day we can take those old motives to the cross, where His power triumphs. We walk in step with the Spirit, not the old sinful nature. We are no longer its slave; we are living by the Spirit. And living by the Spirit brings life and peace.

Lord, I am nothing without Your mercy! I want to live every day with a thankful heart, not relying on Your mercy, but just grateful for it. In Jesus' name. Amen.

Steve Wingfield

Day 5

Do nothing from selfish ambition or conceit, but in humility count others more significant than yourselves. Let each of you look not only to his own interests, but also to the interests of others.

—Philippians 2:3–4 (ESV)

Do nothing from selfish ambition. If we love our neighbor as ourselves (the great commandment, second only to loving God), our motives will be concerned for their good also.

Christ's life was dedicated to others. He came to save everyone, even His enemies. He came not to advance His own career but to do His Father's will. We know that He was tempted in every way we are. So He knows what it means to have the demands, desires, and ambitions of self wiggle into any situation. Any selfish dreams and ambitions that might have tempted Him were denied as He pursued His Father's plan. He did not even have a place of His own that He could call "home."

As Christ's representatives and partners in His mission, we want to look out for the people around us. We want to have the eyes of Christ, that can see not just the outside of a person but also the inside—who a person truly is. Christ in us will also see who a person can be. That's really what God has called us to do, not to judge people but to see something in them that maybe they don't even see themselves. Our motives should always be to lift people up and help them be everything God wants them to be.

Father, let every day remind me of my purpose. Let others see You though me. Let me be an encourager and motivator in everything I do. Amen.

Day 6

The purpose of my instruction is that all believers would be filled with love that comes from a pure heart, a clear conscience, and genuine faith.

—1 Timothy 1:5 (NLT)

All we do should be guided by motives of love. Jesus' commandment was that we love one another as He has loved us. He laid down His life for us; we lay down our lives, our own goals, dreams, ambitions, agendas, and egos for the sake of others. We will not take money, status, power, career honors, possessions, authority, respect, popularity, or anything else the self craves along to heaven with us. Nor can we stash away those treasures so they'll be waiting for us in heaven. The treasures and honors that are building for us in heaven are treasures bestowed by God, not the world.

Even greater than the motive of faith is the motive of love. That one motive should guide all we do. It will come from a heart that harbors the pure love of God. That's what I want. I don't always get it right, but that's my ultimate goal. I want the heart of God living in me and through me, and I want to do everything I can to point people to Him.

Our faith must be genuine and sincere. We want to live out that faith, believing what God says and trusting him to use our lives for His purposes. Through our faith in God, His heart guides our motives. Genuine agape love does not have ulterior motives. It seeks what's best for others as God's heart guides it.

Lord, I want Your heart living in and through me so that I can point people toward You. Help me set my desires for treasures in heaven, not here. Amen.

Steve Wingfield

DAY 7

Dear friends, do not believe every spirit, but test the spirits to see whether they are from God, because many false prophets have gone out into the world.

—1 John 4:1

IT IS NOT ONLY THE SPIRITS AROUND US THAT WE MUST TEST; we must also test our own spirit against the Word of God. That is the standard we want to follow. Not modern-day culture or anything else that presents itself. Above all else, we are to be God's holy people, honoring Him and living lives worthy of our calling.

"Being righteous doesn't mean being perfect or never making mistakes. It means developing an inner connection with God, repenting of our sin and mistakes, and freely helping others." I don't know who originally said that, but I think it's a good word. Those are the motives that we want to harbor in our hearts.

We ask the Spirit's help in examining and purifying our motives. This old hymn by James E. Orr is a good one to make your prayer today:

Search me, O God, and know my heart today,
Try me, O Savior, know my thoughts, I pray;
See if there be some wicked way in me;
Cleanse me from every sin, and set me free.

Lord, take my life, and make it wholly Thine;
Fill my poor heart with Thy great love divine;
Take all my will, my passion, self and pride;
I now surrender, Lord, in me abide.
—James E. Orr, "Search Me, O God"

Lord, I pray now more than ever that You would help me discern the spirits that surround me. I know that if I examine my motives, You will help purify them for Your glory. Cleanse me today, as every day, and make me whole. In Your name, amen.

Notes and Prayers

_____

_____

_____

_____

_____

_____

_____

_____

_____

_____

_____

_____

_____

_____

_____

_____

_____

_____

_____

_____

Steve Wingfield

ORDERLINESS

Orderliness is the difference between being effective or ineffective with your time and efforts.

—Paul Weaver

DAY 1

For God is not a God of disorder but of peace.

—1 Corinthians 14:33

THE VERY WORD "ORDERLINESS" BRINGS A SENSE OF CALM AND PEACE. God is a God of order and peace. We see His order in the intricacies of creation. None of us ever wonder if the sun will come up tomorrow in the western sky or if summer might be followed by spring next year. We can trust tide charts because God has ordered the movements of the sea and the moon.

The more we discover, the more we are awed by what He has created. Did you know that all living things are made up of the same DNA arranged in different patterns? Think about the order commanded by mathematical principles. Those principles hold true throughout the universe and cannot be compromised or adjusted. And God has named every star. He keeps track of every one.

There's a great deal of chaos in the world today. It's a broken world, poisoned by Satan. Followers of Christ are not to be conformed to this world but to Christ's kingdom. Don't let this world tell you how to live. Pattern your life as a citizen of heaven. Follow the example our King has set for us. As you think about the trait of orderliness, ask the Spirit to show you where and how you can gain more order, and peace, in your life.

Father, thank You for the order with which You have designed the universe. Reveal areas in my life where I can bring peace and order. Give me the wisdom to know how to effect positive change. In Jesus' name, amen.

Prayers on ORDERLINESS by Sara Ferrell.

Day 2

Everything should be done in a fitting and orderly way.

—1 Corinthians 14:40

PAUL'S LETTERS TO THE BELIEVERS IN CORINTH included many instructions for conducting their meetings. Why all these instructions? Because "everything that is done must strengthen all of you" (1 Corinthians 14:26 NLT). The bottom line about orderliness in our lives is that it benefits us and those around us. It saves time and money. It fosters a sense of harmony and reduces stress. It increases efficiency and productivity.

Don't underestimate the importance of organization. Having things in order is key to being a good leader. You want to be prepared and not caught off guard. Surprises are probably not going to happen as often if you're organized, but when they do, you'll better handle the unexpected. When things are in order and somebody asks you for something, you know where it is. Everything has a place, and everything is in its place. Your calendar will be organized, too, and you won't be missing deadlines or missing meetings altogether. Orderliness is one protection against overlooking details and messing up on projects.

The church at Corinth had been given the Good News and freedom of the gospel, but to nurture each believer and further Christ's message they needed order in their meetings. What has been given to you and how are you handling it? Your responsibility as a leader is to care for whatever has been put in your trust. To do that properly and to the best of your ability, you've got to be organized.

Father, help me to develop my organizational skills so that I can be an effective leader and valuable team member. Teach me to be structured and efficient so others have confidence in my reliability. In Jesus' name, amen.

Steve Wingfield

Day 3

Turn my eyes from looking at worthless things; and give me life in your ways.
—Psalm 119:37 (ESV)

DECLUTTERING OUR SPACE. Books on the subject have hit the bestseller list, and for a fee, "experts" will come into our homes or businesses to help us organize, downsize, and declutter. But long before all of this became a national topic, God's Word held wisdom for us about the worthless things in our lives.

"Worthless things" refers to idols and warns against the futility of worshiping things that can give you no life. It's tempting to skim over passages about idol worship and say we have no idols in our house. Might there be idols filling up our houses and our offices? Have we collected so much "stuff," tangible and intangible, and crammed our lives so full because we are looking to those things to give us life, to make us feel important, productive, or effective?

We've all collected and are hanging onto worthless things. These things bog us down, distract us, and detour us. Mark 4:19 gives us Jesus' warning about weeds growing up in our lives, the worries of this life, the lure of wealth, and the desire for other things choking out God's work in us.

Bringing orderliness to our lives means we'll need to sort out what gives us life, what we really want to do in this life, and where our ultimate goal and purpose lies. This wise and honest prayer from David must be our own.

Father, I do not want to allow anything into my life that may become an idol or distract me from You. Show me any worthless things that have taken my attention, and remind me that fulfillment and contentment can only be found in You. In Jesus' name, amen.

Day 4

Therefore, preparing your minds for action, and being sober-minded, set your hope fully on the grace that will be brought to you at the revelation of Jesus Christ.
—1 Peter 1:13 (ESV)

SUPPOSEDLY, THE AVERAGE PERSON HAS ABOUT FIFTY THOUGHTS PER MINUTE running through their head. Our thoughts can be just as disorderly as our desks, our calendars, and our surroundings. Again, we can go to the Scriptures for a training manual on how to order our thoughts. Remember, Paul says we are to let God make us into a new person by changing the way we think. His Word lays that out for us.

> *Be discriminating in what thoughts you allow to enter and stay in your head. Welcome true, noble, right, pure, lovely, admirable, excellent, and praiseworthy thoughts. Reject those thoughts that do not meet this checklist* (Philippians 4:8).
> *Keep God's Word firmly in your mind* (Deuteronomy 11:18).
> *Go on the offensive against arguments and ideas that present obstacles to knowing God* (2 Corinthians 10:5).
>
> *Have the same attitude toward others that Christ has* (Romans 15:5).
> *Think realistically, according to heavenly realities, not the world's* (Colossians 3:1).
> *Ask the Spirit to renew your thoughts and attitudes, and then follow his lead* (Ephesians 4:23).
> *Fix your mind on God; it will bring peace.* (Isaiah 26:3).

Follow God's guidelines of order in your thinking. He can defeat that chaos and make us new people by changing the way we think.

Father, sometimes the responsibilities I have been given and the expectations placed on me by others and myself consume my thoughts. It is easy, at times, to feel overwhelmed. Help me to take my thoughts captive in obedience to Christ and to declutter my mind so I can focus on You. In Jesus' name, amen.

Steve Wingfield

DAY 5

So be careful how you live. Don't live like fools, but like those who are wise. Make the most of every opportunity in these evil days. Don't act thoughtlessly, but understand what the Lord wants you to do.

—Ephesians 5:15–17 (NLT)

ORDERLINESS IN YOUR LIFE WILL HELP TO PREPARE YOU to live wisely and intentionally, making the most of every opportunity you have to live as the Lord guides you. Disorder, whether it's in the state of your desk or your too-busy and frantic schedule, will keep you from living out the commands of this verse.

Be prepared for every opportunity. Paul also wrote to Timothy, a young pastor, and told him to be prepared to preach the Word of God whether the time is favorable or not. Peter tells us to always be ready to explain the hope we have. God opens many opportunities for us, but how often we have said, "The time is just not right." We've lost a moment that God intended us to use.

We have been assigned to a mission; we're to carry on Christ's work of guiding people back to God. We need a clear vision of our identity as Christ's representatives and as stewards of the opportunities God gives us to further the mission. Orderliness is a matter of stewardship as well. That includes stewardship of our time and the opportunities God gives us.

Father, thank You for the opportunities You give me to share the hope we have in Christ. Give me discernment and organization when planning my schedule so I can always be ready when those opportunities arise. In Jesus' name, amen.

Day 6

He makes the whole body fit together perfectly. As each part does its own special work, it helps the other parts grow, so that the whole body is healthy and growing and full of love.

—Ephesians 4:16 (NLT)

HERE IS ONE MORE EXAMPLE of the order with which our God operates: He has given each of us certain gifts, and within His church we all complement each other. This verse from Ephesians gives us a beautiful picture of God's design for His followers to be interconnected, giving and receiving life from each other.

Now, let's go from that universal view to the view of . . . my desk. There are all kinds of research and studies that link the organization of your desk to your attitude, efficiency, and productivity. To be honest, at times, my desk does not look like I am an orderly person. But I have a team around me who help me keep orderliness in my office.

If orderliness is not a strong point for you and you know it, bring people into your life who will help you maintain organization, properly keep track of deadlines, and address your responsibilities. Many marriages have learned that each spouse's role in day-to-day responsibilities is best not defined by traditional roles but by the gifts each person possesses. Put that same thinking to work at the office and do whatever it takes to bring order to your leadership. The success of your leadership depends on it.

Father, equip me to bring order to my leadership, whether in my home, office, or church. Help me to recognize my strengths and weaknesses, to use my strengths to help the body grow, and to welcome assistance to overcome my weaknesses. In Jesus' name, amen.

DAY 7

All things have been created through him and for him . . . And in him all things hold together.

—Colossians 1:16, 17

IN SCRIPTURE, WE GET GLIMPSES OF GOD'S ORDER in the garden of Eden and His command to Adam to work and keep the garden. We see it in His precise instructions about many things, including Noah's ark and gathering the animals, the building of the tabernacle, sacrifices, and worship. We see it in Jesus' earthly life, in incidents like His directions to the disciples as He prepares to feed five thousand people and His instructions on where to meet Him after the resurrection. We see it in Jesus' mission, to bring peace between God and man and repair that broken relationship. And we see it in the glimpses we have of the new heavens and new earth coming.

The verse for today is amazing. Stop for a moment and try to grasp the depth of what the Word is saying. In Christ, everything is held together. He is the hope for the broken, chaotic world. If you want your life to be in order, my friend, you need to know the God of order and peace and harmony. Colossians 1:10 tells us that the more we get to know God, the more we will grow, not only in orderliness but in every aspect of life as a child of God.

Hold tight to the Vine. Walk close to your Master. Open yourself every day to the power and guidance of His Spirit who will bring order and peace to your journey.

Father, guide my steps today and every day, and help me to know You on a more intimate level. Bring order and peace and harmony to my, sometimes, chaotic world. In Your name, amen.

Notes and Prayers

_____

_____

_____

_____

_____

_____

_____

_____

_____

_____

_____

_____

_____

_____

_____

_____

_____

Steve Wingfield

Ownership

One true mark of a leader is taking full responsibility for outcomes and results.

—Paul Weaver

DAY 1

God, for whom and through whom everything was made, chose to bring many children into glory. And it was only right that he should make Jesus, through his suffering, a perfect leader, fit to bring them into their salvation.

—Hebrews 2:10 (NLT)

BEFORE WE TALK ABOUT THE IMPORTANCE OF TAKING OWNERSHIP, let's get the big picture clearly in mind. That all-encompassing fact is this: God has taken ownership of you and me. We have been ransomed from slavery in the kingdom of darkness to be brought into Christ's kingdom of light. The ransom was costly.

God claimed us as His own, declared us to be His children and His heirs. Jesus is leading us to glory, to the glory of our final home and to the glory God planned to be *in us*. He is the author and perfecter of our faith. This is all God's master plan, and He will not abandon His work. It is all happening *now*. He is at work in every step His children take on their journey home.

And this is all because of His great love, kindness, and mercy. It's nothing we have done; we can't boast of accomplishing any of this on our own. God has taken ownership of me. He has taken ownership of you. The lives we are living are the work of His hands and are being shaped to bring Him glory and accomplish His purposes.

Lord, help me by example to show love, kindness, and mercy to my family, friends, and all people as I go through this life. Amen.

Prayers on OWNERSHIP by Perry Chupp.

Day 2

But remember the LORD your God, for it is he who gives you the ability to produce wealth, and so confirms his covenant, which he swore to your ancestors, as it is today.

—Deuteronomy 8:18

GOD HAS TAKEN OWNERSHIP OF US. As part of His plan, He's given us responsibilities. Just as parents give children responsibilities to help them grow up and be a contributing part of the family, so has God given us work to do, to grow us up and to do the work of God's family.

We have been entrusted with Jesus' mission: to carry the message of God's grace to the world. We have been given gifts that enable us to serve others in individual and unique ways. For some of us, those gifts are abilities like speaking, writing, networking with others, and other talents. Some have been given abundant resources and out-of-the-ordinary opportunities to use for the kingdom. Jesus said that "From everyone who has been given much, much will be demanded; and from the one who has been entrusted with much, much more will be asked" (Luke 12:48). We will be held accountable for what we have done with what we've been given. On the day I have to give an answer to God for what I did, I want Him to say, "Hey, good job!"

We need to take ownership of what God has entrusted to us. Whether it's talents or opportunities or resources, own the responsibility of using it well for the kingdom. As you own it, you are going to give it everything you've got, because you are working for the Lord.

Father God, help me to use the gifts and resources You entrusted to me. May I continue to bless others by the way I have been blessed. Amen.

Steve Wingfield

Day 3

Work hard to show the results of your salvation.

—Philippians 2:12 (NLT)

OUR EFFORTS DO NOT BRING ABOUT OUR SALVATION or our transformation. God has already done that act of redemption and the Spirit is the one who changes us. But we are to take responsibility and make it evident that we have indeed become sons and daughters of the King, that we are citizens of Jesus' kingdom, and that we are people of new hope and new allegiance. When we refuse to walk in step with the Spirit, when we doubt and distrust and ignore the promises God has given us, when we shirk our new mission as representatives of Christ, then we are not owning our new life, new identity, new purpose, and new reality.

So take ownership of your new life. "Grow up" in your salvation or "put it on," as Paul wrote. Like dressing ourselves in the morning, we need to take responsibility to dress ourselves in our new identity. A snazzy new outfit may hang in your closet, but if you never put it on, it will not benefit you. We must choose each day to live in the new life of our identity in Christ.

John said if we claim to know God but don't live according to His commandments, we are liars. If we do not live by the great hope we say we have, we are avoiding taking ownership of all that our salvation has given us. The old is gone. The new is here. Take ownership of the gift you've been given and work hard to live it out.

Father, thank You for the free gift of salvation. Having faith to face each day as a new day. Knowing that You are there by our side. Amen.

Day 4

Either way, Christ's love controls us. Since we believe that Christ died for all, we also believe that we have all died to our old life. He died for everyone so that those who receive his new life will no longer live for themselves. Instead, they will live for Christ, who died and was raised for them.

—2 Corinthians 5:14–15 (NLT)

TAKING OWNERSHIP MEANS THAT WE TAKE RESPONSIBILITY, work hard, and strive toward certain outcomes. While God's gifts of mercy, forgiveness, and eternal life are exactly that, a free gifts, He also asks that we invest in this new life, too.

Here are just a few words from some of the New Testament letters to Christians: make every effort, work at, put on, put off, flee, resist, use them well, get rid of, run with endurance, hold on to, be on guard, stand firmly, press on.

Yes, God asks us to pour ourselves into the life, identity, and purpose He has given us. He has given us many promises about what He will do in our lives. Peter says that doing so will help us escape the corruption of this world and make us more like Christ. God has laid out what He is doing. Now He wants us to step up and live as His redeemed people. His Word tells us it takes effort. We have got to invest ourselves in this life.

I pray that I can continue to show the love of Jesus in helping those in need. Guide and direct my steps. May we continue to be blessed with good health and safety. Amen.

Steve Wingfield

Day 5

Praise the LORD, for he has shown me the wonders of his unfailing love. He kept me safe when my city was under attack.

—Psalm 31:21 (NLT)

YES, THERE ARE DAYS WHEN OUR HANDS ARE TIRED AND OUR KNEES ARE WEAK. Our minds are frazzled and our hearts are discouraged. Where do our thoughts go then? The enemy will attempt to take advantage of every crack in our city walls. God, in his unfailing love, has provided for us in His plan. David knew it. He wrote his gratitude into many of the psalms. Psalm 31 includes today's verse and other lines about the great goodness the Lord has for those who come to Him for help and protection.

The Bible is a book of hope for you, my friend. In the Word, you'll get to know God better and better. You will see more and more of His plan for you and the great goodness He has for you. You will find that He does supply everything we need in our walk through this world, and in our leadership and our ownership of what God has entrusted to us. Jesus encourages us to ask, seek, and knock. We find what we need in Him. Peter assures us in 2 Peter 1:3 that we'll have all the resources we need to live a life dedicated to God's purposes. He is the Shepherd providing for His sheep. When your city is under attack, His unfailing love will not abandon you. You can count on that.

Lord, thank You for walking with me through the dark valleys whenever I take a wrong turn. Thank You for Your unfailing love. Amen.

Day 6

Whoever conceals their sins does not prosper, but the one who confesses and renounces them finds mercy.

—Proverbs 28:13

TAKING OWNERSHIP ALSO MEANS THAT WE ARE ACCOUNTABLE for those times we mess up. As the wisdom of Proverbs says, attempting to find excuses or blame others for our missteps is taking a path that will not prosper me.

I am so thankful that my God also has a plan for those days I do mess up. When I make a mistake, I don't have to live in bondage to it. I can ask God to teach me from my error, to give me more wisdom and strength, and then go forward. If I have sinned, 1 John 1:9 assures me that He is faithful and just. I can trust Him to hold to His promise. He will forgive me and cleanse me. He not only cleanses my record of black marks but also works in me to clean out more of the old me and put His own character in place. Like the Apostle Paul, we can forget what is behind and press on toward the goal.

On the flip side, we can also celebrate when we get it right. We praise Him for His help, for the guidance of His Spirit, for all that kindness and goodness He showers on us. The ultimate ownership is God's. He is committed to the final result: bringing us home to Him to share in His glory.

Thank You, Lord, for the many times we mess up, all we have to do is ask and we are forgiven. Thank You for Your faithfulness, Your promise that all those things are behind us and we can move on with a clean record. Amen.

Day 7

Do not be deceived: God cannot be mocked. A man reaps what he sows.

—Galatians 6:7

DON'T LET THE DECEIVER, the enemy of your soul, convince you that God's laws of sowing and reaping can be circumvented or prevented. We will reap according to what we sow. If what we sow is dishonesty, a lack of forgiveness, no accountability, insincerity, and selfishness, then we can fully expect those seeds we have scattered will grow into a harvest we'll have to deal with in the people we lead. Such seeds scatter and sprout quickly. On the other hand, so do seeds of honesty, forgiveness, accountability, sincerity, and kindness (to name a few examples).

We will also reap according to *how* we sow. Paul in 2 Corinthians 9:6 tells us that if we sow sparingly, we will also reap sparingly. As a leader, you cannot expect to see a flourishing crop of desirable character traits springing up among your coworkers if you have not planted plenty of seeds. If you sow generously, you'll be rewarded with an abundant crop. That law works in our personal lives, too.

Galatians 6 goes on to say that if we sow to please the Spirit, to walk in step with Him, then our result and outcome will be eternal life. But if it is our sinful nature that is controlling the seed we scatter as we walk through life, the result and outcome will be destruction.

Father God, thank You for forgiving us beyond what we deserve. Help me to show more love and kindness. Continue to walk with me in sowing the good seeds that You would be pleased in all I do and say. Amen.

Notes and Prayers

_____

_____

_____

_____

_____

_____

_____

_____

_____

_____

_____

_____

_____

_____

_____

_____

_____

Passion

Living with passion is the best way to make a life and not just a living.

—Paul Weaver

Day 1

So whether you eat or drink or whatever you do, do it all for the glory of God.
—1 Corinthians 10:31

I AM A COMPETITIVE PERSON, AND PEOPLE KNOW THAT. I like to celebrate and enjoy. If you know me, you know when I take on a project, I'm all in. The word "passion" often has sexual connotations, but we are now focusing on the more general definition of living life or pursuing a goal or leading an organization to the full. Passionate living is what Jesus was referring to in John 10:10, when He said He came to give us life in all its fullness, life abundant and rich and satisfying. That's living with passion for life.

More than any other area of my life, I want to be passionate about my life for Christ. I want to make a difference for His kingdom. In order to do that, I'm going to have to give everything that's in me. Lay it all on the line. I'm doing that because I'm passionately in love with Jesus. I want the words on my tombstone to say, "He died crazy in love with Jesus." I want to die empty. And when I see Him, I want to be able to say, "Lord, I gave it everything I had."

Jesus, from the day I awake until I lay my head to rest, empower me to obediently pursue You at work, at home, at church, and in my interactions with the stranger and enemy. Amen.

Prayers on PASSION by Beau Hummel.

DAY 2

Earth has nothing I desire besides you.

—Psalm 73:25

MY FRIEND, TODAY TAKE TIME TO IMAGINE what your life would be like without God's guidance, strength, and presence. We get caught up in "life" happening, and we take much for granted—until those things are lost to us. Then we discover that we can live without our possessions; yes, we even can live without our loved ones, although that is a far greater and more painful journey. But I can never live without Christ.

This is my greatest passion—to live my life in Christ to the fullest. His presence is one thing that will *always* be with me and will not fade away, betray, fizzle, or disappoint. I'm committed to Him. I want to pour my life into representing Him well.

I'm not saying this to boast. I only want to share (as Asaph wrote in Psalm 73 NLT) "how good it is to be near God!" I want to tell of the wonderful things He's done and the strength He provides. I hope you, too, have found that He is worth pouring your life into.

We all have other passions in life—our families, pet projects, the people and organizations we lead. As we think about *passion* this week, sort out your priorities. Bring clarity into what you hold most essential in life and where your passion is driving you.

Jesus, my schedule is so full, just not full enough of You. Forgive me for placing my interests, my activities, and others before my pursuit of You. I pray Your Spirit fills me with passion today that chooses to pursue You above all else. And may my schedule one day be evidence of my new passionate pursuit. Amen.

Steve Wingfield

Day 3

Since, then, you have been raised with Christ, set your hearts on things above, where Christ is, seated at the right hand of God.

—Colossians 3:1

COLOSSIANS 3 GIVES US A STARK CONTRAST between the old life and the new, sinful passions and godly passions, the earthly and the heavenly. We don't have to read Colossians 3 to know where sinful, earthly passions take a person. We can see it in the world around us: immorality, greed, malice, deceit, cheating, and selfishness. The sinful passions of this world lead to such behavior and even worse, like murder. While many people would never murder another person, how many have attacked, with intent to kill, another person's reputation or status?

When Christ is in us, when our passion is to be God's holy people growing in the likeness of Christ, then the picture is one of a life filled with mercy, kindness, humility, gentleness, patience, forgiveness, love, and peace. Then our hearts are set on doing and saying *everything* as a representative of Christ (Colossians 3:17).

What produces such a passion? What changes us from the grip of old passions to the new? It is Christ, coming to live in us; he is what drives our passion (Colossians 3:11). That passage ends with this (verse 16 NLT): "Let the message about Christ, in all its richness, fill your lives." When that happens, my friend, our passions take a huge turn and pursue another path, with intense, powerful emotion and commitment.

Father, thank You for the reminder that the presence of Your Spirit is that near and even more as He lives in me. Help me lean into You, listening to You, and, with passion, pursue your presence above all other pursuits in my life. Amen.

Day 4

See what great love the Father has lavished on us…
—1 John 3:1

It is our great thanks to God the Father that fires our passion to live as his holy people. Isaiah 9:7 (NLT), within a prophecy about Christ, includes the assurance that "the passionate commitment" of the Lord will make everything happen. God is passionately committed to redeeming His world. He is committed to bringing us out of an empty life and giving us a full life, and He paid an exorbitant price to do so (1 Peter 1:18–19). Just as Colossians 3 speaks of "clothing" ourselves with the new character God has given His people, Isaiah speaks of God clothing Himself, wrapping Himself in a cloak of divine passion (Isaiah 59:17 NLT).

His divine, committed passion has lavished great love on us. He loved us first, before we even knew Him. He is so passionate, so committed to redemption, that He became the sacrifice for what *we* have done. He has come to live with us and give us new lives. He showers us with good and perfect gifts. He made us His children so we could enjoy our inheritance and share in all He has.

We were created anew to live for His glory. May His passionate commitment to us call forth our own, and may our thanks to Him be shown in everything we say and do.

Thank You, I pray that I may begin to passionately pursue Your son and model my life after His. Give me the humility required to hear Your Spirit as He leads me to pursue others around me just as Your Son pursued me first. Amen.

Steve Wingfield

Day 5

My goal is that they may be encouraged in heart and united in love, so that they may have the full riches of complete understanding, in order that they may know the mystery of God, namely Christ.

—Colossians 2:2

Passion influences. Passion energizes. Passion encourages. Passion *spreads*. It can be caught, like a virus. Passion is essential because without it, discouragement, exhaustion, and frustration set in. Not only for the team or organization, but for the leader, too. In contrast, people who dig in with passion lead, even if they do not have the title or position of *leader*. The passionate motivate and energize.

If you've been to a Christmas candle-lighting service, you've seen this illustrated in a small way. One candle lights another. Each of those lights another. And on and on, until the entire room is ablaze with light. Passion can be something like those candles.

Not everyone will "catch" your passion, of course. But passion in any endeavor must begin somewhere, with someone. It is motivating and energizing. Without that flame, any project, business, or organization is going to slog along, struggling to keep life going, often faltering and very possibly failing.

The passion of others can refresh and nurture yours, too. On a spiritual level, this is such an important principle. It is one reason God has given us that Spirit-connection to other lives-in-Christ. We encourage each other.

Father, thank You for the gentle reminder today that regardless of where I am, my role at work, or the state of my home, I am always in a position to influence someone. Give me the courage to remain humble and follow you to the places YOU would have me serve as the greatest influencer for what you are doing in this world today. Amen.

Day 6

Never be lacking in zeal, but keep your spiritual fervor, serving the Lord.
—Romans 12:11

PASSION LEADS TO GROWTH AND EXCELLENCE. That intense, compelling commitment to something leads us to strive to give it everything we've got and then strive even more to increase what we have to offer. Passion is that drive to give something the very best, the full force of who we are and what we have; and the natural outcome is personal growth.

Again, I think of the passionate commitment of God, giving Himself for us, giving us what we need to live that rich, satisfying life. He gives fully, abundantly, far beyond what we imagine.

In turn, we want to grow in our walk with Him and excel in serving Him. I don't want to do a slipshod job for the One who gave His all so that I could have this life. I don't want to get lazy or follow Him reluctantly or half-heartedly. I want to give it my all. Jesus said, "Love the Lord your God with all your heart and with all your soul and with all your mind and with all your strength" (Mark 12:30). That's loving with passion, the most important commandment.

Paul knew exactly what Jeremiah was talking about when he said, "God's word burns in my heart like a fire, like a fire in my bones! I can't hold it in!" (Jeremiah 20:9, paraphrased).

Father God, I am in awe of Your perfection. I am a sinner in need of Your forgiveness and grace, but I also know the Holy Spirit lives inside of me. God, it is my passion to have Your Spirit drive me to excellence in all I do as Your perfect plan unfolds in my life. Amen.

DAY 7

His master replied, "Well done, good and faithful servant!"
—Matthew 25:21

C. T. STUDD, THE BRITISH MISSIONARY, gave up most of his worldly goods and comforts to serve on mission fields. He wrote:

> *Let us not glide through this world and then slip quietly into heaven without having blown the trumpet loud and long for our Redeemer, Jesus Christ. Let us see to it that the devil will hold a thanksgiving service in hell, when he gets the news of our departure from the field of battle.*

We are on the field of battle under the banner of Jesus Christ. I'm not working just to get a paycheck. Whatever I do, I do for the Lord. He gave me this new life. It belongs to Him. I want to represent Him well in everything I do, wherever I go, and with whoever I'm relating to. I want to blow the trumpet long and loud for my Redeemer.

This principle is very helpful in directing and fueling our passion, reminding us exactly how we want to live. For my part, I remind myself constantly that I want to represent Christ well, in whatever I say and do. I have that goal always in mind and pursue it with passion.

He has created this new life we're living. He has good plans for us and work for us to do. Let's be fervent in fulfilling our purpose and calling.

Father, I long for more of You living in me and flowing through me that by the authentic love, joy, peace, patience, kindness, goodness, faithfulness, gentleness, and self-control I show to those around me, it may become increasingly evident that You are the ultimate center, leader, and passion of my existence both now and forevermore. Amen.

Notes and Prayers

_____

_____

_____

_____

_____

_____

_____

_____

_____

_____

_____

_____

_____

_____

_____

_____

_____

_____

_____

Steve Wingfield

PATIENCE

Have patience and enjoy the journey because there is no destination;
it's all about the journey.

—Paul Weaver

DAY 1

Whoever is patient has great understanding, but one who is quick-tempered displays folly.
—Proverbs 14:29

I'LL BE HONEST WITH YOU; patience is the trait I struggle with the most, pray most about, and work at the hardest. A couple of years ago, I walked into a church, and the church secretary said, "I saw you yesterday." I asked her where she had seen me, and she said, "In my rear-view mirror." And what she saw told her she had better get out of my way. Yes, my need for patience shows up most often in my driving. I've never cursed other drivers or given obscene gestures, but apparently what is going on inside me shows on my face.

Patience is a virtue, and it's one that can be learned and controlled. It is up to me, and it is up to you, to choose patience. I don't want circumstances or other people's actions to dictate how I respond to things. Sometimes I just have to take a deep breath and step back and collect my thoughts and practice patience.

I like the term "practice" because that means you keep working at it until you get it to where you want it to be. I hope you choose to work on implementing patience. I choose to. I am working on it.

Dear God, guide me on the path to patience, choosing it again and again, day by day. Amen.

Prayers on PATIENCE by Arthur Wingfield.

Day 2

Therefore, as God's chosen people, holy and dearly loved, clothe yourselves with compassion, kindness, humility, gentleness and patience.

—Colossians 3:12

My goal is to represent Christ well in all I do. This desire guides my decisions, words, and behavior. He is my example, and I want my life to reflect Him.

Think of how often Jesus must have had to practice patience. Crowds followed Him everywhere and often stayed for long hours. Nicodemus came to see Him at night. The Pharisees constantly harassed Him with their questions fashioned to discredit and trap Him. Even His inner circle of friends just didn't "get it" sometimes. He often had to take more time to explain to them what He meant, or they exhibited attitudes and behavior that were so out of line with everything He had been teaching. I have a feeling I would have been aggravated many times if I were in Jesus' shoes. His compassion kept Him patient with these lost sheep He had come to rescue.

You know, you can let people tweak you, or you can choose not to. Patience helps us relate to other people in a good and godly way. We read in the book of Proverbs that "A person's wisdom yields patience; it is to one's glory to overlook an offense" (Proverbs 19:11).

Wisdom yields patience. Overlooking an offense includes forgiveness. Jesus' compassion kept Him patient. All of the Lodestar traits are interwoven. All of them are meant to make me a better me; make you a better you. And I desire those qualities that make me a better representative of the Lord to whom I belong, the Lord I love and serve.

Help me to be patient with others, Holy Spirit, filled with compassion and resisting frustration. Amen.

Steve Wingfield

Day 3

So letting your sinful nature control your mind leads to death. But letting the Spirit control your mind leads to life and peace.

—Romans 8:6 (NLT)

PATIENCE SEEMS TO COME EASILY FOR SOME PEOPLE. For others, like me, it is a daily struggle. Two things that will make a huge difference for us in this battle are prayer and the help of the Holy Spirit. If we commit ourselves to the Holy Spirit's leading, patience is fruit He brings into our lives. The list of qualities of the Spirit-led life includes peace and self-control, too, things we do not find where impatience rules.

Galatians 5 tells us that our sinful nature is constantly in conflict with the Spirit. It wants to take us down the path opposite of where the Spirit would lead us. But the sinful human nature is no longer the master of sons and daughters of God. We are not "obligated" to obey that old nature. In other words, I no longer can say, "That's just the way I am." Jesus broke the power of sin in our lives when He died on the cross. Now, we choose a new guide—the Spirit of Christ.

The battle will always be there, and that is why prayer for the Spirit's help and guidance is so important. Ephesians 6 tells us about the armor God has given us so that we can stand firm in the battles, and the passage ends with "And pray in the Spirit on all occasions with all kinds of prayers and requests" (6:18). He will answer our prayers when our desire is to keep in step with Him. I can guarantee it.

Compassionate Savior, let me turn from my excuses and begin a journey toward godly patience and love. Amen.

DAY 4

For whatsoever things were written aforetime were written for our learning, that we through patience and comfort of the Scriptures might have hope.

—Romans 15:4 (KJV)

THE MORE WE READ OF GOD'S WORD, the more we understand His plans and the more alert we are to see how He is working those plans right now. God's Word helps me put things in my life in perspective. Those little irritations that have pumped impatience into me take on different proportions. When the Spirit starts showing me God's view of things, peace replaces impatience.

God's Word holds the comfort of assurance that He is in control. He has a plan for all of His creation. He has His eye on things, and everything He has planned will come to pass. He cares about the details of my life, even things I don't pay much attention to, and works in everything for my good. He is my Shepherd, and I have all that I need. He'll never leave me or forsake me. He wants me to point others to Him and to show them who He is and what He can do in a life. He is the Alpha and Omega. He holds the beginning and the end.

There is so much more! Reading all these things in Scripture adjusts my attitude. It opens up the scope of my vision. Hearing what God has to say to me can somehow shrink those things that make me impatient. Or, maybe, it's not that those things shrink, but that God and His glorious plan grow larger and larger in my sights.

Heavenly Father, bring my eyes to the right places in Your Word, so I might see what You will grant me for being patient. Amen.

Day 5

But you, Lord, are a compassionate and gracious God, slow to anger, abounding in love and faithfulness.

—Psalm 86:15

How patient God has been with me! Patience is one of God's attributes. How blessed we are because of it! God is love, and 1 Corinthians 13 describes an *agape* love originating from God. Notice the first attribute listed? That's right: patience.

It is only because of God's patience that we have His mercy and forgiveness. He could have simply done away with His creation that wandered so far from His plan. But he did not. He had a plan of salvation in place even before time began. He is still patient, offering people the chance to come back to him.

He is so patient and compassionate with His children! I can't count the times he has had to get me back on track, help me up, or straighten me out. He's had to administer a little discipline now and then—sometimes, more severe discipline—but always as a patient, loving father. His plan was not only to save me but to keep changing me into the person he created me to be. He's patiently doing that.

As his child, he is teaching me to be like him. With His great love and patience for the lost, should I not also be patient and loving toward them? As a recipient of His great patience with me, should I not also be patient with my brothers and sisters? And because His plan covers the beginning and end of everything, should I not even be patient in all circumstances?

Patient Lord, I thank you for your unwillingness to give up on me, and I ask your guidance to show the same patient love to others. Amen.

DAY 6

We do not want you to become lazy but to imitate those who through faith and patience inherit what has been promised.

—Hebrews 6:12

CHARLES STANLEY SAID, "Our willingness to wait reveals the value we place on the object we're waiting for." I don't know about you, but this thought helps me at times when I feel impatience rising inside me. *What do I value the most? What is my highest goal?*

When I'm creeping along behind a car doing 45 in a 55-mph zone, I'll be honest with you—I want to get where I'm going and I want to be on time. I value that. It is important to me to be where I said I'd be and when I said I'd be there. I'm waiting to get there, and I do place high value on promptness. But is that what I value most? What I most want for my life is to be an excellent representative for Christ. I want to reflect him in everything I am, everything I do, and everything I say. So, I look to my example. Jesus experienced all kinds of hindrances, annoyances, and outright opposition to his ministry, but his mission was to save souls and bring the kingdom of heaven to earth. His patience during his ministry, and even now, amazes me.

I am privileged to give my life to being his representative. So, I will keep practicing my patience.

Dear Jesus, remind me daily to practice being patient and to be a faithful representative of You. Amen.

Steve Wingfield

Day 7

May the Lord lead your hearts into a full understanding and expression of the love of God and the patient endurance that comes from Christ.

—2 Thessalonians 3:5 (NLT)

As you practice your patience, I encourage you to take the Sword of the Spirit into the battle with you. The Word of God is the weapon the Spirit uses to fight for you. Believe me, it is truly alive, active, and powerful (Hebrews 4:12), like a fire, a hammer that smashes a rock (Jeremiah 23:29), and sharper than a two-edged sword (Hebrews 4:12). The two-edged sword was used by Roman soldiers in intense, hand-to-hand combat. It was necessary when the enemy was right on you, in life-and-death combat.

If impatience is something you struggle with, pray for help. Then start writing down all those Scriptures that the Spirit points out to you. Proverbs and Ecclesiastes have many. The New Testament letters stress patience repeatedly. Write the Scriptures, mark them, record them—whatever works for you. Then, in the intense battles between impatience and Spirit patience, the Spirit will use this Sword to change the tide of the war. With the Word of God, the Spirit can protect you and repel the enemy of impatience.

I pray for you and me both, that we will be strengthened with all his glorious power and we'll have all the patience we need to represent him well.

Gracious Father, arm me with your Word and fill me with determination to show patience, compassion, and forgiveness. Amen.

Notes and Prayers

_____

_____

_____

_____

_____

_____

_____

_____

_____

_____

_____

_____

_____

_____

_____

_____

_____

Leadership is 80 percent about you and 20 percent about your team.

—Paul Weaver

DAY 1

But the wisdom that comes from heaven is first of all pure; then peace-loving, considerate, submissive, full of mercy and good fruit, impartial and sincere.

—James 3:17

IN HEBREW, THE WORD *PEACE* REFERS TO A LIVING, vibrant wellbeing. It has nothing to do with your situation on the outside. It has everything to do with your condition *inside*. As we have seen consistently through the Lodestar study, our condition on the inside determines what comes out in words and actions. Our character builds not only our reputation but, more importantly, also builds the environment in which we live, work, and socialize. As a leader, you have more influence than any other person on the culture and climate of your organization.

James tells us that God-given wisdom is peace-loving. This wisdom *pursues* peace, both personal peace and peace within the organization. We all know what havoc can result when there is no peace within and between coworkers: there's disorder, disloyalty, deceit, grumbling, distrust, even increased absenteeism.

Key to your leadership is your own peace, a peace within. It must start there, within you. That peace within you will move out and affect those you lead. If you do not have that peace, the disorder and dis-ease will also move out and affect your team. If you do not feel that peace within, ask the Lord to speak to you this week and give you his peace.

Father God, Creator of heaven and earth, I humble myself before you. Come and give me your peace. I receive it through the power of God and praise you. In the name of Jesus, amen.

Prayers on PEACE by Barbara Wingfield.

Steve Wingfield

Day 2

For to us a child is born, to us a son is given, and the government will be on his shoulders. And he will be called Wonderful Counselor, Mighty God, Everlasting Father, Prince of Peace.

—Isaiah 9:6

You can be in the middle of serene nature and not be in peace. Or you can be in the bustle of a city or the roar of a battlefield and have peace. What makes the difference?

Jesus. He is our peace.

Jesus could fall asleep in a storm. He could face more than five thousand people and not be anxious about it. Everybody in Jairus's house was mourning, weeping and wailing, and Jesus said, *"Calm down. It's gonna be okay."* The demon-possessed man charged him, and he stood there as the Prince of Peace. In the Garden of Gethsemane, his words were "Peter, put your sword away." On the cross, he prayed, "Father forgive them."

He is the Prince of Peace. His life showed a peace that is unmatched. And he is the One who will bring peace to us. The child was born *to us, for us.* He holds the key to our peace. In Luke 1:79, we read Zechariah's prophecy about the baby to be born "to give light to those who sit in darkness and in the shadow of death, and to guide us to the path of peace" (NLT). God's tender mercy made this possible. He doesn't want his children to live in anxiety and discord and dis-ease; he wants to give them peace. Jesus came to show us the way.

Lord God, thank you for giving Jesus, for his life, example, forgiveness, for his light and guidance for me today. Because of Jesus, amen.

Day 3

"I have told you these things, so that in me you may have peace."
—John 16:33

THE SAME PROPHECY THAT DECLARED THE COMING MESSIAH to be Prince of Peace also said he would be a Wonderful Counselor, Mighty God, and Everlasting Father, and his government *and its peace* would never end.

We have a Wonderful Counselor. When you need hope, comfort, and assurance, read Jesus' words to all disciples in John, chapters 14, 15, and 16, and his prayer for us in chapter 17. He was counseling and preparing his disciples then, and he counsels and prepares us today. His Holy Spirit lives in us to teach and guide us. What better counselor could we find?

He is Mighty God. We need a mighty God, don't we? He is the living God. That's why we can hope and trust in him, the mighty Creator who is Lord of all. He is everlasting. We do not place our hope in a God who will disappear, fade away, or die. He holds the beginning and the end and everything in between. He is the Almighty, and there is no other.

This is where we have placed our trust—in this omnipotent, everlasting God who lives with us personally as Counselor and Guide. This God came to earth *to us, for us*. He came to guide us to the path of peace. When you follow him on this path, your life and your leadership are transformed.

Mighty God, I need you. Be Lord, be victorious in my thoughts and actions. I praise you for coming so that in you I may have peace. In the name of Jesus, amen.

Day 4

Through him God reconciled everything to himself. He made peace with everything in heaven and on earth by means of Christ's blood on the cross.

—Colossians 1:20 (NLT)

THE CROSS IS GOD'S PLAN FOR PEACE. Sin had put humanity far from God and made us his enemies. Somehow, our peace with God needed to be accomplished. But we could never build a peace with God ourselves. God did it. He made peace with us before we even wanted it. He loved us before we even cared.

You can take a vacation to try to capture a little slice of peace. You can go to the drugstore and buy tranquilizers to calm you down or give you sleep, but you aren't finding real peace. The only place you'll find it is in the God of all peace.

Jacob wrestled with God. His heart was changed and he became Israel. He went from being a conniving deceiver to a man through whom God's kingdom was established. When you accept God's peace through Jesus Christ, your heart is changed. You are, first of all, granted peace with God. Sin is no longer a barrier between you and the Almighty. Your sin has been paid for. Then you are given all of his assurances, his promises, and his presence to provide his rich resources for your walk through this world.

Jesus came to show you the way to peace. He is the God of all peace. Don't look for it anywhere else.

Dear God, thank you for making a plan to rescue me from my sin. Help me know and remember your promises, be thrilled by the presence of your Spirit, and trust you. In the name of Jesus, amen.

Steve Wingfield

DAY 5

A heart at peace gives life to the body.
—Proverbs 14:30

A HEART AT PEACE. In Philippians 4 we find promises of a peace that is beyond our comprehension. The first thing Paul gives us are three simple things to do instead of worrying.

1. *Pray about everything.*
2. *Tell God what you need.*
3. *Thank him for all he has done.*

The result of this, God's Word promises, is that we "will experience God's peace, which exceeds anything we can understand" (Philippians 4:7). It will be a peace that can't be explained from human reasoning or logic, but it will stand guard around our hearts and minds as we live in Christ Jesus.

The second thing to do is to focus our thoughts. According to God's Word, if we focus our thoughts, and if we keep focused on the true, honorable, right, pure, lovely, admirable, excellent, and worthy of praise, and if we keep walking in step with the Spirit, "Then the God of peace will be with you" (2 Corinthians 13:11).

Christ is the One who gives us strength. When we depend on him instead of our own strength, we find we can do and be content in all things (Philippians 4:11–13). God will supply all our needs from his glorious riches—given to us through Christ Jesus (Philippians 4:19). It is the same peace that David celebrated in Psalm 23: "The Lord is my Shepherd. I have all that I need!"

I pray that the God of all peace gives you that *heart at peace.*

Lord God, you are the God of grace and peace. Cleanse my thoughts through the blood of Jesus. Your Spirit is giving me power. In the name of Jesus, amen.

Day 6

Pursue righteousness, faith, love, and peace.
—2 Timothy 2:22

As children of the God of peace and followers of Jesus Christ, we are called to live in peace. Jesus said peacemakers will be blessed. In almost every letter of the New Testament, the apostles wrote, "Do everything possible to live in peace with everyone." Their opening lines included "May God give you more and more grace and peace."

We are not to repay evil for evil, but instead return blessings and good for evil. Don't fight over traditions in the church, wrote Paul in Romans 14. Don't let arguments destroy what God is doing but work for peace and mutual edification. Even in cases of one spouse leaving another, "God has called us to live in peace" (1 Corinthians 7:15).

The disciples were often disturbed. They argued among themselves. They wanted to go to war. They wanted to burn down a village. How many times does your presence declare war? Take inventory of your days. Are you a peacemaker? Are you pursuing peace and building up others instead of warring with them?

If you find yourself going to war with the outside world, it's time to settle the war on the inside. What's expressing itself on the outside is only the fruit, and something has to be done about the root before the fruit can be changed. The only thing that changes the root—your heart—is walking with the Lord. He is the Prince of Peace.

Father God, I earnestly ask you to help me pursue peace, to build others up and to be an encourager. May peace be the fruit coming forth. I praise you and pray in the name of Jesus, amen.

Steve Wingfield

Day 7

But even if you suffer for doing what is right, God will reward you for it. So don't worry or be afraid of their threats. Instead, you must worship Christ as Lord of your life. And if someone asks about your hope as a believer, always be ready to explain it.

—1 Peter 3:14–15 (NLT)

Following Jesus' teaching and His example of peace will often be counter to culture. His words go against much of the popular business "wisdom" of today, and we will most likely be looked upon as foolish or weak. God wants us to be men and women of peace. He wants to give us that *shalom*, that vibrant, healthy life, and He wants us to represent Him as a God of peace. It is His name we bear. We are His representatives. He wants to be involved in every aspect of our lives and walk with us, and He wants us to deliver His message of peace.

Moses talked with God. Enoch walked with God. Daniel had peace in the lion's den. Daniel's friends saw the fiery furnace but trusted God. The king watched them being bound and thrown into the fire. Then he exclaimed, "I thought we threw three men in there. I see a fourth one walking around who looks like the son of God!" (Daniel 3:25) Paul had peace in jail. We can have peace in any and all situations if we make Christ Lord of our lives.

Lord God, You are the Most High God, my Savior and Lord. In sufferings, You are able to deliver me, be my vindicator. I worship Christ as Lord of my life. In the name of Jesus, amen.

Notes and Prayers

_____

_____

_____

_____

_____

_____

_____

_____

_____

_____

_____

_____

_____

_____

_____

_____

_____

Steve Wingfield

PRODUCTIVITY

The success of every organization is tied directly to productivity. The leader who serves his team by helping them be productive is routinely in the trenches.

—Paul Weaver

DAY 1

Make every effort to add to your faith goodness; and to goodness, knowledge; and to knowledge, self-control; and to self-control, perseverance; and to perseverance, godliness; and to godliness, mutual affection; and to mutual affection, love. For if you possess these qualities in increasing measure, they will keep you from being ineffective and unproductive in your knowledge of our Lord Jesus Christ.

—2 Peter 1:5–9

SOME TIME AGO, SOMEBODY ASKED ME IF I WAS RETIRED. I don't know why they thought I was retired. Maybe to them I looked like I had reached the age of retirement. I said, "Well, define *retired*." Their definition was "doing whatever you want to do when you want to do it." I said, "I'm retired." I love doing what I do. I've always loved doing what I do. And I feel like what I do is productive. I'm in the game.

If you want to stay in the game, you've got to be productive. When you are productive, you look for what needs to be done, and you do it; that's initiative. You motivate others to work toward an end result; that's influence. You look for ways to do things better; that's resourcefulness and development and innovation. Boldness, ownership, passion, flexibility, determination, and many more of our traits all work in synergy to keep you productive and in the game.

Lord, may I live in the awareness that I have "Only one life to live, it will soon be past, only what is done for Christ will last." Amen.

Prayers on PRODUCTIVITY by Brandon Traylor.

Day 2

We do not want you to become lazy, but to imitate those who through faith and patience inherit what has been promised.

—Hebrews 6:12

PRODUCTIVITY IS DEFINED AS EFFECTIVELY GENERATING QUALITY RESULTS. Productivity in manufacturing or marketing or as a machinist, whatever you do, has to be efficient. It's got to generate quality results. You've got to meet deadlines. You can't be overwhelmed by work. You can't be watching the clock all the time.

Productivity takes effort. It takes work. You can't be lazy. Most leaders I know are not lazy; in fact, no leader I know is lazy. Productivity and laziness do not go together. In Ecclesiastes 10:18, we read these words: "Through laziness, the rafters sag; because of idle hands, the house leaks." The wisdom of Proverbs warns repeatedly about laziness. An idle person will suffer hunger, and too much "folding of the hands to rest" will bring poverty and need. "Lazy hands make for poverty, but diligent hands bring wealth" (Proverbs 10:4).

We can't be lazy in our discipleship, either. If a constant folding of the hands to rest controls us, we've become its slave (2 Peter 2:19 and Romans 6:16). But Jesus has broken our slavery to all other things; now we offer our obedience to Him. And He offers us so much more in life! Peter wrote that through God's promises "you may participate in the divine nature, and having escaped the corruption in the world caused by evil desires" (2 Peter 1:4).

Those are powerful statements, my friend. Don't be a slave to laziness. Push on in your faith and fortitude and inherit what He has promised you.

Lord, this world needs more people with dirty fingernails and clean hearts. Amen.

Steve Wingfield

Day 3

You make known to me the path of life; you will fill me with joy in your presence, with eternal pleasures at your right hand.

—Psalm 16:11

PROCRASTINATION WILL SHRED OUR PRODUCTIVITY. When we intentionally delay getting a task done, all too often it will never be finished, or it's finished in a manner that gives it less than our best. Now, we can find many Scriptures warning us against procrastination. Jesus said we're to be dressed for service, always keeping our lamps burning (Luke 12:35). Proverbs 20:4 warns that if we don't plow in season, we'll find nothing at harvest time. Paul wrote in Ephesians 5:15–16 that we are to walk wisely, making the most of every opportunity. Procrastination, instead, lets opportunities slip away.

We procrastinate because we want to avoid something—for now. Perhaps we have some fear associated with what we have to do. Maybe we feel inadequate for the job. Or see it as drudgery and boredom. Or think it's too insignificant to bother with. How do you *feel* about that thing you're postponing? We all know that projects we're excited about get our immediate attention and action. But other things get pushed back.

The Lord has put us on the path of life. If we are conscious of His presence in every moment, we look at all opportunities differently. We see His hand in even small details of our day. He reminds us constantly of His purpose and power. When He calls us to something, He provides what we need for the job. We are living with him, serving him with our lives. Then, every opportunity counts. Every moment is the path of life.

My Lord Jesus, fill me with the joy of Your constant presence with me on this path of life. Amen.

Steve Wingfield

Day 4

Set your mind on things above, not on earthly things.

—Colossians 3:2

PRODUCTIVITY REQUIRES COMMITMENT. If you want to be productive, you've got to keep your eye on the goal and get there. I want to challenge you today to think about the areas in which you are striving to be productive. What end results do you seek? What is your goal?

Our verse today tells us to focus on heavenly realities and values. But we still live earthly lives, and God will hold us accountable for how we use whatever we've been given here. Our commitment is to live here with eternity's perspective on all things. Our real lives are now the lives we live in Christ, lives with eternal dimensions. So when we seek productivity—even if it is productivity in business—is our ultimate goal eternal results?

C. T. Studd, a British missionary who lived his life on earth investing in heavenly realities, wrote two lines that many of us have often heard and quoted. Those lines come from a longer poem that reminds us our lives on this earth must be aligned with God's eternal purposes if we want our productivity to be eternal. Here's just one stanza:

> *Only one life, the still, small voice,*
> *Gently pleads for a better choice*
> *Bidding me selfish aims to leave,*
> *And to God's holy will to cleave;*
> *Only one life, 'twill soon be past,*
> *Only what's done for Christ will last.*

Powerful words. In everything we do, we make the choice between selfish aims and God's holy will. What is the ultimate aim of your productivity?

Lord, as long as I have breath may I stay on the front line of your service. Amen.

Steve Wingfield

DAY 5

Therefore, my dear brothers and sisters, stand firm. Let nothing move you. Always give yourselves fully to the work of the Lord, because you know that your labor in the Lord is not in vain.

—1 Corinthians 15:58

EACH OF OUR LODESTAR BULLETINS GIVES AN OPPORTUNITY to assess specific traits in yourself. *How influential am I? How courageous am I? Am I a diligent person? How much determination do I have?* We offer benchmarks and evaluations to see how we're doing with each character trait in our leadership, but I want to remind you: the utmost value of these traits is measured not in business or societal aspects but in their eternal consequences. *Productivity* is one area where, if we are not careful, we may also fall into the temptation of gauging eternal results by earthly measurements.

For example, can an evangelist gauge his productivity by how many people come to the altar or remain seated after a sermon? If a writer never receives feedback on things she has written for the Lord is she unproductive? Would we say that the missionaries who died at the end of spears in Ecuador in 1956 were not productive because they did not live to see a convert among the Aucas? Do you feel unproductive in the kingdom because you have no numbers and nothing measurable associated with your name? Are you cringing because there are no "quality results" apparent as fruit of your faith?

Paul says that whatever we do for the Lord has eternal results. Nothing you do for the Lord is in vain. Even if you see no measurable results now, your *productivity* is measured in heaven.

Lord, I know the only thing I can take to heaven is someone else. Help me to rescue one more. Amen.

Steve Wingfield

Day 6

But you will receive power when the Holy Spirit comes on you.

—Acts 1:8

OUR LEADER IS ALWAYS IN THE TRENCHES WITH US. He lives with us as the Holy Spirit. It is the Holy Spirit's power that gives us whatever gifts of leadership we have and empowers them to the highest levels. As Jesus said, without Him we can do nothing of eternal value. Only the Spirit can make your productivity generate results that last to eternity.

Our Leader in the trenches with us has given us His vision. He motivates, rewards, is our role model, deals with roadblocks for his people, provides constant affirmation, prunes and gets rid of dead branches, celebrates with us, and provides great compensation.

He is the One who fuels our eternal productivity. The Lodestar bulletin lists three things necessary for productivity: commitment to excellence, intelligent planning, and focused effort. The Spirit who has come to live in us is the Spirit of "wisdom and understanding, the Spirit of counsel and of might, the Spirit of the knowledge and fear of the LORD" (Isaiah 11:2). By this Spirit, God can do "immeasurably more than all we ask or imagine" (Ephesians 3:20).

In Acts 3 we read the story of Peter and John healing a man who had never walked; he was crippled from birth. The healing was by faith in the power of God. The man was able to do something he had never been able to do before. So can you, my friend, when you are living by the power of the Holy Spirit.

Fill me, Lord, with Your Spirit. Amen.

Steve Wingfield

DAY 7

Now it is required that those who have been given a trust must prove faithful.

—1 Corinthians 4:2

IN OUR VERSE TODAY, PAUL IS TALKING about himself as a servant of Christ, entrusted with the message of the gospel. We are likewise entrusted with Jesus' mission. He chose us, not only to save us but also to empower us to be productive. We, too, are commissioned and entrusted with God's message to the world.

Jesus tells us that He empowers His disciples so that they can get things done. "So that you might go and bear fruit—fruit that will last . . ." (John 15:16). When we become His disciples, we're given a new purpose and a new mission in life. We're to bear fruit that has eternal results. But don't think that means you have to be a missionary or a preacher, at least in the usual definition of those vocations. In God's reality, the simplest act done with kindness, goodness, and right motives, makes you a missionary carrying God's message or a preacher delivering a sermon.

So ask Jesus to increase your desire to bear much fruit that will last. As you do, remember that He tells His disciples to ask anything in His name—for His purposes and in His Spirit—and He will do it to bring glory to the Father. His Spirit empowers us and brings productivity in heavenly value, "for it is God who works in you to will and to act in order to fill his good purpose" (Philippians 2:13). And when it is of God, nothing can stop it or shut it down.

Lord, help me to, "Rescue the perishing, care for the dying, snatch them in pity from sin and the grave . . ." Amen.

Notes and Prayers

_____

_____

_____

_____

_____

_____

_____

_____

_____

_____

_____

_____

_____

_____

_____

_____

_____

_____

_____

PUNCTUALITY

Punctuality is vital: it is a telltale sign of a person's character.

—Paul Weaver

DAY 1

For the Kingdom of God is not a matter of what we eat or drink, but of living a life of goodness and peace and joy in the Holy Spirit. If you serve Christ with this attitude, you will please God, and others will approve of you, too.

—Romans 14:17–18 (NLT)

PUNCTUALITY IS A CULTURAL THING. I have been in cultures where schedules and timetables don't hold the importance that they do in North America. In our country, though, the attitude toward punctuality is the one expressed by Paul Weaver's quote: it is a telltale sign of character.

No matter the culture in which we live, we're called to live godly lives, representing Christ in our daily world, and living a life led by the Holy Spirit. This is Paul's overriding concern in chapter 14 of Romans. "For we don't live for ourselves or die for ourselves. If we live, it's to honor the Lord . . ." (Romans 14:7–8 NLT).

The Scriptures have a great deal to say about how we honor or dishonor the Lord by the way we relate to other people. Cultures may vary in some things, but we have principles from the Word that teach us how to life a life worthy of our calling, a life that honors the Lord and represents Christ well. This is our first checkpoint on the matter of punctuality. Do our attitude and actions about time, promptness, and reliability mark us a people of the kingdom of God living in our current culture?

Live through me, Lord. Allow me to be a demonstration of who You are, by serving and respecting those around me. Amen.

Prayers on PUNCTUALITY by Bill Mullet.

Day 2

Do nothing out of selfish ambition or conceit, but in humility count others more significant than yourselves. Let each of you look not only to his own interests, but also to the interests of others.

—Philippians 2:3–4 (ESV)

BE AGREEABLE, ACT IN LOVE, WORK TOGETHER. Don't be selfish and try to impress others. Look out for their interests. Then he holds up our example, Christ Jesus, who was God and yet came to earth to serve. Several verses (12–16) give us the umbrella thought. We need to obey God and live as people in whom He is doing a work—and that includes how we work with other people. In verses 16–18, Paul wrote about pouring out his life for others—and that in so doing, we're making our offerings to God. He finishes up the chapter referring to Timothy as one who "genuinely cares about your welfare," unlike others who "care only about themselves," and Epaphroditus, devoted to others to the point of risking his life for the work of Christ.

All of this stands in contrast to doing things out of selfish ambition and conceit. If you are habitually late to meetings or miss them altogether or are always running behind schedule, is it because of your slavery to your own agenda? That's selfish ambition. Or is it "conceit" that causes inconsideration because you and all the matters you must attend to are more important than any other meeting you're asked to attend? Where punctuality is a habitual problem, it's time to ask the Spirit to examine our hearts for selfishness and conceit.

Lord, grant me strength to be less selfish, and enable me to give of my time, so that I do not rob others of theirs. Amen.

Steve Wingfield

DAY 3

Love is not arrogant or rude.

—1 Corinthians 13:4–5 (AMP)

IF YOU HAVEN'T ALREADY DETECTED IT, tardiness is one of my pet peeves. I'll be honest with you; I just think that being on time is the responsible thing to do. When a person is consistently late or undependable in keeping appointments, they are saying, "My time is more important than yours."

A lack of punctuality is rude. It shows no consideration for others and does not take into account the effect that lateness or not showing up at all has on everyone else's day.

That is a lot of negative words, and you might even detect my negative emotions behind the words. Let's put this in the positive. Punctuality shows respect for others. Even if you are the most scrupulously punctual person, like the person who is always ten minutes early, there are times when something comes up and you cannot avoid being late or missing a deadline. Then the respectful thing to do is to—if at all possible—let the other party know what's happening. If late to an appointment, call and let them know when they can expect you. If you can't make a meeting, let them know as much in advance as possible and reschedule if necessary. Jesus' Golden Rule applies here. Treat others the way you would want to be treated if the situation were reversed.

Punctuality is an expression of respect for the other person and their time. The interesting thing is, if you treat others respectfully, respect will be returned to you.

May Your Spirit remind me to be punctual and treat others as I want to be treated. And help me to be considerate of the time You have given them. Amen.

Day 4

Look carefully then how you walk, not as unwise but as wise, making the best use of the time, because the days are evil.

—Ephesians 5:15–16 (ESV)

PUNCTUALITY IS A MATTER OF STEWARDSHIP—being good managers of our time. For many people, a lack of punctuality is a result of managing their time poorly. Time management is big business these days, but it comes down to this: God has given you this day to use for His purposes and His honor. Are you being a faithful steward of that time?

Some people constantly overschedule, trying to do too much. Some of our most important schedule decisions have to be decisions to say NO. We're to live wisely, and that includes knowing how much we can do and how we can keep our lives in balance. As in so many other areas, quantity does not mean quality. We often sacrifice doing things well for the sake of doing many things. Sometimes, even a project of highest priority is short-changed because we have scheduled too much for that day. Be wise about your schedule. Make sure that pride doesn't push you to overload.

Others who are consistently late or undependable don't have enough structure in their lives to keep them on schedule. These days, we have all kinds of digital help to keep track of where we are supposed to be. This can be helpful, but it can also be overwhelming and confusing. Whatever system you use to schedule, be sure you understand it—and then pay attention to it.

Lord, grant me wisdom from above, so that I can serve You with the time You have allocated me here on the earth. May it glorify Your holy name! Amen.

Steve Wingfield

Day 5

So you must live as God's obedient children. Don't slip back into your old ways of living to satisfy your own desires. You didn't know any better then. But now you must be holy in everything you do, just as God who chose you is holy.

—1 Peter 1:14–15 (NLT)

Punctuality lives side-by-side with dependability. Dependable people strive to be punctual because they know people are counting on them. When we make ourselves accountable to others, we'll be punctual. Our attitude will keep us on schedule. Punctuality keeps productivity rolling along; diligence will plan wisely so that punctuality is possible; and self-awareness makes realistic schedules that can be met. Empathy understands the effect tardiness will have on others. Motivation creates a desire to be punctual. Ownership and being teachable kick in when a person knows they have been lacking in punctuality and they're determined to do better.

These traits are like the body—although each has individual purposes and looks different, they are all related. Weakness in one will affect the entire body of your character. Discipline in one affects the strength of all. So we make every effort to build up these traits. That is the purpose of our Lodestar program. We want to be "more productive and useful" in representing our Lord Jesus Christ (2 Peter 1:8 NLT). Representing Him to the very best of our ability and with the power that works in us, is our highest purpose as we walk through this life. So we strive to use all these traits to the fullest, for His purposes and to His glory.

Lord, You have linked us together in the Church, and in our places of employment. Strengthen me to be a strong link in the chain that brings success to others and glory to You! Amen.

DAY 6

And this is my prayer: that your love may abound more and more in knowledge and depth of insight, so that you may be able to discern what is best and may be pure and blameless for the day of Christ, filled with the fruit of righteousness that comes through Jesus Christ—to the glory and praise of God.

—Philippians 1:9–11

THIS IS MY PRAYER FOR YOU, that you will grow in Christ and in your discernment of "what is best." That applies to all areas of our lives. If the Spirit is already showing you that it's time to work on being more punctual, here are a few encouraging passages (paraphrased):

Ask for wisdom to know what needs to be changed in your life so that you can be more punctual (James 1:5).

In humility, ask for help, both from God and from someone (or a group) to whom you'll be accountable (Proverbs 11:2 and Proverbs 15:31–32).

Depend on God's divine power to help you change (2 Peter 1:3).

Plan and follow the plan diligently (Proverbs 21:5).

Pray for discernment, and take care of important things (Philippians 1:9–11).

The following quote from the Lodestar bulletin is worth reading again.

When tomorrow comes, this day will be gone forever, leaving in its place something that I have traded for it. I want it to be gain, not loss; good, not evil; success, not failure; in order that I shall not regret the price I paid for it.

Purify my heart, Lord, that the fruit of righteousness may grow in abundance to benefit others. And give me the grace to humble my heart so that Christ may be seen in the plans I pursue. Amen.

Steve Wingfield

DAY 7

Let the message about Christ, in all its richness, fill your lives.

—Colossians 3:16 (NLT)

As LONG AS WE'RE THINKING about the hours and minutes of our days, I'd like to encourage you to make these two Scriptures part of your life. Both have to do with showing up at the right time.

In your hearts, revere Christ as Lord.

> *Always be prepared to give an answer to everyone who asks you to give the reason for the hope that you have. But do this with gentleness and respect* (1 Peter 3:15).

> *Therefore keep watch, because you do not know on what day your Lord will come* (Matthew 24:42).

We are waiting, ready, for the fulfillment of all our hope; and while we wait, we will share His message of hope whenever we have the opportunity. God bless you as you stand as His representative in this world.

Fill me with your presence and power to share Your name, the only name whereby we receive salvation for our souls! Thank You for loving us and giving me salvation and redemption by the death and resurrection of Jesus Christ! Amen.

Notes and Prayers

_____

_____

_____

_____

_____

_____

_____

_____

_____

_____

_____

_____

_____

_____

_____

_____

_____

_____

RESOURCEFULNESS

The truth is that opportunities are usually found in unexpected situations, and sometimes these are not pleasant.

—Paul Weaver

DAY 1

By his divine power, God has given us everything we need for living a godly life. We have received all of this by coming to know him, the one who called us to himself by means of his marvelous glory and excellence.

—2 Peter 1:3 (NLT)

THE RESOURCEFULNESS THAT WE HAVE, the skills and ingenuity we're blessed with, are a blessing from our Lord, given for us to use, and as we use them and walk in step with the Spirit, He enhances and grows them.

Amazing grace! God's divine power gives us everything we need for living a godly life. Now, *godly* doesn't mean *perfect*. We don't always get things right. But it does mean a life devoted to following hard after God. That's the life we want to live out as leaders and as Christian men and women in every daily situation.

I want to encourage everybody to keep seeking to know Him more and more, because the closer we get to Him and the more we get to know Him, the stronger we are in our walk with the Lord. He wants us to stand strong for Him, and He's given us the resources to do that. So continue to deepen your relationship with Him. It's the most important thing you can do in this life.

By his divine power, God has given us everything we need for living a godly life. We have received all of this by coming to know him, the one who called us to himself by means of his marvelous glory and excellence (2 Peter 1:3 NLT).

Prayers on RESOURCEFULNESS by Keith Cook.

Day 2

I pray that the eyes of your heart may be enlightened in order that you may know the hope to which he has called you, the riches of his glorious inheritance in his holy people, and his incomparably great power for us who believe. That power is the same as the mighty strength he exerted when he raised Christ from the dead and seated him at his right hand in the heavenly realms.

—Ephesians 1:18–20

GOD HAS GIVEN US HIS SPIRIT TO EQUIP US and strengthen us in our inner being. He wants us to grow and mature. He has given us the power of His Spirit so we can have access to all the resources He's given his children. All the demons in hell cannot defeat us when we rely on the resource of His power.

We have so many examples in the Bible of this inner strength given by God. David, standing up against Goliath; Gideon, leading a handful of men against thousands; Abraham, faithfully on the move, following God's call; Peter and Paul and the apostles, going to the ends of the earth. They all walked in obedience, relying on the resource of His power and strength.

Jesus encourages us to knock, seek, and ask. The door will be opened to us, we'll find what we need, and what we asked for will be supplied. As we think about needed skills and ingenuity and facing unexpected circumstances, we can be certain that when we rely on the Spirit, He is there to supply what we need. Let us not tire in our knocking, seeking, and asking.

God, You have enlightened me through Your Word and given me Your resources and Your power. Right now, fill me, inform me, empower me, and push me! Amen.

Steve Wingfield

Day 3

And my God will meet all your needs according to the riches of his glory in Christ Jesus.

—Philippians 4:19

Like Paul, we can do nothing on our own. But Jesus has all the resources we need for us to succeed as His representatives in this world. This doesn't mean that we can just sit back and wait for Him to pour into us. He wants us to "strain" toward the goal and run the race giving it everything we've got. In our work for Him, He doesn't ask us to strive and work on our own—He supplies the resources we need.

There is one "resource" I want to encourage you to use: obedience born of faith and trust.

Through obedience we are strengthened; we learn that He keeps His promises, that He does supply what we need. Our obedience opens the door for God to work, even though we can't see the goal or even the reason for what he asks us to do.

Charles Spurgeon said, "A man runs a great risk when he steers himself. Rocks or no rocks, the peril lies in the helmsman. The believer is no longer the helmsman of his own vessel; he has taken a pilot on board. To believe in God, and to do his bidding, is a great escape from the hazards of personal weakness and folly."

A life of obedience doesn't cancel our personal responsibility to use the skills and ingenuity the Spirit grows in us. Instead, we're to use our resourcefulness to the fullest as we live out our faith and obedience.

Lord, I know You want to supply all my needs. Whatever great or small task You would have me do as Your servant, I will do it! Amen.

DAY 4

But he said to me, "My grace is sufficient for you, for my power is made perfect in weakness." Therefore I will boast all the more gladly about my weaknesses, so that Christ's power may rest on me.

—2 Corinthians 12:9

GOD'S STRENGTH IS MADE PERFECT IN OUR WEAKNESS. Yet, somehow, we think we've got to shore up our weaknesses and strengthen ourselves. Western culture would have us believe that "God helps them who help themselves" is Scripture. It is not. Jesus came to earth to help those who could not help themselves. We need God's resources, and all we have to do is ask, come boldly to His throne, and we will find the help we need.

God wants us to grow—but to grow in His strength, wisdom, and power, not in our own. If resourcefulness requires thinking outside the box, then reliance on God is our best bet. God's resources are outside of every box. Don't limit your thinking to what is "humanly" possible or practical or logical. Jesus said nothing is impossible with God.

2 Corinthians 4:7 tells us that "we have this treasure in jars of clay to show that this all-surpassing power is from God and not from us." My prayer is that my life and yours would exhibit a power far beyond anything we can drum up on our own. May God's power, His resources, His wisdom, His strength, all shine through our lives. Let us grab for the impossible, expecting great things from Him whose ways do not fit in any box.

Almighty God, please do not let me limit what You want to do through my life for Your glory. Lift me up so I can grab an impossible job that You have picked out just for me! Amen.

Steve Wingfield

DAY 5

Now may the God of peace ... equip you with everything good for doing his will, and may he work in us what is pleasing to him, through Jesus Christ, to whom be glory for ever and ever. Amen.

—Hebrews 13:20, 21

UNLIKE THE DISCIPLES OF JESUS whose world experience was fairly limited, we have access to tools and resources that previous generations never even imagined. You can wear a watch on your wrist that connects you to events happening all around the world. We have tools to search the Scriptures with our computers; within minutes, we can find Scriptures on any subject. As of this writing, the entire Bible and parts of it have been translated into almost 3,400 languages.

You can fly to countries that the disciples did not even know existed. We have unbelievably powerful tools to learn more and more about what God wants in our lives and then to communicate and implement His will. In America, we have been given incredible resources to carry out His mission. The Bible says to whom much is given, much is required, and we should use all of what we've been given for His honor and his glory and the advancement of His kingdom.

I am a channel through which God's grace in its many, many forms flows out to the world. He has equipped us for the mission. 2 Timothy 3:17 says He uses His Word to equip His servants "for every good work." Be resourceful.

Father, may I be a good steward of the resources, talents, and the call that You have given me. May I, every day and in every way, look for new and fresh ways to honor, serve, and channel Your blessings and grace out into Your world. Amen.

Day 6

Don't let your hearts be troubled. Trust in God, and trust also in me.

—John 14:1 (NLT)

NONE OF US KNOWS WHAT WE WILL MEET in the next hours of today or tomorrow or the coming months. God's gift to us of resourcefulness—skills and ingenuity—equips us to get the job done even when we face circumstances we did not expect or imagine. Merriam-Webster's definition of *resourceful* uses this phrase: "Able to meet situations."

Jesus told His disciples that they would meet situations they weren't expecting: they'd be brought before rulers and religious officials and have to answer for their faith. "But," he said, "don't worry about what you're going to say. The Spirit will be giving you the words." Certainly Jesus' words must have created some anxiety for the disciples, but what a promise they were also given.

We have promises just as comforting that make us confident we will be "able to meet situations." Because of these promises, we can go forward in courage and confidence. No matter what we meet, our faith trusts these words, and we can live accordingly.

> *In every situation, God is working for our good.* (Romans 8:28)
> *He is always with us and will never leave us.* (Matthew 28:20)
> *He is always there to help.* (Isaiah 41:10)
> *Even in trouble, we have opportunities for joy.* (James 1:2)
> *Ask for what you need, and you'll receive!* (John 16:24)

Thank You, God, that You know what is coming to confront and confound me. My trust is in You; that You are working for my good and are with me and will not leave me out on a task alone. In Christ, I can do all the things You have for me to do. Amen.

Steve Wingfield

Day 7

But the Lord stood at my side and gave me strength.

—2 Timothy 4:17

Billy Graham said, "The will of God will not take us where the grace of God cannot sustain us." It is the grace of God that equips us to meet whatever is ahead on our journey. As leaders, we have been endowed with traits that enable us to represent Him well in our calling. Our Lodestar program is designed for the purpose of helping you use those gifts to the fullest.

Besides equipping us, He's given us His Word for our guidance, growth, and encouragement. Romans 15:4 says that "whatever was written in former days was written for our instruction, that through endurance and through the encouragement of the Scriptures we might have hope" (ESV). Be in the Word. Treasure it. Hide it in your heart.

> *'Tis so sweet to trust in Jesus,*
> *Just to take him at his Word*
> *Just to rest upon his promise,*
> *Just to know, "Thus saith the Lord!"*

—Louisa M. R. Stead and William J. Kirkpatrick, "Tis So Sweet To Trust In Jesus"

He has assured us of His constant presence and help. We can go courageously and resourcefully down the path on which He's leading us. He will be beside us to meet every situation. Let Him teach you to think outside the box and reach into the impossible with God.

My prayer for all of us is for grace to trust Him more.

Dear Jesus, it is so encouraging to know that You are with me. You have brought me so far and I want to go all the way with You. You are my strength. My heart's desire is to be the servant leader You called me to be. Amen.

Steve Wingfield

Notes and Prayers

_____

_____

_____

_____

_____

_____

_____

_____

_____

_____

_____

_____

_____

_____

_____

_____

_____

_____

_____

_____

Without respect, relationships do not have much of a chance.

—Paul Weaver

DAY 1

Do to others as you would have them do to you.

—Luke 6:31

SCRIPTURES HOLD MANY INSTRUCTIONS on how we are to treat people. As Jesus was teaching, the people he addressed were living under many rules laid down by their religious law. But all of those rules, and all of the Scriptures we have about interacting with others are summed up by Jesus in this one principle: treat others the way you want to be treated.

This commandment from Jesus also means we're to treat *everyone* in this way. In Luke 6:31, this rule is embedded in Jesus' teaching about loving your enemies and doing good to those who hate you. When you're dealing with a person who is militant in his opposition to you, treat him as you would want to be treated. Do the same with those who are downright dislikable. With the competition. Even with people who have lied to you or cheated you or sabotaged your reputation.

Now we're getting into the really difficult part of that Golden Rule. But Jesus says, "Do it. In everything."

Holy Spirit, alert me today when my attitude, words, or actions do not give others the respect that I would want myself. Amen.

Prayers on RESPECT by George Moxley.

DAY 2

Therefore be imitators of God, as beloved children.

—Ephesians 5:1 (ESV)

"SHOW RESPECT EVEN TO PEOPLE WHO DON'T DESERVE IT; not as a reflection of *their* character, but as a reflection of *yours*." I came across that quote, but I don't know where it originated. It is scriptural, though. In the same passage in Luke that gives us the Golden Rule, Jesus says that being good to our enemies is a characteristic of sons and daughters of God. That's what God is like, kind and merciful even to those who are ungrateful and wicked.

This is not how the world usually works, or how our old nature wants to run things! As James wrote in chapter 3 (NLT), when selfish ambition or envy rules our attitudes and actions, we end up with "disorder and evil of every kind."

If we can show a godly respect to everyone, in every situation, it will come only as fruit of the Spirit in our new, changed character. Romans 12:2 tells us not to be conformed to the world's way of acting and speaking, but be transformed according to the way God wants us to be acting and speaking. Ephesians 4:23 puts it this way: "to be made new in the attitude of your minds." Titus 2:12 says that God's grace "teaches us to say 'No' to ungodliness and worldly passions" and to live and think as His children.

Only a Spirit-led character can treat others with esteem and kindness even when they don't deserve it. That is how our heavenly Father operates—on grace.

Dear Lord, You have brought _____ to mind. Show me how to treat him/ her with more respect, because I want Your character to grow in me. Amen.

Steve Wingfield

Day 3

But God is so rich in mercy, and he loved us so much . . .
—Ephesians 2:4 (NLT)

OUR FATHER'S CHARACTER GROWING IN US WILL LOOK MORE AND MORE LIKE HIM. That means we'll be looking at the people and situations we meet today through His eyes and from His perspective. We'll be caring about the things and people He cares about.

Everyone you meet today is as special and loved in God's eyes as you are. It doesn't matter if they're saints or the nastiest person you've ever met—God wants them "to be saved and understand the truth" (1 Timothy 2:4 NLT). It doesn't matter if they hold the highest position in the company or the lowest. God's love for them is so great, He shed His own blood for them. He paid that extreme price to bring them back to Him.

We know from Jesus' words about sparrows and lilies and hair on our head that God cares about every detail in His creation. He cares about every person. There is not one soul outside His grace. We may think someone has not earned our respect or doesn't deserve our respect, but that's not how God sees them. They were created in His image. They are dearly loved, whether they are already safe in His fold or are still lost sheep out in the wilderness.

Who are we, then, to treat any of these beloved of God with disrespect? Instead, we will see them as He does, valued, cared-about souls for whom Christ suffered and died.

Lord Jesus, give me Your eyes to see each person I meet today as You see them and as You love them. Amen.

Day 4

In everything set them an example by doing what is good. In your teaching show integrity, seriousness and soundness of speech that cannot be condemned so that those who oppose you may be ashamed because they have nothing bad to say about us.

—Titus 2:7–8

WE ARE TO BE A MODEL OF GOOD WORKS, integrity, dignity, self-control, and wholesome speech above reproach. God tells us to walk with honor and respect people. Leaders set the tone, lead the way, and nurture the culture of an organization or a team. We model the behavior and attitudes we want in our people. Let those standards we set be godly standards. Because we carry Christ's name, what we model and teach presents Him to the world. We are His representatives.

There's an important contrast here, in the interplay of respect between people. On the one hand, as leaders we want respect, and we know that we must earn it by our leadership. That's how it works. We don't gain respect simply because of a title or position or even authority. Whether or not people respect us depends on our character and leadership.

At the same time, as Christians *we* are to show respect to everyone, whether they've earned it or not, whether they deserve it or not. We show respect to all because God commands it and because how we conduct ourselves tells the world about who our King is. Our King doesn't operate like the rest of the world. He operates on love and grace. *Undeserved* love and grace. We've been recipients of love and grace, and as His representatives, we want that divine love and grace to flow through us to the world.

Lord, above all I want to represent You well in all I do and say. Amen.

Steve Wingfield

DAY 5

And whatever you do, whether in word or deed, do it all in the name of the Lord Jesus, giving thanks to God the Father through him.
—Colossians 3:17

THIS VERSE COMES AFTER SEVERAL PARAGRAPHS that talk about relationships between God's people, members of the body of Christ. It is a beautiful picture of people working together with compassion, kindness, humility, gentleness, patience, and forgiveness. Those wearing these "clothes" will naturally treat each other with respect. All of this is unified by love for each other and by the peace of Christ ruling in hearts.

This is a wonderful vision of God's people supporting and building each other up in loving relationships. As Paul Weaver wrote, "Without respect, relationships do not have much of a chance." Respect is essential in this picture of a healthy church. If respect is lacking, then compassion, kindness, gentleness, and all those other traits are probably also lacking.

After giving this picture of how God's people should live together, Peter reminds us that whatever we do or say, it should be in the name of the Lord Jesus. In other words, even within the church, our small accountability groups, or other groups of believers, we are Christ's representatives. We speak in His name. We represent Him not only to the world but to each other—to those who sit next to us in the pews and share a Spirit-connection in any setting.

Lord, I know words matter and I desire that my words will always be spoken in love and kindness. May this tongue that You gave me always be speak words of blessings. Amen.

Day 6

For I did not come to judge the world, but to save the world.
—John 12:47

AN ENEMY OF GODLY RESPECT FOR OTHERS IS A JUDGMENTAL ATTITUDE. Like the sinful nature that is always fighting what the Spirit does in us, a judgmental attitude will always be wrestling with the attitude of respect the Spirit wants to exhibit in our lives. As we interact with the world who does not believe, we're to be respectful, gentle, and following that Golden Rule. Remember, you were once at the same place they are; God's grace brought you to Him, and His grace extends to all. The temptation to judge is even stronger within the body of Christ, when we look across a congregation and find ourselves judging a person's walk of faith. If you find your thoughts going down that path, remember that the same Spirit who is working in you is always working in that other person.

We have straightforward commands not to judge. We can be "fruit inspectors," but we are not judges. We are partners with Christ in His gospel mission, and that mission is to save people, not judge them. Judgment will come, but it will come later.

Scripture warns us against thinking "too much" of ourselves and being conceited. A judgmental attitude rises up and puts oneself above others. But we have all sinned; we all fall short of God's standards of righteousness. God has forgiven each of us, forgiven a great deal. We are to forgive others in the same way and let His grace flow through us to everyone. *Everyone.* He hasn't given up on anyone. We can't either.

Lord, help me to see the world and every individual as You do. I want to be on a rescue mission to reach the lost. Amen.

Steve Wingfield

DAY 7

Show proper respect to everyone, love the family of believers, fear God, honor the emperor.

—1 Peter 2:17

PETER ADDRESSES SLAVES AND TELLS THEM TO OBEY THEIR MASTERS "with all respect," and not only the kind and good masters, but the harsh and unreasonable ones as well. Paul teaches the same thing. "All who are under the yoke of slavery should consider their masters worthy of full respect, so that God's name and our teaching may not be slandered" (1 Timothy 6:1).

Peter wasn't condoning slavery. He was saying that no matter what situation you are in, "show proper respect to everyone." We find ourselves in plenty of unpleasant situations with unpleasant people. Yet we need to show proper respect and conduct ourselves with dignity and self-control. Why? Because we reverence our Heavenly Father and do not want His name slandered, and because we have a message for the world about love and grace and we do not want to diminish that message by our words or actions.

In our politically explosive climate and the culture wars of today, we each must take an honest look at how we have been speaking, acting, and posting in the current debates. Jesus didn't give us "if" options. He said "Do this. Act this way. Have this attitude. In *everything.*"

It turns out that our guidelines on how we treat people do not depend on the other person's character or attitude toward us. It depends solely on our obedience to Jesus' kingdom laws.

Lord, You are my King and I honor You. You have also instructed me to honor those in authority. Help me always to pray for those in authority. Even when I disagree with their decisions, remind me to pray for them. Amen.

Notes and Prayers

_____

_____

_____

_____

_____

_____

_____

_____

_____

_____

_____

_____

_____

_____

_____

_____

_____

_____

_____

There's no future for leaders who burn the candle at both ends.
We pay a high price, business and personal, for having a schedule completely
full, every day of every week.

—Paul Weaver

Day 1

Come with me by yourselves to a quiet place and get some rest.

—Mark 6:31

IN THIS CHAOTIC WORLD IN WHICH WE LIVE, we need the discipline of rest. You cannot go 24/7 at high speed and escape disaster. Yet, there are people who keep their nose to the grindstone and do not give themselves rest.

Rest is an important part of life. Jesus indicated the importance of rest in Mark 6:31. He and His disciples had been busy with so many people coming to them that they had not even had time to eat their meals uninterrupted. So, they set off by boat, intending to take some "down time." We all need times of rest, healing, and restoration.

Our need for rest is as much a reality of life as is our need for food and water. Just as improper nutrition or impure water will affect us adversely, so will lack of rest. The same is true of our spiritual health and well-being. Our souls need rest and refreshment. The two cannot be separated. Physical rest affects our spiritual health, and rest for our souls affects our physical health.

Whether you're in a leadership position, a busy mother, a person working two jobs, a student working hard to keep up—no matter who or what you are, you need periods of rest in your life, rest for your body and your soul.

Father God, help me to trust You enough to rest in You. Amen.

Prayers on REST by David Wingfield.

Steve Wingfield   Guiding Principles 335

DAY 2

Be still, and know that I am God.
—Psalm 46:10 (ESV)

SUSANNA WESLEY WAS THE MOTHER OF JOHN AND CHARLES WESLEY. She had nineteen children, nine of whom died as infants, yet she found time each day to talk with each child and time to talk to God. She would sit in her rocker and pull her apron over her head; that was the signal to her family that she was praying and was not to be disturbed.

Sometimes, it seems we have little more than a flimsy piece of fabric to stand between us and the noise and activity of our hectic days. But we have to disconnect and quiet ourselves and be alone with God. God wants to be *your* God; to know Him and hear His voice, you have to step back and spend time with Him.

This is a discipline we all should practice. Our connection with our God is our connection to life. We must stay connected to the Vine. From Him flow health, strength, grace, peace, all the fruit of the Spirit, and more. Psalm 23:2 is a metaphor for the rest and revitalization our Great Shepherd provides. He leads us to green pastures and peaceful streams.

It is important to plan time to get away for a day or a week to "be still," but it's absolutely essential to throw that apron over your head every day and meet with your God.

My heart is quiet. My soul is still. I wait and listen for You. Amen.

Steve Wingfield

DAY 3

The LORD your God is giving you a place of rest. He has given you this land.
—Joshua 1:13 (NLT)

REST IS A GIFT AND PRIVILEGE OF YOUR SALVATION. When God brought the children of Israel out of slavery in Egypt, He promised them His presence would be with them and He would give them rest (Exodus 33:14). As they stood on the banks of the Jordan and prepared to enter the Promised Land, Joshua told the people, "The Lord is giving you this land as a place of rest."

God has promised us rest, a place of His blessing and provision. "Come to me, and I will give you rest" (Matthew 11:28). We know that God has promised us a final, perfect rest, but He also offers rest to us now as we are already living in His kingdom.

Sin destroys. Sin depletes and deprives. Jesus replenishes. He restores and builds. He gives life. He wants us to rest in Him and His salvation—that place provided by God where we can live in God's presence and under His care.

Your salvation has brought the Spirit to live in you, to help you in all sorts of ways. But you can quench that fire of the Spirit. God doesn't force it on you. Your salvation has also made available to you a deep rest that only God can give. You can also choose to ignore that and keep living in slavery to everything in your day that drives you. But don't! Take advantage of this rest from God. It's life-giving.

Thank You for the good gifts You have given me. Help me to rest within Your giving love. Amen.

DAY 4

Those who live in the shelter of the Most High will find rest in the shadow of the Almighty.

—Psalm 91:1 (NLT)

AS WE READ THE SCRIPTURES, we soon see that giving His people rest is every bit as important to God as giving His people peace, strength, compassion, and mercy. It's one of the first invitations we hear Jesus issue: "Come to me. I will give you rest."

He gives rest for both body and soul. Sleep is a precious gift. I held onto the promise of Psalm 4:8 during dangerous times in Romania. I was in that country during the Revolution. It was chaotic! People were being killed; we would hear gunfire around us; and there were times I wondered if I'd ever see my wife and children again. But in the midst of that, I trusted the promise that God would "make me dwell in safety," and I was able to go to sleep at night even with the sound of gunfire outside the hotel. God put peace in my heart and gave me rest even in the midst of the storm.

When we live in the shelter of the Most High, when we live constantly in His presence, we find a peace and rest beyond logic or understanding. We have wonderful promises in Christ.

What's keeping you awake at night? The Lord will speak His assurance to you if you talk to Him about it and open your ears to Him. He cares about everything that's going on in your life. He is the Great Shepherd, attentive to all your needs and everything that affects you.

God, be my shelter. Be my refuge. I long to rest in the quiet of Your gentle wings. Amen.

Steve Wingfield

Day 5

Then he said to them, "The Sabbath was made for man, not man for the Sabbath."
—Mark 2:27

REST IS A VERY, VERY IMPORTANT PART OF OUR WALK WITH THE LORD. It's very, very important for our bodies and minds. If you are going to be everything that God wants you to be, you've got to find rest.

God set the example. He created the world in six days and rested on the seventh. Then He gave the law through Moses and included strict rules about the Sabbath. A person was not even to carry wood into the house for the fire on the Sabbath. Even the land was to be given a time of rest.

The principle of rest continues to be so important, not because God wants to lay down laws, but because rest is so essential to our well-being. Parents won't allow children to eat ten cookies at one sitting. God doesn't want us running so fast and hard without pausing to rest. It's for our own good. Our bodies need to recuperate, our minds need to be cleared and refreshed, our souls need to reconnect with God and others.

The principle of observing a weekly Sabbath as a day of rest has either been ignored or modified by many people. Yet we have so many warnings in the Scripture about observing Sabbath—again, for our own well-being. Jesus said that the Sabbath was created *for us*. It's worth taking an honest look at our ideas of the Sabbath and asking God to show us how we can be practicing the principle of rest in our lives.

God, shine Your revealing light on my soul. What am I trying to do on my own? Show me how to take rest in Your Spirit. Amen.

Day 6

And so, dear brothers and sisters, I plead with you to give your bodies to God because of all he has done for you. Let them be a living and holy sacrifice—the kind he will find acceptable.

—Romans 12:1 (NLT)

IN ROMANS 12:1, PAUL PLEADS WITH US. He is emphatic about the importance of what we do with our bodies. At other places in Scripture, we read that our bodies have become the temple of the Spirit of God. He is dwelling here! This should give us pause to ask, "What's the condition of the sacrifice I'm giving to the Lord? And in what condition am I keeping the temple of the Lord?" Verse 2 says we are also to let God transform our minds. Our minds need refreshment. They need to have a lot of stuff cleared out. We need times of rest to allow the Spirit to give His temple a good housecleaning.

There are many exhortations of Scripture that we simply cannot accomplish unless we also give ourselves rest. Stay strong, keep alert, run the race with diligence. Even the command to be kind becomes more difficult when you have been deprived of rest. A person who desperately needs rest falls more easily into selfishness, apathy, anger, and lack of faith—to name only a few of the pitfalls. We can each look at our own character and know what qualities falter when we aren't getting proper rest. We are to present our bodies and minds to God. They belong to Him. Are we giving them the best care possible?

God, I give You my best efforts, my worldly strivings, my 110 percents. Let me let go and find my rest in You. Amen.

Steve Wingfield

DAY 7

Let each of you look not only to his own interests, but also to the interests of others.
—Philippians 2:4 (ESV)

WE'VE LOOKED AT PHILIPPIANS 2:4 several times throughout this year. It applies in so many situations. Now, a word specifically to those in leadership positions. Keep an eye on your team's need for rest. Whether you're the CEO of a multi-million-dollar company, the leader of a worship team of three, or you're leading a family through this world, be aware of the need for individuals to rest.

Our Western culture especially pushes and drives. Not all cultures have this characteristic, but we live in a society where accomplishments, hitting goals, and a passion to succeed can quickly consume lives—of both leaders and those they lead. If God's placed you in a position of leadership, He's also given you a responsibility for those you lead. Their welfare demands more than reasonable wages, and you are accountable to God for more than reasonable wages.

Look for ways to promote rest in your organization. It can be something as simple as a cot in a private place for someone to rest during breaks. Or maybe it could be as complex as restructuring certain positions that are overloaded with too much to do in reasonable hours. I've encouraged you all along to create a culture that reflects godly values and builds godly character. Rest is important to everyone—rest of body, mind, and soul. Create a culture that acknowledges the importance of rest and gives opportunity for rest.

Look not only to your own need for rest, but also to the needs of those whom God has put in your hands.

Father, show me how I can help others find rest in You as You have helped me find rest in You. Amen.

Notes and Prayers

_____

_____

_____

_____

_____

_____

_____

_____

_____

_____

_____

_____

_____

_____

_____

_____

_____

_____

_____

_____

RESTRAINT

*Restraint is not only important to have when dealing with our team,
but it is also beneficial to our own health and well-being,
as well as to living a life without regrets.*

—Paul Weaver

DAY 1

A person without self-control is like a city with broken-down walls.

—Proverbs 25:28 (NLT)

RESTRAINT IS THE QUALITY of self-control, managing your emotions and behavior appropriately. Lack of restraint can ruin relationships, reputations, projects and productivity, and, especially, our witness for our Lord Jesus. Proverbs says a person without self-control is like a city with walls that are broken down. That was written in the day when towns walls to keep out the enemy. Without such walls, the people were open to attack and defeat. It was protection. When your city walls are not strong, other people or circumstances around you push your buttons or tweak something in you and things within spill out in anger and frustration. You speak and act without restraint.

You want to be a person who has strong walls of restraint, who is in control of what you say and how you act. If you do that, I promise you, you will be the beneficiary. You will beat back attack and win.

Peter let his walls be breached when He denied his friendship with Jesus. He let fear control his speech and behavior. Much later, Peter wrote a caution to all of us. Be alert. Be on guard. Because your enemy the devil is on the prowl to devour you. (1 Peter 5:8 paraphrased)

Keep your city walls strong. Be alert and on guard against attack. Be a person of restraint.

Lord, I ask You to keep an armed guard around my heart, my mind, and my mouth. Amen.

Prayers on RESTRAINT by Jessica Crawford.

Steve Wingfield

DAY 2

For this very reason, make every effort to add to your faith goodness; and to goodness, knowledge, and to knowledge, self-control . . .
—2 Peter 1:5–6

PETER WROTE HIS LETTERS TO EVERYONE WHO FOLLOWS CHRIST. That is us, too. In the verse above, he encourages us to "make every effort." Work at these qualities. In that list of qualities to pursue, we find self-control, that is, restraint. That verse starts with "For this very reason," so we go back to the verses before it, and we see the promise that God has provided what we need to live godly lives and to "participate in the divine nature, having escaped the corruption in the world caused by evil desires." That's quite a promise. Restraint is one of those qualities we are to develop to live out a godly life.

Restraint will keep us from uttering words we will regret. We've all learned, sometimes painfully, that we can't put words back in our mouths once they're out. We need to control how our emotions affect our behavior. We need to be in control of speech and actions. We can't be flying off the handle or acting irrationally in reaction to anything that triggers our emotions, whether it's firing words in anger or whipping out a credit card for an impulse buy. If we learn and practice restraint, people will know they can rely on us. Instead of being a person who's unpredictable and out of control, we will be seen as trustworthy, stable, and dependable, someone who thinks things through before acting and speaking.

Restraint—it's not just for leaders and businessmen, but for every disciple of Christ.

My heart's desire is to live under Your control. Amen.

Steve Wingfield

DAY 3

His divine power has given us everything we need for life and godliness through our knowledge of him who called us by his own glory and goodness.

—2 Peter 1:3

IT IS INTERESTING THAT PETER INCLUDED SELF-CONTROL in his list of qualities we should make every effort to develop. As we know, Peter was an outspoken person, often blurting things out without exercising restraint. What changed him? The indwelling of the Holy Spirit.

In the letter written by James, the problem of our speech keeps popping up. In James 1:26, James wrote that those who claim to be Christians but don't control their tongue are only fooling themselves. James 3:2 says, "We all stumble in many ways. Anyone who is never at fault in what they say is perfect." I'm not perfect. We all know we don't have it in us to be perfect. Unless we have the Holy Spirit in us. He is the One who is perfect. Then, we do have what it takes *in us.*

For me, any hope of learning to exercise restraint rests solely on being filled with the Spirit of God. Self-control and restraint are fruit of the Spirit in our lives, and I believe His guidance and power provide the only way we'll learn how to wisely manage our emotions, our behavior, and our words.

2 Timothy 1:7 says the Spirit God gave us is one of power, of love, and of self-discipline. That's the power that radically changed Peter. If you are a follower of Christ, you have the same power living in you.

Lord, I want to live in the constant awareness that You are living in me. Amen.

Steve Wingfield

Day 4

For the grace of God has appeared that offers salvation to all people. It teaches us to say "No" to ungodliness and worldly passions, and to live self-controlled, upright and godly lives in this present age.

—Titus 2:11–12

WHO OF US HAS NOT AT SOME TIME SAID WORDS we wish we could take back? We've all had those moments when we are painfully aware of the truth of the many Proverbs that warn us to restrain our tongues.

> *When words are many, sin is unavoidable, but he who holds his tongue is wise* (Proverbs 10:19).

> *The evil man is trapped by his talk, but those who speak rightly escape trouble* (Proverbs 12:13).

> *He who guards his lips guards his life, but speaking without restraint brings you to ruin* (Proverbs 13:3).

> *Guarding your mouth will keep you from calamity* (Proverbs 21:23).

God has good plans for us. He wants us to grow in the likeness of Christ, to have life to the fullest, and to enjoy the life he died to give us. That's His grace at work—to give us new, full life even though we did nothing to deserve it. And in His grace, He makes available to us the power to say "NO" to ungodliness and to say "YES" to the fruit of the Spirit, which includes restraint. Take the wise escape from ruin and calamity, my friend. Say "YES" to the Spirit and learn restraint from Him.

May these words of my mouth and this meditation of my heart be pleasing in Your sight, LORD my Rock and my Redeemer (Psalm 19:14).

Steve Wingfield

Day 5

Being strengthened with all power according to his glorious might so that you may have great endurance and patience.

—Colossians 1:11

THE LODESTAR PROGRAM BULLETIN ON RESTRAINT presents three things that are required: Pausing. Evaluating. Visualizing. The very first thing we must do is pause. We rarely have time to prepare for those things that attack our city walls. We're bombarded with all kinds of situations, speech, and actions from others throughout the day. But if you're a person of restraint, if you're living by a Spirit who gives the power of self-control, you will not immediately react according to whatever emotion has been inflamed.

Pause. And pray. Pray for the Spirit to give you self-control. Ask the Spirit for wisdom and guidance in your response. Acknowledge your weakness. Maybe you even want to name the emotion you're struggling with: "Lord, I want to strike back at her, but I know that is not what You want for me. Help me." Or, "Lord Jesus, my pride right now is rising up and urging me to take this path, but I know it's not the best plan." Yes, call for help!

In your pause, also remember God's Word, His cautions about lack of restraint, His promises to help, and His plans for you. His Word is given to us as a gift. Psalm 91 tells us that His promises are armor and protection. The Spirit will use the Word to rescue us at times like this, when we need to battle the sinful desires within us and avoid disaster by using restraint.

I am so thankful, "That the one who lives in me is greater than the one who lives in the world" (1 John 4:4).

DAY 6

The tongue has the power of life and death, and those who love it will eat its fruit.
—Proverbs 18:21

THERE ARE TIMES THAT it is much better to hold your tongue than to speak. At times, it's better not to act than to jump in and immediately kick into action. Whether we are in leadership positions or not, our actions and words have a ripple effect. What we do and say is never contained in one isolated, insulated moment in time. And our actions have consequences.

The second thing restraint must do is evaluate. What will result from my actions and words? Who will it affect? How will it affect *me* if I let my emotions rule? How far will the ripples of my action spread? Will this bring glory to my Lord and King? Will it spread His light? Writing about the power of the tongue, James told us to consider how the destruction of a great forest fire is set ablaze by a single spark. What fire might soon be ablaze if I say what I'm thinking right now or if I act on that impulsive urge? We depend on the Spirit for wisdom. Ask Him to give you the discernment and insight to know how your actions will affect others.

Most of all, consider what your actions and words should be as a representative of Christ. C.S. Lewis wrote, "Don't shine so that others can see you. Shine so that through you, others can see him." That is our purpose here in this world, to let the light we have been given shine so brightly that others see Christ.

Lord, I want my light to shine brightly for You. Help me to say and do the right thing at the right time. Amen.

Steve Wingfield

Day 7

Finally, be strong in the Lord and in his mighty power.

—Ephesians 6:10

THE THIRD THING RESTRAINT MUST DO IS VISUALIZE. We have used a number of metaphors this week. Use them to visualize what your restraint or lack of restraint will mean. Picture a city with walls broken down, open to attack and defeat. Then imagine a city with strong, high, impregnable walls. Visualize a small spark, leaping quickly to become a roaring forest fire. Visualize saying "NO!" to pride, hurt, envy, and all the other emotions that urge you to jump in immediately with hasty words and actions. When you say "YES!" to the Spirit, visualize His power working in you, strength flowing through you to stand strong. Picture God's grace and power bursting through the clay of your being, His light shining into the world in which you live your daily life.

Most of all, visualize your Lord and King. He was falsely arrested and accused, beaten, and sentenced to die, and "yet He opened not His mouth" (Isaiah 53:7 NKJV). He was obedient to God's plan, to the very end. He stayed on mission. Jesus Christ ran this race, modeling it for us. Visualize how He would handle the situation that is now threatening your city walls.

And then, dear friend, visualize finishing your race and winning the prize. The prize is so much more than any fleeting satisfaction your emotions might demand right now. Be strong in the Lord and in His mighty power! You *can* be a person of strong and wise restraint—through Christ, who will give you His strength.

Lord Jesus, stand beside me and give me the strength of Your restraint. Amen.

Notes and Prayers

_____

_____

_____

_____

_____

_____

_____

_____

_____

_____

_____

_____

_____

_____

_____

_____

_____

Steve Wingfield

SELF-AWARENESS

If you want to know what is holding you back from being a great leader,
ask yourself this question: "Can I handle the truth?"

—Paul Weaver

DAY 1

But when he, the Spirit of truth, comes, he will guide you into all truth.
—John 16:13

YOU HAVE TO KNOW YOURSELF TO BE A GOOD LEADER. This principle is unavoidable. To know yourself, you've got to be honest about your strengths and your weaknesses. That could be threatening at times. Self-awareness does take both humility and courage. Humility will ask for feedback and be willing to take it; humility shows a willingness to admit we're wrong or weak or annoying in some area; and humility desires change and growth. It takes courage to open ourselves to being transparent (another Lodestar trait). But with self-awareness will also come other traits like compassion, empathy, and teachability. And self-awareness is absolutely necessary to live life with integrity.

We have a guide in this path to self-awareness. The Holy Spirit lives in us to guide us to truth about many things, including truth about ourselves. He will also give us the humility and courage to seek self-awareness. This week, ask Him to lead you further along the path of knowing yourself.

Heavenly Father, You know my strengths and my weaknesses. I ask, Lord, through the power of the Holy Spirit that You give me the strength to look at myself accurately and address my weaknesses. Help me to have the courage to open my heart and my eyes to address those weaknesses and seek Your guidance and wisdom in being more Christ-like in my thoughts, attitudes, behaviors, choices, and motives. Amen.

Prayers on SELF-AWARENESS by Mike Little.

Day 2

I pray that the eyes of your heart may be enlightened in order that you may know the hope to which he has called you, the riches of his glorious inheritance in his holy people, and his incomparably great power for us who believe.

—Ephesians 1:18–19

KNOWING THE RICHES OF OUR SALVATION, all that has been given to us because of Christ, is so important for us to know accurately who we now are. With Christ, the old is gone, the new has come. We want to walk in our new identity, in our new lives, in our new purpose.

As we work at self-awareness, we also need to work at living with the awareness of what God says is true about us. This is absolutely essential. The world will try to tell us one thing, but God has the truth for us. Our self-awareness as children of God means we walk in the knowledge that we are loved with an eternal love, that He has given us new life and is changing us to be like Christ, that His mercy and forgiveness are constant, and that we have unlimited resources in His strength, power, and guidance. Our strengths are gifts from Him, and our weaknesses are areas where His power will work.

Help me, Lord, to find my identity in You. Help me to see my strengths and weaknesses and to have the desire and discipline to walk closer to You. I ask for Your forgiveness for being more concerned about myself, than You, and others. Thank You, Lord, for loving me and providing me with grace. Thank You for being so generous with Your wisdom. I know You will provide what is needed if I will be obedient. Amen.

Steve Wingfield

Day 3

Guide me in your truth and teach me, for you are God my Savior, and my hope is in you all day long.

—Psalm 25:5

MOST OF US LOOK IN THE MIRROR AT LEAST A FEW TIMES A DAY. Are we seeing what God is seeing? At the end of the day, I'm accountable for my words and actions—to God first, then to whoever is over me, and to myself. If I don't have an accurate understanding of my feelings and motives, I'm going to live in confusion, shame, and lack of self-control. But looking in that mirror and asking God to help me know myself better, I'll humble myself before Him and allow Him to work in and through me.

I am certain of this: that everything good in me is not of myself but is from Him. All my hope truly is in Him. So, I ask Him to guide me and teach me, to understand and know myself so that I can walk more faithfully in His paths.

Lord, so many times I fall short of honoring and loving You and others. Many times my behaviors and motives are obvious to me, yet the root cause is confusing. You designed me, Lord, and You know when I fall short and what is needed for me to have inner peace and direction. Help me to see myself as You see me, give me the strength to look in the mirror and see my shortcomings, and the power and strength to seek You, Lord, for correction and direction in my life. You are the source of my power and strength. My only hope is in You. Thank you. Amen.

Day 4

Instead, speaking the truth in love, we will grow to become in every respect the mature body of him who is the head, that is, Christ.

—Ephesians 4:15

IN PURSUIT OF SELF-AWARENESS, we look to other members of the body of Christ to help us grow. We often have blind spots, especially when we're looking at our own character. Ephesians tells us we've put on a new life, and we're to speak truth to each other because we are all members of one body, a body that will be healthy and growing if there is honesty, love, and helping one another.

Wise leaders look to brothers and sisters in the body of Christ for help in better knowing themselves. We must first have the courage and sincerity to be transparent, we must be honest and courageous enough to look inward. Then we must have the wisdom to accept the truth and the diligence to improve where we need to improve. Teachability, humility, determination, focus—all these traits enter into our growing self-awareness. And all of them are dependent on our willingness to be a part of a living body, the body of Christ.

Father, I want to thank You for the many people You have brought into my life who have provided insight, encouragement, and support. I ask that You provide people to help me better understand myself and be prepared to serve You and others. I need the courage to look in the mirror and confess to You and ask for Your forgiveness when I know I have fallen short. I ask, Lord, that You reveal to me when I'm out of alignment with the direction You want from my life. Please open my eyes and my heart to change. Only You, Lord, can reveal the truth. Amen.

Steve Wingfield

Day 5

Do not conform any longer to the pattern of this world, but be transformed by the renewing of your mind. Then you will be able to test and approve what God's will is—his good, pleasing and perfect will.

—Romans 12:2

Self-awareness as a follower of Christ—an *accurate* understanding of who you are—depends on breaking from the world's way of thinking. As in every other area of our minds, Satan tries to work through our culture's messages to twist and corrupt our perception of ourselves. The world's way of thinking brings defensiveness, bends to our egos, and holds on to negative thoughts. But worldly patterns should no longer have a part in our understanding of ourselves. Our self-awareness is most clear when we listen, instead, to God's thoughts about us.

In your pursuit of self-awareness, if you detect patterns of the world popping up, counter them with statements from God's Word. Let the Spirit of God remind you and show you even more of all that God has freely given you. Let the Spirit use His Sword to demolish the old ways of thinking and make way for the renewing of your mind and transformation.

Father God, Your Word tells us not to love the world or the things in the world. When I look through the lens of this truth, I see that I fail too many times. Too much of my life has been about power, position, and things. Forgive me, Lord, for being self-centered. Serving the world will not produce any lasting benefits. Help me, Lord, to love You with all my heart, soul, and mind, and to love my neighbor as myself. Thank You, Lord, for Your Word. Thank You for your Spirit that encourages me to seek Your wisdom. Amen.

Steve Wingfield

Day 6

Do not conform any longer to the pattern of this world, but be transformed by the renewing of your mind. Then you will be able to test and approve what God's will is—his good, pleasing and perfect will.

—Romans 12:2

OUR VERSE TODAY IS THE SAME AS YESTERDAY'S. Before renewal can come, we need to be able to see our character clearly. We also need to see clearly who and what God says we are. Then, renewing our mind means lining up our thinking with God's thinking. We soak up and absorb what God says about this new life He's given us. We work hard at fleshing it out in our daily lives. Aligning our thoughts with God's has transformative power.

That renewal will enable us to walk more faithfully, with His strength and power and according to His resources. We'll see God's will more clearly. We'll understand *His* character better. His plan for our lives will become more distinct. Our lives will be increasingly conformed to His will and plan.

Renewal is the work of the Holy Spirit. He is renewing us day by day, through all the details of our lives. He breaks the grip the world has on our feelings and thinking. He shows us our character and points the way God wants us to go.

Lord, I ask for confidence to trust You in everything, and never trust myself. Help me to see when I fail You. Transform me. I want to be aware of my shortcomings, and I know that only You know me completely, and only You can provide the transformation that I need. I pray Your will and not my own. Amen.

Steve Wingfield

DAY 7

How great is the love the Father has lavished on us, that we should be called children of God! And that is what we are!

—1 John 3:1

THE BOTTOM LINE IS THAT WHO AND WHAT GOD SAYS we are is the truth. The Spirit of God lives in us to show us all that He has given us. If you are having trouble seeing this clearly, why not first pray for that enlightening of the eyes of your heart (Ephesians 1:18), and then begin writing down all of those Scriptures that convey things that God says about you. Just to start you off, here are a few. We won't write out the Scriptures here, but it will help you if you write them out for yourself. God says we are:

> *Sinners, deserving condemnation but given a clean record*
> *Forgiven*
> *His children and His heirs*
> *The sheep of His pasture*
> *His ambassadors, citizens of His kingdom, His holy people*
> *Given everything we need to live a godly life*
> *Strengthened in our inner being by His power*
> *Loved with an everlasting love*

Once you start searching and collecting these statements of God about *you,* you will find them everywhere throughout Scripture. The Spirit will lead you, showing you everything God has given you. Whatever and whoever the old was, it's gone. The new is here. Walk in self-awareness of who you are, child of God.

Father God, I am so grateful to be a part of Your family. You have blessed me in so many ways and for that I am thankful. I commit today to use all You have given me to further Your kingdom. I want to live the rest of my life for Your plans and Your purpose. Amen.

Notes and Prayers

_____

_____

_____

_____

_____

_____

_____

_____

_____

_____

_____

_____

_____

_____

_____

_____

_____

_____

Steve Wingfield

Self-Control

*Self-control—measured responses and choosing words and actions
that fit the occasion—is one of the marks of a great leader.*

—Paul Weaver

Day 1

But be transformed by the renewing of your mind.

—Romans 12:2

RESTRAINT IS KEEPING SOMETHING UNDER CONTROL. It is a discipline. Think about the discipline an athlete goes through. A swimmer, for example, trains her body so that it can function at the highest level in swim competitions. Parents discipline their children to mold their character and behavior. God disciplines his children to yield a "peaceful harvest of right living for those who are trained in this way" (Hebrews 12:11 NLT).

Self-control is disciplining all aspects of ourselves that are still tempted by the old nature: our thoughts, our words, our actions, and our attitudes. It's a discipline to re-shape them, or as one anonymous writer put it, "Self-control is transforming desires to please self into desires to please God."

The Apostle Paul wrote at length about his own struggles to do what he knew was right, and Galatians 5 tells us that this war will go on until God's plan of salvation is completely finished. The sinful nature and our new nature are constantly fighting each other. We are all too familiar with the battles. But that's no reason for discouragement. We have plenty of encouragement and hope in the Word of God. He has promised to empower you by His Spirit to live in victory.

Father God, it is my biggest battle—to overcome negative mindsets I've learned but I want to respond in this day as YOU would. Therefore, give me Holy Spirit self-control when I am tempted to shoot off at someone without thinking! Amen.

Prayers on SELF-CONTROL by Jonas Borntrager.

Day 2

For the grace of God has appeared that offers salvation to all people. It teaches us to say "No" to ungodliness and worldly passions, and to live self-controlled, upright and godly lives in this present age, while we wait for the blessed hope— the appearing of the glory of our great God and Savior, Jesus Christ.

—Titus 2:11–13

OUR VERSE TODAY FROM THE BOOK OF TITUS gives us a clear picture of self-control, disciplining ourselves in order to transform our desires to please self into desires to please God. Or, as this verse puts it, saying no to the old way of thinking and feeling and acting, and saying yes to God. That is the salvation that God offers, freedom from the old slavery.

Even though we would like to deny it (and modern thought tries to ignore this truth) we are slaves to whatever controls us. But Romans 6 tells us we have a choice in the matter; we can offer ourselves "to sin as an instrument of wickedness," or, as people who have been brought from death to life (Amen!), we can offer every part of ourselves to Him as instruments of righteousness.

The first step is offering ourselves to Him, giving ourselves over to His control. My prayer is that in the course of our Lodestar studies, we are bringing all of ourselves to Him and saying, "Here, Lord, take all of these traits You've gifted to me and empower and use them for Your purposes."

Yes, I can choose to say NO to ungodly, unhealthy responses and YES to God's way. Enable me to pause and think before I speak in a negative way. I want my life to reflect the character, honesty, and grace of Jesus Christ. Amen.

Steve Wingfield

Day 3

For the Spirit God gave us does not make us timid, but gives us power, love, and self-discipline.

—2 Timothy 1:7

In reality, the self-control found in those who follow Christ is not "self" control. The disciplining of our thoughts, words, actions, and attitudes to transform them goes far beyond what we can do by "self."

When we ask Christ to come into our heart, He does! He dwells with us by His Holy Spirit. Someone asked me what it means to be "filled" with the Holy Spirit. It means we come under His control. As we grow in our walk with the Lord, we walk more and more in step with the Spirit, with more and more of our thoughts, words, actions, and attitudes guided, molded, and changed by Him.

The Holy Spirit's presence in us is a gift of God's grace, and when we accept that gift and allow Him to work in us, He brings wisdom, discernment, self-control, love, and more—all in exceedingly abundant supply, more than anything we could ask or imagine.

The discipline of Spirit self-control can be enjoyed. Sometimes it may be painful and a hard battle—we do have to work with the Spirit as He teaches and empowers—but we are blessed by the Spirit. He is gentle and patient as He teaches us the best way to live, and His discipline produces that "peaceful harvest of right living" that Hebrews promised.

It's hard to deny my selfish responses in tight, threatening situations. It's not automatic, it's not natural. But it's the new me I want to develop to live a self-controlled, upright life. Help me today, to respond in Christ's love and power and with Your sound composed mind. Amen.

Day 4

But the fruit of the Spirit is love, joy, peace, forbearance, kindness, goodness, faithfulness, gentleness, and self-control. Against such things there is no law.
—Galatians 5:22–23

Galatians 5:24 says that those who are in Christ have crucified the old nature, and verse 25 speaks of walking in step with the Spirit. We aren't magically endowed with self-control. We read in many other verses that we need to strive for it, disciplining our thoughts and actions. But the energy and power to carry out this long and arduous battle is the power of the Spirit—and that is the same power that raised Jesus from the dead and will one day resurrect us.

We've got a great power at work for us. He is stronger than any other force that comes against us, from without or within. We no longer need to be slaves to our old sinful nature or what the world would call "human nature." You've heard that excuse, "Oh, it's understandable; it's just human nature to get revenge." Those indwelled by the Spirit have access to a power stronger than that old sinful nature.

So stay strong in the battle. His power is at work in you as you keep on disciplining your thoughts, words, actions, and attitudes.

> *Father God, Your great Person is working within me. Let this be my prayer today:*
>
> *"Lord, Your gentleness," (when tempted to impatience)*
>
> *"Lord, Your peace," (when tempted to be unsettled)*
>
> *"Lord, Your faithfulness," (when tempted to walk away from needs of others)*
>
> *"Lord, Your kindness," (when tempted to be hasty and unkind)*
>
> *"Lord, Your self-control," (when tempted to speak thoughtlessly the first thing that enters my mind)*

Steve Wingfield

Day 5

Trust in the LORD with all your heart and lean not on your own understanding; in all your ways submit to him, and he will make your paths straight.
—Proverbs 3:5–6

YOU ARE GOD'S CHILD. He lives in you and wants to help you live in control of your life. Spirit-led self-control empowers you to stand strong in any and all situations. Circumstances will not control you; God within will control you. He has promised never to forsake us. We can put our trust in Him as we learn more and more what it means to be under His control and thus be self-controlled.

Relying on the Spirit produces a calmness in our lives. I believe God wants us to live that way, to get to the point where our moods don't shift with every wind that blows around us. We are certain of His presence, His power, and His provision for us.

One emotion that gets the best of many people is fear. Throughout the entire Bible, we hear God or His messengers say, "Do not fear." Deuteronomy 20 holds a precious promise: "Do not be afraid as you go out to fight your enemies today! Do not lose heart or panic or tremble before them. For the LORD your God is going with you! He will fight for you against your enemies, and he will give you victory!" (NLT)

That is a promise for today, too.

Oh, thank You for going ahead of me and around me all day today. I will not live in fear but in the conscious presence of You with me and confidence in Your work within me. I am Your child, and this day I lean not on my own understanding but on You and Your Word alive in me. Amen.

Day 6

Take the helmet of salvation and the sword of the Spirit, which is the word of God.

—Ephesians 6:17

WHEN PAUL WROTE ABOUT THE ARMOR GOD PROVIDES US for the battles we face, the Word of God is compared to a sword, the Sword of the Spirit. The Spirit takes the Word of God and uses it to fight for us against lies the devil whispers, against our old nature's desires, against the messages of the world that bombard us. The psalmist wrote that he had hidden God's Word in his heart as a protection against sin.

You want to know what God thinks? Go to His Word. Wondering what His plan is, or even who He is? Get into his Word. Looking for His plan for your life? The answers are in His Word. There's comfort in the Word, and encouragement, and joy. And the Holy Spirit will use the Word to help you discipline your actions, thoughts, words, and attitudes. God breathed this gift to us. Open the gift and use it and delight in it.

I delight in Your Word, Oh God. If it had not been for Your Word, I would have perished in my afflictions. How I love Your statutes, for by them You have preserved my life! (Ps. 119:93). Today, I pick up the Sword of Your Spirit You've given me. Help me to recall Your words, hidden away in my heart when a need arises. To repeat that inspired Word, to shoot down all the fiery darts Satan will try to shoot at me. Your Word is sharper than any two-edged sword! Amen.

Steve Wingfield

Day 7

For the grace of God has appeared that offers salvation to all people. It teaches us to say "No" to ungodliness and worldly passions, and to live self-controlled, upright and godly lives in this present age, while we wait for the blessed hope— the appearing of the glory of our great God and Savior, Jesus Christ.

—Titus 2:11–13

The discipline of self-control is a life-long process. Perhaps that's why so many of the New Testament letters emphasize it. The first chapter of 2 Peter includes great steps to self-control. God has given us everything we need for life and godliness. If we live by his promises, we can "participate in the divine nature, having escaped the corruption in the world caused by evil desires" (2 Peter 1:4). "So make every effort to . . ." and he lists attributes we need to work at developing, self-control being one of them. God wants us to add those things to our lives; they have all been made available to us; we just have to take advantage of them. At other places in his letters, Peter urges us to be alert and watchful, on guard against the enemy who is always on the prowl. To do that, must have a disciplined mind.

This progression of growth is what we are to work on, so that we can live self-controlled, upright, and godly lives while waiting for Jesus Christ to appear again on earth.

Oh, great and awesome Father God, thank You for making me Your personal project—to conform me to the image of Your Son, to develop self-control, to remain calm in Your care, to help me. Use Your Word to discipline my thoughts, actions, words, and attitudes. Amen.

Steve Wingfield

Notes and Prayers

_____

_____

_____

_____

_____

_____

_____

_____

_____

_____

_____

_____

_____

_____

_____

_____

_____

_____

_____

The key is to take time to connect. Relationships make or break us. Good relationships result in the growth of people and companies. Bad relationships cause problems and consequences that mire us down today and haunt us tomorrow.

—Paul Weaver

DAY 1

Finally, all of you, be like-minded, be sympathetic, love one another, be compassionate and humble.

—1 Peter 3:8

SENSITIVITY IS ABOUT KEEPING YOUR EYES, ears, and heart open. If you are sensitive to those with whom you interact, you heed the counsel of Scripture to keep your mind alert, paying attention to what you see and hear. Then, your heart responds to what you've seen and heard. Sometimes action is appropriate and necessary; at other times, what you see, hear, and feel will act *in* you, aiding your flexibility, patience, generosity, self-awareness, and many other desirable characteristics as a godly leader.

Sensitivity—open eyes and open heart—is, in fact, an essential component of nearly all our Lodestar character traits. Without sensitivity, we won't be compassionate. Wisdom depends on information gleaned by sensitivity. Discernment requires sensitivity. Sincerity without sensitivity becomes ferociously selfish. Without sympathy and tender hearts, all the Lodestar traits become robotic at best. Nearly every quality we desire and pursue and hope to use in godly leadership is in some way dependent on our sensitivity. The needs of others must touch our hearts.

Most of Jesus' teaching and the letters of the apostles focus on our relationships with other people. We serve, not rule. We edify and share the burden of others, not judge and condemn. Ask for the Spirit's help in being sensitive to all those God puts in your path today.

Lord, I am thankful for Your sincere love which continues to overwhelm me. Amen.

Prayers on SENSITIVITY by David Wingfield.

DAY 2

As a prisoner for the Lord, then, I urge you to live a life worthy of the calling you have received.

—Ephesians 4:1

LET'S START THINKING ABOUT SENSITIVITY by focusing on the one thing we absolutely must always be sensitive to—God's calling on our lives. This will be the foundation on which we build our lives. Whether that call is to a life-long vocation or to act, in one specific situation, as He would have us act, our ears must always be open to hear, and our heart must be willing to respond.

What is God's calling on your life? How do we know what it is? The Scripture will always speak to us. Sometimes the words are plain: "You have been called to . . ." The Spirit will also speak, teaching and guiding the children of God. And God often uses other hearts who are committed to Him to help us along the way. We need to keep our ears open to hear what He is asking of us. If we are truly seeking, we will find.

Then, we need to respond. Three times, the book of Hebrews tells us, "If you hear his voice, do not harden your hearts" (Hebrew 3:15). God extends His call, but He has given us the choice of accepting His invitation to be part of His work here on earth—or to harden our hearts and say NO to what He asks of us.

He gave His life for me. He paid an extreme price to give me the gift of life. My life is now His, and now I want to be sensitive to whatever He calls me to do.

Test me, Lord. Examine my motives and give me the courage and power to change where I lack sensitivity. Amen.

Steve Wingfield

Day 3

But the Advocate, the Holy Spirit, whom the Father will send in my name, will teach you all things and will remind you of everything I have said to you.

—John 14:26

JESUS SAID THE SPIRIT WILL TEACH US "ALL THINGS," and all of us can benefit from the Spirit's guidance in being more sensitive to others, especially since we know how important this is in our relationships.

Our relationship with Christ is key. The closer we get to Him, the more we can depend on His Spirit developing sensitivity in us. He will bring understanding and insight. Paul Weaver's quote this week holds truth about both our interactions with others and our relationship with God. We must take time to connect. Strong relationships will promote our growth, or the lack of relationship will be our undoing. And the one relationship that is the foundation of all others is our relationship with God.

Walking in step with Jesus on our journey is walking in step with His Spirit teaching us and guiding us. The disciples learned from Jesus every day as they saw their teacher interact with the crowds and the individuals who came to Him. We will learn, too, as we walk with Him. If we are earnestly seeking to learn, He'll show us how to read people, understand what they need, and be willing to offer ourselves to help meet those needs. Take the time to connect with Him, and He'll teach you how to connect with others.

Lord, search me and know my heart . . . See if there is any wicked way in me and lead me in the way everlasting (Psalm 139:23–24). *Amen.*

Steve Wingfield

DAY 4

But if anyone has the world's goods and sees his brother in need, yet closes his heart against him, how does God's love abide in him?

—1 John 3:17 (ESV)

AS CHRIST'S FOLLOWERS AND REPRESENTATIVES IN THIS WORLD, we are called to have tender hearts of compassion. We're called to look beyond the masks people wear and see the struggles in every life. Our verse for today from 1 John 3 speaks of needs of worldly goods. But every person has needs that go deeper than material possessions, even deeper than the need for food and clothes. Jesus asks his disciples to see the needs of their brothers and sisters—all of them, the material, the emotional, the spiritual. And then, we are not to close our hearts to those needs, but to love as Jesus loved.

Jesus gave up His life because He loved. Literally. He gave up a home and His reputation. He gave up comfort. He rejected any temptation to build a career for His own benefit. He sacrificed approval of the religious structure around which all of Jewish life was centered. His days were given to serve the purpose of His Father. He gave all of His life because he loved so much. How much of our lives are we willing to give up to be Jesus' representative now in our world? Will we give up our dreams? Goals? Agendas? Comfort? Time? Image?

Some of His last words on this earth are words that ring loud and clear even today: "Love each other as I have loved you" (John 15:12).

Father God, I want to be free, help me to stay close to You and to do right so that others can see You in me. Amen.

Steve Wingfield

DAY 5

The Spirit of the Lord is on me, because he has anointed me to proclaim good news to the poor. He has sent me to proclaim freedom for the prisoners and recovery of sight for the blind, to set the oppressed free, to proclaim the year of the Lord's favor.

—Luke 4:18–19

JESUS READ THE PASSAGE FROM ISAIAH as an announcement of His mission. The same Spirit who anointed Him also works in you and empowers you to carry on His mission in the world. Sensitivity to the needs around us—being aware of and responsive to the broken, the hurting, those trapped and burdened—is a gift that God wants us to use to touch lives that need Him.

As partners in Christ's mission, we also need to be sensitive to what God is saying to us. I know that when I listen to His voice and I obey His voice, I'm a much better me. The gift of being able to speak into someone's life is a true gift, and we need to honor that privilege of touching lives in the name of Christ.

Jesus' sensitivity to the needs around Him was evident in so many ways—His weeping over those who rejected Him, His compassion that kept Him ministering to the crowds when He needed food and rest, and His tender care of the flock God gave Him. Many of His words in John chapters 14, 15, and 16, shared with His disciples on the night of His betrayal, show us His tender heart for His disciples of all time. And in chapter 17, His earnest prayer for us.

I pray He will keep us sensitive to all those needs around us.

Lord, I want to be Your love with skin on. Amen.

DAY 6

Be kind to one another, tenderhearted, forgiving one another, as God in Christ forgave you.

—Ephesians 4:32 (ESV)

BE SENSITIVE. OPEN YOUR EYES AND HEART to what the Spirit is doing in others. It is a strategy of the devil to make us quick to judge and condemn a person's faith or Christian walk. We see the splinter in their eye, forgetting the huge log in our own. Critical and judgmental attitudes bring discord and break the bonds the Spirit would use to strengthen and protect us. If the enemy can use those few thoughts of criticism of brothers and sisters in the body of Christ, he will. He will use such thoughts (and spoken words) to do as much damage as he can.

Rather than judging others, look for the Spirit's work in their lives. The same Spirit who is so patiently teaching and molding you is also at work in them. Just as children learn and mature in different ways at different rates of growth (both mentally and physically), so do the children of God. We are growing into Christ-likeness at different paces, growing in different ways, but all children of God are in the hands of the Holy Spirit. Open your eyes to that, and keep your heart tender toward others. Be kind to each other; be patient and forgive each other. The work is ongoing! He is committed to bringing many sons and daughters to glory, and He will do it.

Lord, help me to guard my eye gate and my ear gate for the filth of this world. May I be filled with Your Spirit. Amen.

Steve Wingfield

Day 7

Being confident of this, that he who began a good work in you will carry it on to completion until the day of Christ Jesus.

—Philippians 1:6

THROUGHOUT THIS WEEK, YOU MAY HAVE REALIZED your lack of sensitivity in one area or another. The Spirit may be speaking to you, leading you to a greater understanding. That is really what we are saying when we focus on sensitivity. We want to be increasingly open to the Spirit of Christ within us, who will teach us all things. I really think this is what the Spirit does in us: opens our eyes and ears and moves our hearts.

You have been possessed by Christ, as Paul put it, "possessed for perfection" (Philippians 3:12). His Spirit is not going to abandon you; He'll teach you and guide you—even in this difficult area of being more sensitive! Be open to Him. Be sensitive to and patient with the work He is continuing in other lives, too.

We are Christ's representatives. His life and mission carry on in the world through us. I want to complete my part of the mission well. That is my heart's great desire. All of the Lodestar leadership traits we've looked at are tools Christ can use for His glory. He did not give you the gift of leadership for your own glory. To use your abilities for that purpose will be hollow and unsatisfying and have no eternal value. To let Christ imbue His power through these traits, for His mission and to bring Him glory and honor—that will be the most fulfilling and exciting life you can have, beyond anything you can imagine.

Lord, I want to do Your will, speak to me. Amen.

Notes and Prayers

_____

_____

_____

_____

_____

_____

_____

_____

_____

_____

_____

_____

_____

_____

_____

_____

_____

_____

> *If our rhetoric and our motives are not in alignment, the motives will always surface sooner or later. When that happens, trust with our teams will be broken, and fear and doubt enter our culture.*
>
> —Paul Weaver

DAY 1

We speak as those approved by God to be entrusted with the gospel. We are not trying to please people but God, who tests our hearts.

—1 Thessalonians 2:4

I HOPE AND PRAY THAT MY LIFE EXHIBITS SINCERITY. My heart's desire is to be a person of sincerity. Here's how that desire shapes my life. I love people. I want to live out my belief system and let people know that's who I am. Sincerity is connecting with people genuinely and truthfully, focusing on their needs—even above my own.

I want my word to be my bond. Sincerity is a part of what makes you and me believable. It's what makes Christianity believable. Especially in this culture. Christianity is so misunderstood today by so many people. Unless we exhibit truth and sincerity and live it out, we're not portraying the gospel. I want to represent Christ well in all that I say and all that I do. I want to exhibit my relationship with Christ genuinely, as a way of life. Truth is vitally important.

We need to be sincere. We've been entrusted with the gospel of Christ. As His ambassadors, we simply cannot have hypocrisy and phoniness and deceit as a part of our lives. I want to be and live worthy of the trust He's given me.

Oh Jesus, help me to be real. May my words and actions show that I live what I say. Amen.

Prayers on SINCERITY by Frank Shelton.

DAY 2

Test me, LORD, and try me, examine my heart and my mind.

—Psalm 26:2

YOU KNOW, THERE IS SOMEONE WHO KNOWS ME BETTER THAN I KNOW MYSELF. He knows you better than you know yourself, too. That's why we go to Him for truth and wisdom—especially for truth about ourselves. Because, as I'm sure you know, we are sometimes blind to our own faults. Psalm 19:12 asks, "How can I know all the sins lurking in my heart? Cleanse me from these hidden faults" (NLT).

We will ask ourselves hard questions this week. *Am I trying to give or get in my relationships? What motives are driving my relationship with this person? Do I manipulate or even lie to make things go my way? Am I pretending? Are my desires and needs always uppermost in my mind, or do I put the desire and needs of others first? How sincere am I—really?*

As a start, let's make these two verses from Psalms our prayer, asking the Holy Spirit to test our hearts and examine our sincerity. He knows where we might be living with some pretense or hypocrisy or hidden motives. Then, let's be courageous and obedient, and ask Him to show us how we'll need to change and to give us the power to do it.

Be courageous and ask for the Spirit's help this week. Then the cleansing will come.

Lord, I wanna walk my talk and I want to talk my walk. May people see Jesus in me, but I pray I will also communicate His love to others by what I say. Amen.

Steve Wingfield

Day 3

Dear children, let us not love with words or speech but with actions and in truth.
—1 John 3:18

ACTIONS SPEAK LOUDER THAN WORDS. Unless your words are backed up by actions, they don't mean much. "It is not by telling people about ourselves that we demonstrate our Christianity. Words are cheap," wrote Jonathan Edwards. "It is by costly, self-denying Christian practice that we show the reality of our faith."

Talk is cheap. It is easy to *say* something. It's much harder to actually carry through and *do* it. I want my word to be my bond. When I say I'm going to do something or be somewhere, I want to carry through with that. Sometimes unforeseen things turn up that interfere with plans, but then I always try to let people know why I can't show up.

The man who says, "I hate lies," and yet is known to tweak the truth to his own advantage will not have anyone believing his words. They'll be wondering about the Christ he serves, too, if he professes to be a Christian. The woman who says, "I care," yet never gives up her own schedule to help out someone in need is also just loving "with words and tongue," as John put it. The truth is that she doesn't care enough to act in accordance to what she says.

We each need to ask Him if we've been throwing out cheap talk that is only pretense and manipulation.

Lord, give me a sensitive ear to Your voice and a sensitive heart to the needs of others. Amen.

DAY 4

Now that you have purified yourselves by obeying the truth so that you have sincere love for each other, love one another deeply, from the heart.

—1 Peter 1:22

THERE ARE TWO PARTS TO THE VERSE FOR TODAY. We'll look at the first part today and the second tomorrow. There are also two uses of the word *love* in this verse. In the English language, we use the word *love* for many different things. I love my wife. I love hunting. I love beans, cornbread, and creasy greens on a cold winter day. But the original Greek has different words for *love,* depending on the relationship.

The first use in this verse ("sincere *love* for each other") is the Greek word *philia,* the bond between friends. Peter wrote that purifying ourselves by obeying the truth leads to sincere *philia.*

Obeying the truth. That's necessary, my friend, if we want sincerity in a relationship. Jesus said the truth will set us free, and in our relationships, commitment to the truth cleanses and frees us from hidden agendas, comparisons, and selfish competition that lead to envy, manipulation of others, and hypocrisy. Truth guides us as we strive to get things aligned correctly. Truth guards us against sinful desires within as we check our motives, speech, and actions. Truth brings sincerity to our relationships—and keeps us operating in sincere *philia.*

Commitment to the truth. Commitment to the One who is Truth. That's what gives us the freedom to be sincere—courageously doing what is right and genuinely expressing our feelings and thoughts.

Will You promise to supply all my needs? I want a sensitive heart and open hands to help meet the needs of others. Amen.

DAY 5

Now that you have purified yourselves by obeying the truth so that you have sincere love for each other, love one another deeply, from the heart.

—1 Peter 1:22

AGAPE LOVE IS A PERFECT LOVE, one that goes beyond all other loves. Jesus used this word when He commanded that those who follow Him should love others the way He loves us. *Agape* love is the mark of His disciples. For citizens of Christ's kingdom, *agape* love will take all character traits and elevate them to heavenly traits imbued with the Spirit of Christ.

In Colossians, Paul wrote about God's people putting on the "clothes" of compassion, kindness, humility, gentleness, patience, and forgiveness. "And over all these virtues put on love, which binds them all together in perfect unity" (Colossians 3:14). This is, again, *agape* love. When we operate in that kind of love, all of these traits work together, each supporting and enhancing the others. Then, everything you do in sincerity, kindness, empathy, and courage takes on heavenly dimensions. Your productivity, initiative, diligence, and patience (and all the other traits) operate on spiritual levels, not just earthly levels.

The love of Christ in us brings true, pure sincerity to our relationships. I want to be a person who is filled with the love of Christ.

Lord, I will go where You want to go; I want to do what You want me to do. Help me to trust You and walk in obedience to Your plans and Your purpose for my life. Amen.

DAY 6

Love must be sincere. Hate what is evil; cling to what is good.
—Romans 12:9

I DON'T LIKE EVIL ANYWHERE—in the home, the church, the workplace, on the street, in traffic. Not anywhere. I want to hate what is evil and cling to what is good. Proverbs 6:17–19 talks about seven things the Lord hates: "haughty eyes, a lying tongue, hands that shed innocent blood, a heart that devises wicked schemes, feet that are quick to rush into evil, a false witness who pours out lies, and a person who stirs up conflict in the community." Those things are all deceptive, disruptive, and evil. Several verses after Peter's instructions to practice *agape* love toward each other, he listed things we must get rid of: malice, deceit, hypocrisy, envy, and slander. These lists show us places we go to when we are not sincere in our relationships. We end up practicing all of this that is evil and ignoring what is good. Don't be lured to those places by sinful motives lurking in your heart. Ask the Spirit to cleanse you with His truth.

Stay away from evil around you. Cling to what is good, and represent that to the people you are talking to, those you relate to, and those you work with. Be sincere, focus on the good, and pursue it.

Sincerity avoids drama and conflict—and evil. Sincerity seeks good. The goal is allowing God to love people through you. A pure heart and a good conscience coupled with faith in the Spirit's power in you will help you to relate and love sincerely.

Lord, I want to see people not just for who they are but help me to look beyond that and see who they can be in Christ. Amen.

Steve Wingfield

DAY 7

So I say, walk by the Spirit, and you will not gratify the desires of the flesh.
—Galatians 5:16

WHAT HAS THE SPIRIT BEEN SAYING TO YOU THIS WEEK? If your prayer has been for Him to test you and lead you into more sincerity, then listen as He speaks, and follow Him. Don't be discouraged if you have realized there are areas in which you have been hypocritical, deceitful, and insincere or if the Spirit has shown you that you do not have pure motives. Galatians 5 tells us that the sinful nature will always be at war with what the Spirit wants to do in our lives. But the Spirit was given to those who belong to Christ to teach, guide, and change us. His Spirit is constantly changing us into His image. The Spirit is the first installment of the glorious destiny God has promised us.

Whatever the Spirit has been saying to you this week, follow His leading. He will guide you to the truth. His power will enable you to obey the truth, hate evil, and cling to what is good. Living by the Spirit allows His power to bring His fruit into our lives—fruit we can never produce by our own will and power. His power will enable you to love sincerely and be a trustworthy representative of Christ and His gospel.

Lord, I ask You at the end of this week to help me represent You well. When I don't get it right, may I be quick to ask Your forgiveness so that others will see You in me. Amen.

Steve Wingfield

Notes and Prayers

_____

_____

_____

_____

_____

_____

_____

_____

_____

_____

_____

_____

_____

_____

_____

_____

_____

_____

Steve Wingfield

Ultimately, we are given our resources from our Creator, including not only our monetary assets but our area of giftedness as well. Stewardship is investing in others and giving freely rather than thinking only of ourselves.

—Paul Weaver

DAY 1

Each of you should use whatever gift you have received to serve others, as faithful stewards of God's grace in its various forms.

—1 Peter 4:10

YOU ARE A STEWARD. God has entrusted certain things to you. He has given you resources and gifts to use. You are a steward of those resources. Like it or not, that's who you are, who God wants you to be.

God has given us abilities, talents, and intellect to minister to others. He's given some of us positions of influence and leadership. He's given us material goods. He's entrusted this beautiful earth to us. He's given us, well, all of life, from sunup to sundown. He has given us time, each day we live. He has put the gospel of Jesus Christ into our hands, showering us with mercy, kindness, and forgiveness. Are we only recipients of that, or are we opening the greatness of God's grace to others? He has given us access to His resources of strength and power and wisdom. How are we using all of that?

What has He put into your hands to be used for His kingdom? He has given you *every good thing* you have. Consider how you can manage it all well, my friend.

Heavenly Father, I want to be a good steward of what You have entrusted to me. Give me opportunities this week to use my abilities, talents, and intellect for Your kingdom. Give me the courage to give away what You have given to me. In Jesus' name, amen.

Day 2

The earth is the LORD's, and everything in it, the world, and all who live in it.
—Psalm 24:1

WHATEVER HAS BEEN PUT IN OUR HANDS IS NOT OURS. It belongs to the Lord. It's on loan to us to use according to His plans. We need to live with that awareness. Nothing is ours. What we have belongs to the Lord and is given to us to handle wisely and for His purposes, as His overseers, and His stewards.

One day when I was at the farm on Lodestar Mountain Inn, a man stopped by and asked if I was the owner. "No, I'm not," I answered. "This property belongs to the Lord. I'm just a steward of what He has put into our hands." I really believe that's how the Lord wants us to live.

If we hold too tightly to what we have, claiming our ownership, we'll find that it soon owns us. But when we live with the knowledge that everything belongs to God, including our very lives, then we will not be owned by any amount of material prosperity.

I was taught a long time ago that if you don't have sticky fingers, the Lord will allow a lot of stuff to pass through your hands. If He knows you are a good steward of what He entrusts to you, He will place even more in your hands. I challenge you to use whatever God has given you. He loans it to you for the purpose of serving and glorifying Him.

Father, I want to be more generous and open with everything I have. I give You my life, my resources and my relationships, thank You for entrusting all of that to me. In Jesus' name I pray, amen.

Steve Wingfield

Day 3

Be shepherds of God's flock that is under your care, watching over them—not because you must, but because you are willing, as God wants you to be.

—1 Peter 5:2

Once we step into the area of responsibility of leadership as a follower of Christ, I believe God puts us at a different level of standards and judgment. This leadership may be of the church, of a business, of a team, or of a family. As leaders and those with influence, God has given us the position of overseers to shepherd those we lead.

It is not *our* congregation, *our* business, or *our* family. It is God's flock and is now entrusted to us as overseers and shepherds. Even if those we lead are not yet believers, Christ paid the price for them, and He's entrusted us to carry on His mission to call sinners back to God.

Where has God placed you? As shepherds of the flock God has put under our care, our shepherding must follow the model of the Great Shepherd. Our thinking, actions, and character will be patterned after Him and His shepherding. That's what the Holy Spirit will do in our lives: transforming us to shepherd others in the same way He cares for us.

When the Great Shepherd returns, you will receive a crown of glory that never fades. It is a solemn charge to take care of God's flock. I want to encourage you to be a faithful steward of the resources He has given you to do His work.

Lord, give me the wisdom I need to lead well the people under my care. Give me the understanding and patience I need to be the best leader and example I can be to those around me. Amen.

Day 4

I tell you, use worldly wealth to gain friends for yourselves, so that when it is gone, you will be welcomed into eternal dwellings.

—Luke 16:9

PEOPLE YOU WILL NEVER MEET IN THIS WORLD will be in heaven because you have been a good steward of what God put in your hands. Maybe you supported a missionary or our evangelistic ministry or an organization distributing bibles and someone came to faith in Christ through that. Those people who have died before you, in the providence of God, will be a part of the welcoming committee when you get to heaven. I believe that God's going to connect those dots. Then you will know what fruit has been produced by your stewardship in this life.

As I sat at Billy Graham's funeral, I had a vision of thousands upon thousands upon thousands of people who had come to faith in Christ through his ministry over the years. Many of them had died and were already in heaven, and when he walked in, I believe there was a great celebration. Luke's gospel especially includes many teachings on storing up treasures in heaven, and stewarding our worldly resources to build our heavenly accounts that will last forever. This is a part of our responsibility concerning whatever God gives us, to use it to help others get to heaven, too.

God, show me where You want me to give and serve to make a difference in peoples' lives for eternity. Connect me to the right people, organizations, and churches that I can partner with to further Your kingdom. In Jesus' name I pray, amen.

Steve Wingfield

DAY 5

Now, a person who is put in charge as a manager must be faithful.
—1 Corinthians 4:2 (NLT)

THOSE WHO ARE ENTRUSTED WITH THE MANAGEMENT OF ANYTHING MUST BE FAITHFUL. We would readily agree with that. Let's look more closely at *faithful*. Dictionaries tell us that to be *faithful* means we'll be loyal, constant, and steadfast. Are you being faithful with that entrusted to you? Are you *loyal*? Is your highest goal and deepest desire to serve Christ and Christ alone?

We cannot serve two masters. If we try, we're like waves of the sea, constantly changing direction. I hope and pray that nothing, *nothing* else comes between you and your loyalty to our Lord. "Let us offer through Jesus a continual sacrifice of praise to God, proclaiming our allegiance to his name" (Hebrews 13:15 NLT).

Are you *constant*? Are you focused on God's purpose and plan for you, living out the life He has called you to as His representative, His ambassador, His heir, and His steward? Are your eyes and ears glued to that calling?

Are you *steadfast*? Are your roots going ever deeper into Christ? "Hold tightly without wavering to the hope we affirm" (Hebrews 10:23 NLT); keep your eyes on our Champion and the unshakable kingdom of God.

God has entrusted us with so much, and Jesus said if we're given much, much will be required of us. Be loyal, be constant, be steadfast.

Lord God, I want to be loyal, constant and steadfast. I realize that I can't do that on my own, so help me in even the smallest area of my life to be faithful. Keep my eyes firmly fixed on You and what You are doing in the world around me. In Jesus' name, amen.

Day 6

So I am willing to endure anything if it will bring salvation and eternal glory in Christ Jesus to those God has chosen.

—2 Timothy 2:10 (NLT)

In order to be good stewards, we need to identify our goals. If stewardship is "administering and managing efficiently and effectively," we need to know the ultimate goal of managing the resources we've been given. Remember, we are stewards of the Lord. We represent Him; we're His ambassadors here until Christ comes back to earth. So we must take *His* purposes and goals as *our* purposes and goals.

God said He made everything for His glory, including the new lives He's given us, part of His new creation. Nature points to God's glory. We are to be living to bring glory and honor to God. He wants everything to point people to Him. He wants everyone to come back to Him, to be saved by Jesus' sacrifice.

The apostle Paul wrote of his life being poured out as a sacrifice to God, with the one purpose of bringing the gospel to many people and seeing people brought to faith in Jesus Christ. God has poured out, too, "poured out His love into our hearts through the Holy Spirit, whom He has given us" (Romans 5:5 BSB). God has poured out His life into the life He's given us.

Lord, use me. Help my life to reflect You and give Your glory. Give me opportunities to pour Your love into others. Lord, I'm willing to give You every area of my life to use as You see fit. In Jesus' name, amen.

Steve Wingfield

Day 7

As a prisoner for the Lord, then, I urge you to live a life worthy of the calling you have received.

—Ephesians 4:1

PAUL OFTEN REFERS TO HIMSELF AS A PRISONER or slave of the Lord Jesus Christ. Today, we resist using such words. *Slave* and *prisoner* are not much to our liking. But the fact remains that we are all devoted to something or someone; there is that one thing in our lives that controls our thoughts, compels us to action, and determines our path. Let it be Jesus Christ, my friend.

Such a passion consumes us. After all, we were bought with a heavy price. We were given honored and lavish standing in God's family as His sons and daughters, His heirs. With all that came a calling to live a life according to our Father's plans and purposes. As part of that calling, He asks us to be wise stewards of the resources He puts into our hands. As a matter of fact, He's promised He will equip us with everything we need. If He asks us to do something, He'll make sure we're prepared, supplied, and outfitted for it. The Apostle Paul wrote to the young pastor Timothy: "Be strong through the grace that God gives you in Christ Jesus" (2 Timothy 2:1 NLT). That is how we can live this life—with God's grace giving us everything we need.

Father God, You have blessed me in so many ways and for that I am thankful. I commit today to use all You have given me to further Your kingdom. I want to live the rest of my life for Your plans and Your purpose. Amen.

Notes and Prayers

_____

_____

_____

_____

_____

_____

_____

_____

_____

_____

_____

_____

_____

_____

_____

_____

_____

_____

TEACHABLE

Our minds are like sponges. Keep filling yours with good, wholesome information, and never stop pouring into it. Whatever you pour in is ultimately who you will become.

—Paul Weaver

DAY 1

Poverty and disgrace come to him who ignores instruction, but whoever heeds reproof is honored.

—Proverbs 13:18 (ESV)

I THANK GOD FOR PEOPLE WHO ARE WILLING to come and speak into my life and help me to become better than I currently am. What does the Bible have to say about having a teachable spirit? We don't have to read very far in Proverbs to find verses that speak of the value of learning, discipline, instruction, and growth. We must be teachable to grow and to live well. But it is also very plain that being teachable is next to impossible unless you have a humble spirit.

Pride and self-centeredness are powerful enemies of teachability. We need to be open to somebody speaking into our lives, whether it be the Holy Spirit, a mentor, a team member, a family member, or even a stranger. God designed us to learn and grow and become wiser as a result of life experiences and interactions with others. Humble spirits will thank God for those who speak into their lives because they know there is always more for them to learn and more ways in which they can grow.

Lord, give me a humble spirit to increase my receptivity to instruction and correction from You and others. Amen.

Prayers on TEACHABLE by Dr. Wayne Schmidt.

Day 2

In the same way, you who are younger, submit yourselves to your elders. All of you, clothe yourselves with humility toward one another, because, "God opposes the proud but shows favor to the humble."

—1 Peter 5:5

BEING TEACHABLE IS A QUALITY YOU NEVER OUTGROW. You never "arrive" at a place where it is no longer necessary. 1 Peter 5:5 and Titus 2 both advise the younger generation to respect the older, but Peter added *"all of you . . ."* All of us, younger or older, are to clothe ourselves with humility toward one another. What that says to me is that we are to be learners all of our lives.

Earlier in his letter, Peter wrote that Christians should live in harmony with one another, loving as brothers and sisters, compassionate, and humble. We are to walk in humility and always be open to learning something new be it from an older person or a younger person.

Years ago, Ralph W. Neighbour Jr. wrote a book called "The Last Seven Last Words of the Church: We Never Tried It That Way Before." Those are also the seven last words of a leader. If a leader is not pliable and teachable, his or her leadership will wither away for lack of growth.

It doesn't matter if you're young or old, male or female, new to your leadership role or a patriarch of the company, young in the faith or an aged saint—the Spirit of Christ connects us all as part of one body, each part giving and receiving life to and from other parts. That give and take depends on humble teachability.

Father, may I be clothed with the humility to fully experience Your grace, so I will be a lifelong learner who lives in harmony with others. Amen.

Steve Wingfield

DAY 3

Looking to Jesus, the founder and perfecter of our faith.
—Hebrews 12:2 (ESV)

THE NORMAL CHRISTIAN LIFE IS A LIFE OF MATURING AND GROWING. Throughout the letters of the New Testament, we find many passages that talk about growing in our faith, growing in our spiritual identity, and growing in effective discipleship. The ultimate, over-arching plan of God is that we grow up to be His true son or daughter, like Jesus, our big brother.

Maybe you can remember trying to emulate an older brother or sister. Or as a parent, you noticed how younger children learn quickly from their older siblings, picking up ways of speaking, characteristic actions, and attitudes. Jesus said, "Take my yoke upon you and learn from me . . ." (Matthew 11:29). That is, "let me teach you." He said we're His disciples if we remain faithful to His teachings. Being faithful, that is being teachable. We learn from Him. Our words begin to sound more and more like Jesus talking. Our actions and reactions begin to look more and more like the ways in which He would act and react. Our spirits become more and more like His.

Our discipleship is daily and constantly saying "Yes, Lord. Yes. Yes." Like younger siblings, our desire is to be like Him. We let Him shape us. That is God's plan: to bring many sons and daughters to glory. And Jesus is the One we look to as the perfecter, the finisher, the completer of our faith. The One who says, "Learn from me. Let me teach you."

Jesus, as I humbly and continually learn from You, may I be more and more like You, the founder and perfecter of my faith. Amen.

Steve Wingfield

Day 4

Dear brothers and sisters, when troubles of any kind come your way, consider it an opportunity for great joy.

—James 1:2 (NLT)

WHEN FAITH IS TESTED, we have an opportunity to cultivate endurance. The effect of standing fast through it all is that we'll be "perfect and complete, needing nothing" (NLT). What a promise!

The old barn that was going to be reconstructed at the Lodestar Mountain Inn would become the central event center. We saw God's hand in giving us this wonderful barn, and we had big dreams for it. The first day of the "barn raising" was an exciting day. But not many weeks later, a windstorm came through and completely destroyed the framing that had gone up. A total loss. When I posted the news and the photos of the wreckage on Facebook, several of the first responses asked, "What can we learn from this?"

We need wisdom in our trials. We needed wisdom in dealing with the loss of the barn. James says we can ask our generous God and He will give us the wisdom we need. We need to ask, and we need to keep learning what He wants to teach us. Sailors learn their skills on stormy seas, not smooth, calm waters.

My friend, God says He is always with you, holding your hand. A wise, loving Father, He is teaching you, His child, through every experience in your life. His purpose is for you to become all that He plans for you to be. I hope you live with that faith and hope.

Holy Spirit, I look expectantly for You to teach me in times of trial, considering it an opportunity for great joy. Amen.

DAY 5

But the Advocate, the Holy Spirit, whom the Father will send in my name, will teach you all things, and will remind you of everything I have said to you.

—John 14:26

QUENCH. IT'S A STRANGE SOUNDING WORD WHEN YOU SAY IT OFTEN. That's the word used in 1 Thessalonians 5:19: "Do not quench the Spirit." *Quench* means to put out, to extinguish, as in extinguishing a fire. *Do not put out the fire of the Spirit.* The fire of the Spirit burns within you, my friend. The Holy Spirit lives in you to teach you, guide you, and mold you. He will teach you all things, if you will be teachable. And we have so much to learn. If we made a list of all the passages from the New Testament letters alone that urge us to learn and grow, we would fill pages. Here's just a sampling of things we need to learn:

> *To put on the full armor of God* (Ephesians 6)
> *To devote ourselves to good works* (Titus 3:14)
> *To walk in a manner worthy of your calling* (Ephesians 4:1)
> *To discern what is pleasing to the Lord* (Ephesians 5:10)
> *To be obedient children* (1 Peter 1:13–15)
> *To preserve the unity of the Spirit* (Ephesians 4:13)
> *To rely on God and not worry* (Philippians 4:6–7)
> *To give thanks in all circumstances* (1 Thessalonians 5:18)
> *To persevere under trial and standing the test* (James 1:12)

Be teachable. Don't put out that fire!

Holy Spirit, instead of quenching You, may I humbly invite You to burn brightly within me to mold and guide me. Amen.

Day 6

Get all the advice and instruction you can, so you will be wise the rest of your life.
—Proverbs 19:20 (NLT)

WISE PEOPLE LISTEN TO OTHERS AND LEARN. Seek out those relationships that can help you grow. In this, as in all other areas, the Spirit will help you. Ask for the Spirit's help in finding those connections that will build you up in your faith and spur you on. It may be a mentor or an accountability group. You need people who will pour into your life. And the Spirit will help you make those connections.

It was the Spirit who spoke to Philip and sent him down an unexpected, unplanned road. Along the way, Philip met an Ethiopian, an important official in the queen's court. The Ethiopian was reading Scripture but could not understand it. He needed someone to teach him, and he was humble enough to acknowledge that and welcome Philip's guidance. As a result, the good news about Jesus went to Ethiopia.

Like selecting what you read and put into your mind, be intentional about building relationships that can teach you. Select wisely who will help you learn, grow, and mature.

The most important relationship to nurture is your relationship with God. We've seen how the Trinity teaches us: the Father, who loves and teaches His children; Jesus, the One who teaches us to be like Him; the Spirit, who lives with us to teach, guide, and mold us. "All the while, you will grow as you learn to know God better and better" (Colossians 1:10 NLT). That is my prayer for you.

Lord, connect me with godly people who will spur me on to love and good deeds. May I intentionally build relationships that teach me to mature in You. Amen.

Steve Wingfield

Day 7

May God give you more and more grace and peace as you grow in your knowledge of God and Jesus our Lord.

—2 Peter 1:2 (NLT)

PETER OPENED HIS SECOND LETTER TO EVERYONE who belongs to Christ with the prayer that grace and peace would grow in believers' lives as they got to know God better and better. He then went on to write about God's great promises and plans for us, and *therefore* or *for this very reason* (2 Peter 1:5), we are to make every effort to grow in specific character traits: goodness, knowledge, self-control, perseverance, godliness, brotherly kindness, and agape love. Doing so will increase our effectiveness and productivity as Jesus' disciples.

For me, that means I need to make every effort, to work hard at developing these things if I want to represent Christ well in this world. I need help because even though this is my heart's desire, I know I don't always get it right. I need to have a teachable spirit, one that receives instruction and wisdom from God and from other Christians the Spirit brings into my life. I need to be open to others speaking into my life and to what the Spirit wants to teach me. I thank God that He has planned for this. When God promises that He will supply all we need for living a godly life, that includes people from whom we can learn and gain wisdom.

I want to be the best representative of Christ I can possibly be, so I'll work hard at it. I'll be teachable. I pray you will be, too.

God, may I grow in Your grace and keep in step with the Spirit so that I may know You better and represent Christ more fully. Amen.

Steve Wingfield

Notes and Prayers

_____

_____

_____

_____

_____

_____

_____

_____

_____

_____

_____

_____

_____

_____

_____

_____

_____

_____

Steve Wingfield

Thoroughness

*Many of the difficulties we have in life are due to not being thorough
with our plans and actions. When we are thorough and pay
attention to the details, life is much less chaotic.*

—Paul Weaver

Day 1

*Teach me, LORD, the way of your decrees, that I may follow it to the end. Give
me understanding, so that I may keep your law and obey it with all my heart.*
—Psalm 119:33–34

"No man with a sense of God could fail to do his finest work, even on
the smallest detail." Those are words from Dr. Elmer Towns, my friend and
mentor. Thoroughness, attention to detail, and accuracy in everything we do
is not a matter of simply being efficient, pleasing the boss, or getting the job
done right. It is a matter of honoring the Lord. We find this explanation in a
strange place—in Paul's instructions to slaves.

> *Slaves, obey your earthly masters in everything; and do it, not only when
> their eye is on you and to curry their favor, but with sincerity of heart and
> reverence for the Lord. Whatever you do, work at it with all your heart, as
> working for the Lord, not for human masters, since you know that you will
> receive an inheritance from the Lord as a reward. It is the Lord Christ you
> are serving.*
>
> —Colossians 3:22–24

I want the details of my everyday life to show my reverence for Him.
So I'll be paying attention and being sincere and thorough in *whatever* I do,
doing it with all my heart.

*Lord, keep before me my love for You, and may I always live in the awareness that
I am doing what I do for You. Lord, I want to do my best. Amen.*

Prayers on Thoroughness by Dr. Wayne Schmidt.

Day 2

"Well done, my good servant!" his master replied. "Because you have been trustworthy in a very small matter, take charge of ten cities."

—Luke 19:17

JESUS TOLD A STORY ABOUT A NOBLE WHO LEFT THE COUNTRY and put his money into the hands of his servants to manage. Our verse for today from Luke tells us that being responsible and faithful in the small things builds habits within us that make us responsible and trustworthy in much bigger matters, also.

Thoroughness is a habit that can be developed. Pay attention to the "small" things, to things that might seem insignificant. Sloppiness in the small things leads to sloppiness in larger things. If we don't take care with those very small matters, our nonchalance quickly grows and spills over into other areas. Soon, we're taking shortcuts or doing the job "good enough" to get by, even in larger, more important matters. In everything you do, do it as unto the Lord. That's one of the first verses many of us learned as children, and this perspective makes a huge difference in our attentiveness to doing a careful and thorough job.

How we go about our day, whether it's delivering mail or preaching to a stadium of people is a reflection of our desire to do everything as unto the Lord and out of reverence for Him.

Lord, I know we are in a battle and our adversary, the devil, wants to defeat me. I am thankful that You rescued me from his grip on my life. The chains have been broken and I have been set free to serve You. I choose to serve You with everything in me. Amen.

Steve Wingfield

DAY 3

Everyone who competes in the games goes into strict training. They do it to get a crown that will not last, but we do it to get a crown that will last forever.

—1 Corinthians 9:25

WE CAN GET SO BUSY AND RUN THROUGH OUR DAYS SO FAST that we forget about heaven's realities. We forget that Jesus is there, interceding with the Father for us. We forget that we are going to be accountable to God for what we are doing today, and how we are doing it. Jesus said that we'll have to give an account for every careless word, and that what we are doing or not doing even to "one of the least of these," we are doing or not doing for Him. Our sights are clouded (the enemy has a hand in this), and our glimpses of heavenly reality, which is far more important than anything called "reality" here on earth, are obscured.

Remember that we are running a race for a prize. And that heavenly prize is one that lasts forever. Everything on this earth will eventually disappear. But our rewards in heaven will last forever. Our work here is looking toward that crown. Am I doing my work for the approval of the Lord who awards eternal crowns?

As you go about your *whatevers* today, ask the Lord for a glimpse into heaven's glory and an awareness that today you are already living toward that forever.

Jesus, I am thankful that You are seated at the right hand of God praying for me. Help me live in the reality that You are cheering me on as I run this race. Amen.

Steve Wingfield

Day 4

The Lord directs the steps of the godly. He delights in every detail of their lives.
—Psalm 37:23 (NLT)

GOD IS THOROUGH IN HIS WORK. He has placed us in a creation with amazing and delightful intricacy and detail. He ordered the universe. He keeps track of all the stars, every sparrow, the tides, and even the hair on your head. Every part of your body works in conjunction with the rest of your body—even your little toe. He keeps an eye on all the details.

His plan of salvation is thorough and complete. Christ became like us "in every way" and yet did not sin so that he could be our perfect High Priest and bring us to God. His one sacrifice "made perfect forever those who are being made holy" (Hebrews 10:14). Forgiveness is complete. He forgets no one. His salvation is for the whole world. He died for everyone, and His patience waits now so that everyone has a chance to hear and repent.

He provides for us in every way. He equips us thoroughly for the work He calls us to do. He defeated every power that would hold us captive. He gives us armor for the battle, the bread from heaven that sustains us, and the water of life. He steps into every situation and works for our good.

He will complete the work He started in us. His plan will be finished and complete. He is the beginning and the end. We build our hope on His unfailing love.

Lord, I am thankful for Your unfailing love and I claim Philippians 1:6, "Being confident of this, that he who began a good work in you will carry it on to completion until the day of Christ Jesus." Amen.

Steve Wingfield

Day 5

Love the LORD your God with all your heart and with all your soul and with all your strength.

—Deuteronomy 6:5

WE NEED TO BE ALL IN. When Jesus said "Follow me" to you and to me, he was asking for every part of us, not just bits and pieces, here and there. He wants our hearts, souls, strength, mind, and bodies. He asks for 24/7, 365 days, not just Sundays and a few hours each week. Scripture is clear. We must make a choice. We cannot serve two masters. Our treasures and our hearts will lie either with Christ or elsewhere. Jesus said whoever is not with Him and working with Him stands against Him and is working against Him.

We see this call to be thoroughly devoted to God throughout the Psalms. David often uses phrases like "with all my heart." Psalm 119:2–3 declares that joy comes to those who search for God "with all their hearts. They do not compromise with evil" (NLT). That speaks of a thorough devotion. Seeking with *all* their hearts. *No* compromise.

> You have charged us to keep your commandments *carefully* (119:4 NLT)
>
> Oh, that my actions would *consistently* reflect your decrees! (119:5 NLT)
>
> I will put them (your instructions) into practice *with all my heart.* (119:34 NLT)
>
> I *closely* follow your word. (119:67 NLT)

Everything we do for the Lord will matter. Everything. He is paying attention to the details and using them for His purposes. We should do likewise.

Lord, I am reporting for duty and to the best of my ability. I am all in. Amen.

Steve Wingfield

Day 6

And whatever you do, whether in word or deed, do everything in the name of the Lord Jesus, giving thanks to God the Father through him.

—Colossians 3:17 (ESV)

WE CANNOT DO A SHABBY, HALF-HEARTED JOB. If we represent Christ here on earth, everything we do is stamped with His name. In Acts 5, we read about the apostles being severely reprimanded by the Jewish religious leaders and then flogged before they were released. The apostles rejoiced "that God had counted them worthy to suffer disgrace for the name of Jesus" (v. 41 NLT). I want to be worthy of bearing the name of Jesus. I want my words and deeds to honor that name and represent Him well.

We do well to ask the Spirit's help each day as we check ourselves. How did I do today? In my words and deeds, did I represent Him well? Where do I need to ask forgiveness or make adjustments? Where do I need to ask Him to teach me more? Here again, an accountability group can help you. The Spirit will be teaching you each day and showing you the truth.

In everything we say and do, we must be thoroughly committed to being worthy of bearing His name.

Lord, this old hymn is my prayer, "Give of your best to the Master; Give of the strength of your youth; throw your soul's fresh, glowing ardor into the battle for truth."

[Howard Benjamin Grose (lyric) and Charlotte Ailington Barnard (music), "Give Your Best To The Master."]

DAY 7

Through the power of the Holy Spirit who lives within us, carefully guard the precious truth that has been entrusted to you.
—2 Timothy 1:14 (NLT)

AS WE CARRY ON CHRIST'S MISSION HERE ON EARTH, we've all been given specific things to do. I am an evangelist. You might be a youth pastor, or a NASCAR driver, or a parent entrusted with the training of precious lives and souls, or a builder of homes. In every place Christ is using each of us right now, He wants us to be thorough in our work. We belong to Him; no matter what we work at today, we are working for Him.

Prepare yourself each day as His representative. Dress for the job, according to Colossians 3:12. Always be prepared to explain your faith and hope, according to 1 Peter 3:15. Walk in step with the Spirit and do good whenever the opportunity presents itself as James 4:17 advises. Romans 6:13 tells us to offer "every part" of ourselves to God as instruments for His work. Every part. Thoroughly committed.

We have been entrusted by God with the gospel of Jesus Christ. He has put it into our hands. Every bit of your life. In every little detail, every brief moment, every chance encounter, may you be *thoroughly* committed to this calling, so that one day, you will hear the most important words of your life: "You have been faithful. Well done, and welcome home."

Lord, I want to be a faithful witness for You. May I use every available means to reach every available person. Help me remember that if I sow and don't reap, someone will reap after me and if I reap having not sown, may I always thank You for those who sowed before me. Amen.

Notes and Prayers

_____

_____

_____

_____

_____

_____

_____

_____

_____

_____

_____

_____

_____

_____

_____

_____

_____

_____

_____

_____

_____

TRANSPARENCY

Leadership is about building bridges of relationships;
without them we cannot move forward.

—Paul Weaver

DAY 1

Nothing in all creation is hidden from God's sight.
—Hebrews 4:13

MANY PEOPLE LIVE IN FEAR OF GOD'S ALL-SEEING EYE, having the idea that God is up there watching, waiting for us to step out of line. But my response is that He loves us so much that He can't take His eyes off us. That is a comfort to me.

Nothing in all of His creation is a secret before Him. He sees and knows everything. God knows the secrets of every heart. We are open books to him. He knows the good and the bad, the weaknesses and the strengths, the sorrows and the joys. He knows the things I might not even want to admit to myself, and He loves me anyway.

God wants us to live with transparency, openness, and honesty. He's designed us in such a way that this kind of life is the path to great joy and freedom. Our best life—whether we are in a leadership position or not—calls for transparency.

Dear heavenly Father, I am so grateful that You see me and You know me just as I am, with all of my faults, foibles, and failures. Yet, You love me just as much as You love Your Son, Jesus. Thank You for loving me, not for who I am, but for whose I am! In Jesus' name, amen.

Prayers on TRANSPARENCY by Babbie Mason

Day 2

He knows the secrets of every heart.

—Psalm 44:21 (NLT)

TRANSPARENCY DEMANDS SELF-AWARENESS. That is obvious. To clearly communicate so that you're known and understood, you're going to have to have self-awareness. You will have to understand yourself first. You also need honesty to be transparent. You will need to be truthful. Transparency requires courage. It is often a scary thing to let people know exactly how you feel or where you stand. Sincerity, accountability, and self-control all play a role in transparency, as do many other Lodestar traits.

None of these traits are stand-alone. None of them function at any level without the support of other traits. Struggling or putting out the Spirit's fire in one area will affect all others. Maybe you feel great hesitation to be transparent because you do not have the courage to stand firm in your identity. God knows every part of you, every fiber, every thread. He knows where you are struggling, and He says, "I am here to help you."

He already sees everything in your heart; be open to Him, ask Him to show you, *to teach you* what is necessary to change, and then to strengthen you in your inner being to be obedient to what He has shown you.

Dear heavenly Father, the world has convinced me that it is easier to blend in with everyone else than to stand out in my own uniqueness for Your glory. Thank You, God, for the courage to see that my uniqueness is a part of Your plan and purpose. In Jesus' name, amen.

Day 3

If we walk in the light, as he is in the light, we have fellowship with one another.
—1 John 1:7

SECRECY DIVIDES. Hiding things shuts us off from others and creates a loneliness. We cannot build bridges to others if we do not want to be known and understood. If we don't build bridges, then, as leaders, we cannot move forward. In our personal lives, we also cannot move forward if we are not transparent in our relationships.

Hiding behind facades is a strategy of the devil. It keeps us from fellowshipping with others. It keeps us from being teachable, compassionate, sincere, and empathetic. Bridges of relationships will never get built if we cannot be transparent.

Spend a few minutes today rejoicing in and savoring the wonder and amazing grace of God in building bridges of relationship with us. He has been so transparent; He's even told us that He wants us to know Him more than He wants any ritual of worship. To love Him with everything we've got is the greatest commandment. He communicates clearly with us through His Word and His Spirit who connects us to His thoughts. Our heavenly Father has modeled a transparency for us. He is building bridges so that our relationship with Him can move forward, so that *we* can move forward toward the lives He wants us to have. We, His children, can follow that model. Build those bridges. Be transparent.

Dear heavenly Father, ever since the beginning of time in the Garden, man has been hiding—hiding from the light of the truth, hiding from You. Please give me the courage to be open, honest, and transparent with You. That is the only way to become the person You want me to be. In Jesus' name, amen.

DAY 4

Therefore each of you must put off falsehood and speak truthfully to your neighbor, for we are all members of one body.

—Ephesians 4:25

BEING OPEN AND HONEST WITH EACH OTHER is a trait of the new life born of the Spirit in us. It connects us to others in the body of Christ. This connection is a two-way street, and our being transparent encourages transparency in others. It also opens up the channels of sincerity, compassion, forgiveness, and unconditional love. Those in the body of Christ are meant to share in the troubles of others and in so doing, provide strength and comfort. We are meant to encourage and help others in their struggles.

If we wear our masks of having it all together, though, we will not be approachable, we will not be seen as someone who can comfort, listen with compassion, or speak into another person's life.

Those who have struggled with depression, for example, can best understand someone else's struggle with depression. Those who have lived through divorce or abandonment can empathize with others who experience the same. Those who have lost children are most compassionate toward others in similar circumstances. The tears and wounds in your life and, yes, even the consequences of sins that you have suffered can be used by God to minister to others. Your story can show others the goodness of God.

Dear heavenly Father, I confess. I have been guilty of a great "cover up." Too often I have tried to conceal my imperfections and weaknesses from others. May my hurting neighbor's healing begin the moment I show my own scars. In Jesus' name, amen.

Steve Wingfield

Day 5

And whatever you do or say, do it as a representative of the Lord Jesus, giving thanks through him to God the Father.

—Colossians 3:17 (NLT)

Our transparency is also necessary in our relationships with others not yet in the body of Christ. Remember, in everything we do, we are representatives of Christ, and I want to always represent Him well.

When we build relationships through honesty and openness, others see truth. That draws people. In our relationships with non-believers, God can use our struggles, weaknesses, sorrows, and joys to connect us with those who still need to hear the message of Christ. No one builds bridges with those who are in hiding, appearing to be "perfect." Honesty about our hearts and lives can draw others to us and give us an opportunity to talk about the new life Christ has given us.

We are to live as Christ lived on this earth. "Whoever claims to live in him must live as Jesus did" (1 John 2:6). Jesus commanded us to love others as He did—openly, honestly, transparently, with humility, gentleness, and patience. Whether sisters and brothers in Christ or those who are enemies of Christ, in our relating to them, we are representing the Savior of the world. In our calling to do that, there is no place for falseness, secrecy, or pretending to be someone we're not.

Dear heavenly Father, thank You that I have a story of how You changed my life. Help me to use my God-story as a magnet, drawing others to You. In Jesus' name, amen.

Day 6

Whoever conceals their sins does not prosper, but the one who confesses and renounces them finds mercy.

—Proverbs 28:13

WE LEAK. That's borrowing from D. L. Moody, who once was asked why he prayed so often to be filled with the Holy Spirit. "Don't you believe God has filled you with his Spirit?" he was asked. "Yes," replied Moody, "I believe he's done it, but I leak." We all leak. We all mess up sometimes. That's why God gave us 1 John 1:9. He reassures us that if we confess our sins, He'll forgive them and do a scrubbing job in our hearts. Years ago, Bill Bright taught me the concept of spiritual breathing. We exhale and confess to the Lord. We inhale, and pray, "*Lord, fill me afresh with your Spirit.*" Like our need to breathe constantly, this spiritual breathing is a necessary, constant practice.

James 5:16 tells us to confess our sins to each other (transparency) and pray for each other. But how can we pray unless we know and understand each other so that we may be healed? Healing is what we all desire after we have messed up. Transparency is essential to this process.

Dear heavenly Father, thank You that I am free—free from the bonds of sin, the shame of the past, and the guilt of the present. All because of Jesus, I have a clean slate, a fresh start, and a brand new life. Absolutely nothing is better than that! In Jesus' name, amen.

Steve Wingfield

Day 7

To the Jews who had believed him, Jesus said, "If you hold to my teaching, you are really my disciples. Then you will know the truth, and the truth will set you free."
—John 8:31–32

Our security always rests in the love of Christ. We can say, "The Lord is my light and my salvation—so why should I be afraid?" Our life, our confidence, our hope all rest in God alone, not in what man thinks of us. Remember Jesus' words about his flock: He knows each one of His sheep, and He holds them securely, forever. Know that you—just as you are—are loved and held by the Lord of all. Nothing can separate us from that everlasting acceptance and love.

We live in a world that competes. But in Christ's kingdom, there is no competitive comparison among brothers and sisters. Ego has no place. Gifts are given by the Spirit, and each is to use gifts they have as the body works together as a whole. God designed you and put you where you are. In this new life you've been given, you are His masterpiece, created in Christ Jesus to do the work He has for you.

Don't let the enemy ensnare you in any of His traps. Living out who you really are is a great freedom. God bless you.

Dear Father, the problem with PRIDE is that "I" stands right in the middle of it. Help me to remember today that "I have been crucified with Christ and I no longer live, but Christ lives in me. The life I now live in the body, I live by faith in the Son of God, who loved me and gave himself for me." (Galatians 2:20). In Jesus' name, amen.

Notes and Prayers

_____

_____

_____

_____

_____

_____

_____

_____

_____

_____

_____

_____

_____

_____

_____

_____

_____

_____

_____

_____

TRUSTWORTHINESS

Without trust, relationships are short-lived. As leaders and parents, we cannot be successful long-term if we are not trustworthy.

—Paul Weaver

DAY 1

Urging you to defend the faith that God has entrusted once for all time to his holy people.

—Jude 1:3 (NLT)

ENTRUST MEANS "TO ASSIGN RESPONSIBILITY FOR DOING SOMETHING" or "to put something into someone's care or protection." God entrusted us with His message to the world, a message of forgiveness and hope. He has also entrusted us with the means to accomplish this mission—His unlimited resources and the unique gifts He has given each of us.

We are called and equipped by Jesus to be fishers of men. Paul wrote in 2 Corinthians 5 that God gave us a wonderful message of reconciliation to him, and so we are his ambassadors, "making his appeal through us." In Spurgeon's words, if we are saved, "the work is but half done, until you are employed to bring others to Christ. You are as yet but half formed in the image of your Lord unless you have commenced in some feeble way to tell others of the grace of God."

We don't all have to be evangelists. In any profession or walk of life, we can tell others about the goodness of God. Recall Peter's urging to be ready at every opportunity to explain why we have a wonderful hope and confidence. God has entrusted this message to us. Are we trustworthy ambassadors?

Lord Jesus, thank You for entrusting and equipping me to share Your Good News. Teach me as Your ambassador to trust You for the confidence I need to tell others about You. Give me the words I need today to point someone to You. Amen.

Prayer on TRUSTWORTHINESS by Dr. David Jones.

Day 2

For we are God's handiwork, created in Christ Jesus to do good works, which God prepared in advance for us to do.
—Ephesians 2:10

You might be tempted to think that God has not entrusted you with much, that He has not made you a missionary, a powerful speaker, or an especially gifted professional of any kind. Don't be deceived by the lies of the devil and his demons. They would love to get you off track and have you think that what you say and do each day is insignificant and unimportant to God.

Nothing you do for the Lord is ever useless. Even a cup of cold water to a thirsty person is important. Jesus talked about sorting out the sheep and the goats, based on things they did or did not do. Both groups asked Him, "*When* did we see you hungry or naked or sick or in prison?" None of them realized at the time that their actions were so significant.

The small things matter. It is all the small moments that build a life, create character, and make you an ambassador of Christ. You are sent out on your mission field every day, touching whatever lives intersect yours. The way you live speaks as powerfully as eloquent words. God has gifted you with exactly what you need to accomplish the job He's given you. God has entrusted you with His message for the world. Whatever He commands you to do, be trustworthy. *Everything counts.*

Lord, help me to trust You for the courage I need today to share Your Good News. Teach me to rely on You and understand the small things in life do matter. Open a door today for me to share Your love with someone who is lost. Amen.

Steve Wingfield

Day 3

To all who are victorious, who obey me to the very end, to them I will give authority over all the nations. They will have the same authority I received from my Father, and I will also give them the morning star!
—Revelation 2:26, 28 (NLT)

GOD HAS ENTRUSTED YOU AND ME WITH A LIFE-AND-DEATH MESSAGE. What information is more valuable to anyone than the news of how to save your soul, beat death, and have a new life? It is an amazing, overwhelming thing to consider. We have this "fearful responsibility to the Lord" (2 Corinthians 5:11 NLT).

His plan is to bring out the best in His children, to make them more and more like Him—actually, to get them ready for even more responsibility. Remember that He is doing a work in you, and He won't abandon it until it is complete. His work is to change us into His likeness. We were created to be like Him.

In both 2 Timothy 2 and multiple references in Revelation, we learn that those who are victorious, those who overcome, and those who endure and obey Him to the very end will someday reign with Christ, with all the authority He has. They will inherit the kingdom prepared for them and be given authority over nations.

Our imagination can't even scratch the surface of what all that means, but God has His plans for His children. And in the meantime, He has given them a life-and-death mission here on earth. Be faithful. Endure.

Heavenly Father, help me to trust You for the strength I need today to persist and endure in sharing Your love. Make me a blessing and encouragement today to someone who is lost and hurting. Thank You for entrusting me with Your life-saving Good News. Amen.

DAY 4

That is why we labor and strive, because we have put our hope in the living God, who is the Savior of all people, and especially of those who believe.

—1 Timothy 4:10

SHEEP IN CHRIST'S FLOCK CAN BE THE MOST SECURE PEOPLE IN THE WORLD. We are secure in our status with the Lord. No one, Jesus said, can snatch His sheep out of His hand. Because of His sacrifice for us, we know we're in good standing with God, and we can come boldly into His presence at any time, with requests, fears, doubts, praises, or just for a chat. We've been adopted as His dearly loved children. The barrier between us and our holy, holy God is gone.

We are also secure in His power and promises. If God is for us (and He is!), no one can stand against us, not even the spiritual forces of darkness and evil. He holds us; He has given us armor to protect us. His promises assure us that He will see us through this earthly journey and bring us safely home to Him.

Our hope for the future lies in an inheritance that will not change or fade away (as earthly inheritances do), in riches piled up that will not rust or decay and no one can steal, and in an eternal peace and perfection of life as God intended His children to have. Our hope is in a living God.

Heavenly Father, thank You for the secure hope I have in You. Thank You, that You have given me everything I need to share that hope with others. Thank You for rescuing me when I was lost in my sin and help me to tell others how they too can be rescued. Amen.

Steve Wingfield

DAY 5

So letting your sinful nature control your mind leads to death. But letting the Spirit control your mind leads to life and peace.

—Romans 8:6 (NLT)

ANOTHER QUALITY NECESSARY FOR TRUSTWORTHINESS IS SELF-CONTROL. About a month ago, we spent a week meditating on self-control as Christ's representatives. It is Spirit-control that gives us the power to discipline our thoughts, words, and actions. We need that discipline if we're going to be worthy of the trust Christ has placed in us as His ambassadors. Self-control that depends on the Spirit's control guides us in knowing when to speak and when to keep quiet, when to act and when to refrain from acting.

"Walk by the Spirit, keep in step with him," wrote Paul in Galatians 5. If we let the Spirit guide us in every part of our lives, we won't get attitudes and behaviors that are inappropriate for those God has entrusted with His message. We will know God's will and follow it.

The Holy Spirit living in you is the "first deposit" of everything God wants to do in you, His new creation. He has also a guarantee that God will give you everything He has promised. He has a direct connection to God's own thoughts. So let the Spirit lead you and mold you. Hide the Word of God in your heart so the Spirit can use it. Don't stifle His power in your life. Turn your self-control over to him, and He'll make you a trustworthy steward of what God has entrusted to you.

Heavenly Father, thank You that Your Holy Spirit lives in me and guides me. Teach me how to rely on Your presence in my life and not rely on myself. Use me today to lead someone to You. Amen.

Day 6

So we tell others about Christ... That's why I work and struggle so hard, depending on Christ's mighty power that works within me.

—Colossians 1:28, 29 (NLT)

Consistency is the third attribute required in being trustworthy. Consistency is, well, *not* being a hypocrite. It is making our actions match up with what we profess. Since what we do is an outflowing of what is really in our hearts, we can see that consistency is a matter of soil. That is, the soil in Jesus' parable in Luke 8 about a farmer who scattered seeds onto four different kinds of soil.

In Jesus' parable, the seed is the Word of God. The fertile soil, in which the seeds take root and grow, is an honest and good heart. God wants to plant His Word in people with good-soil hearts, so that they cling to the Word "and patiently produce a huge harvest" (Luke 8:15 NLT). Good-soil hearts are committed to deep roots and growth. God has entrusted us with the Word of God. He wants to plant in us and then see an abundant harvest. We must be faithful and steadfast in our commitment to share the message about Christ, pouring patience, perseverance, and diligence into our calling as His ambassadors.

As Paul wrote, I want to work hard, with all the energy God gives me, to be a constant, steadfast, and trustworthy steward of the message of Christ. Good soil, holding God's Word close, and producing a huge harvest.

Heavenly Father, help me to be consistent in my walk with You. Teach me to trust You more and to place my confidence in You and Your Word. My heart's desire is to be a trustworthy steward of Your Good News. Help me to faithfully point people to Jesus. Amen.

Steve Wingfield

Day 7

You are a chosen people. You are royal priests, a holy nation, God's very own possession. As a result, you can show others the goodness of God, for he called you out of the darkness into his wonderful light.

—1 Peter 2:9 (NLT)

OUR MEDITATIONS HAVE FOCUSED ON BEING TRUSTWORTHY STEWARDS of the message and resources God has entrusted to us. We have not touched on trustworthiness in human relationships. Yet, we have. The qualities of character we exhibit in our interactions with others spring from our commitment to being God's holy people and showing others the goodness of God. We clothe ourselves with the Lord Jesus Christ, as Romans 13:14 describes it, and that takes care of our trustworthiness in human relationships. That makes us honest and gives us self-control and generosity and humility and the other traits we've discussed.

It doesn't work the other way around. Being trustworthy in earthly relationships doesn't make us God's holy people or trustworthy representatives of Christ. Being generous doesn't make us God's children. It is our relationship with Christ, living our lives by faith in the Son of God, that gives us these Spirit-empowered character traits.

The Lodestar program is all about character-based leadership. If you're a follower of Christ who happens to be in a leadership role, the most powerful leadership will flow out of Christ's character at work in you.

Heavenly Father, I want to trust You in every aspect of my life and to teach others to do the same. Teach me to rest in You knowing You live in me. I want to represent You well so that people will see Your presence in my life. Help me to lead like Jesus. Amen.

Notes and Prayers

_____

_____

_____

_____

_____

_____

_____

_____

_____

_____

_____

_____

_____

_____

_____

_____

Becoming a wise person is not an event; it is a lifelong journey.

—Paul Weaver

DAY 1

Wisdom is a tree of life to those who embrace her; happy are those who hold her tightly.

—Proverbs 3:18 (NLT)

GOD GAVE SOLOMON WISDOM. He also gave him wealth, riches, and honor more than any king who had come before him. God used Solomon's wisdom in a major way. He can use it in your life in a major way.

If you have wisdom, you will be able to apply knowledge and clear judgment accurately to life situations, and who doesn't want to do that? We want to be able to sort out whatever situation comes our way, making good choices and working out conflicts. Without wisdom, we're going to make foolish decisions and waste our time and energy on all kinds of meaningless endeavors, possibly endeavors that end up in devastation.

Listen to Solomon's descriptions of what wisdom brings to your life: Whoever finds wisdom finds life. You'll understand what is good, right, and fair. Wisdom brings discretion that protects and guards you. It leads you down the right paths and keeps you from the wrong paths that lead to destruction and darkness. "Whoever finds me finds life and receives favor from the LORD" (Proverbs 8:35 NLT).

Father in heaven, I acknowledge that I need Your wisdom. Lead me to be quick to humble myself and call out to You. Open my eyes to see areas where I have relied on my own ideas. I want to find life and receive the favor You have for me and those around me. I pray in Jesus' name. Amen.

Prayers on WISDOM by Michelle Wingfield Curlin.

DAY 2

Search for [wisdom] as for hidden treasure.

—Proverbs 2:4

THE WORD *TREASURE* SEEMS TO BE ONE THAT IS UNDERSTOOD BY EVERYONE. How many of us as children have played at hunting treasure? How many of us as adults are still on a treasure hunt?

Solomon accumulated immeasurable material wealth. You can read about it in 1 Kings 10:14–29. And his kingdom shared in the wealth—silver was as common in Jerusalem as the stones in the streets. Yet he declared there was one thing more precious than anything else: wisdom. It is a treasure to be searched for.

This tree of life produces fruit that is better than fine gold, wrote Solomon. It is far more precious than rubies. Nothing you desire can compare with wisdom. I want you to think about that for a moment. Envision finding your treasure. What do you dream of someday having or accomplishing? Whatever it is, it doesn't compare to finding wisdom. That is the treasure we are to seek. It's the one thing King Solomon wanted, even more than wealth, power, or defeat of his enemies. He knew he needed wisdom above all else.

We need wisdom, too, my friend. It will bear vital fruit, guard and protect us, and bring us life.

Lord, You are the Creator and Sustainer of all life. You understand me and all my ways much better than I do. Teach me to live with this awareness every moment. Grow my appetite for the true treasure that is found in You and revealed in Your Word. In Jesus' name, I pray. Amen.

Steve Wingfield

Day 3

The fear of the LORD is the beginning of wisdom, and knowledge of the Holy One is understanding.

—Proverbs 9:10

SOLOMON GOT IT RIGHT. When he became king, he knew that he needed the Lord's help to rule well. He came to the Lord in humility. Even after he had established himself as the wisest, richest king in the country's history, he still held that humility before the Lord. He built a lavish temple, but at the dedication service, his prayer acknowledged, "Oh, Lord, we can never build a temple worthy of you!"

"With humility comes wisdom" (Proverbs 11:2). Humility is a necessary attitude in gaining wisdom. C. S. Lewis wrote, "A proud man is always looking down on things and people; and, of course, as long as you are looking down, you cannot see something that is above you." Humility knows it can learn from others. Wise men learn from others and become wiser still (see Proverbs 9:9).

Humility also looks up to God. He is the source of all wisdom. If we're looking for wisdom, it's got to be built on the foundation of reverence for the holy Creator of the universe and of wisdom itself. He has given us the invitation. He will give us wisdom if we ask.

Lord God, thank You that You have invited me to ask for wisdom and promised that You will not shame me when I ask. I feel my need for wisdom more every day. Please pour out Your wisdom for each situation that I am facing and give me faith to trust You as I obey. In Jesus' name, I pray. Amen.

DAY 4

Trust in the LORD with all your heart, and do not lean on your own under-standing. In all your ways acknowledge him, and he will make straight your paths.

—Proverbs 3:5–6 (ESV)

SOLOMON'S PRAISE AND EXALTATION OF WISDOM was focused on wisdom that comes from God, one of the "good and perfect" gifts He delights in giving to those who come to Him and ask. The wisdom from above can be trusted to be a tree of life, to protect and guard, to lead in right paths. God-given wisdom is a treasure of incomparable worth.

We recognize there is another "wisdom" touted by the world, and we need to be alert and on guard against it. We read about this conflict in James chapter 3. Earthly wisdom gives rise to selfish ambition, envy, disorder, and evil practices. This is the wisdom of this world: we must look out for number one, do whatever it takes to achieve our worldly goals, ferociously protect our rights and what is ours. But the wisdom from above is exhibited in a good life and deeds done in service and humility. This wisdom is pure, loves peace, and is considerate, submissive, merciful, impartial, and sincere. This is the wisdom God freely and abundantly gives to those who seek it.

The wisdom from above will protect you from the deceptive, destructive wisdom of this world. Seek and trust the Lord's wisdom. Acknowledge you need Him, His guidance, and this great treasure.

Father in heaven, show me where I do not trust You with all my heart, and give me the courage to acknowledge You in all my ways. You are always trustworthy. You are the Good Shepherd who walks ahead of me, making my paths straight. I pray in Jesus' name. Amen.

Steve Wingfield

DAY 5

So that they may have the full riches of complete understanding, in order that they may know the mystery of God, namely, Christ, in whom are hidden all the treasures of wisdom and knowledge.

—Colossians 2:2–3

IN CHRIST WE FIND THE RICHES AND TREASURE that Solomon found so desirable. All the wisdom from above dwells fully in Him. 1 Corinthians 1:30 tells us that God unites us with Christ Jesus for *our* benefit. He becomes our righteousness, our holiness, our redemption. And our wisdom. God's plan to redeem and renew His creation—and us—reaches fulfillment in Christ Jesus. Christ brings us into an eternal life that knows heaven's realities; we are already living that life. Christ defeated death and sin and broke our bondage to our sinful nature and to the fear of death. Christ is our Great Shepherd, providing all we need and leading us safely home to God. Christ provides the wisdom we need as we walk through this world. His Spirit guides us to the truth. His wisdom protects us from the insidious "hollow and deceptive philosophy, which depends on human tradition and the elemental spiritual forces of this world rather than on Christ." (Colossians 2:8).

It is His Spirit and His wisdom which gives us an advantage over those who do not know Him. I'm not being arrogant. Scripture is very clear: Christ is our wisdom, and all the fullness of God dwells in Him. Christ is worth everything, my friend! He is everything to us. He is the great, rich treasure God has given to us.

Thank You, Lord, that "all treasures of wisdom and knowledge" hidden in Christ can protect me from being deceived in this confusing world. Make my spirit sensitive to Your leading today. In Jesus' name, I pray. Amen.

Day 6

Whoever walks with the wise becomes wise, but the companion of fools will suffer harm.

—Proverbs 13:20 (ESV)

I HAVE NO DOUBT SOLOMON WROTE these words with human relationships in mind. When we hang out with the wise, our own tree-of-life wisdom is nourished and grows. The opposite is also true. Companions of the foolish will find themselves in unfortunate predicaments and on paths that lead into darkness. Wisdom chooses her close companions carefully.

But Solomon did not yet know the joy of walking daily with the One who has the fullness of wisdom from above. We, though, are privileged to do that. Ephesians 1:8 (NLT) says God has "showered his kindness on us, along with all wisdom and understanding." He has made His wisdom accessible to us through Christ. And so we can walk with the wisest of the wise and learn from Him.

Jesus said to His disciples that hearing His words and putting them into practice is like being wise and building your house on a rock where nothing can shake or destroy it. He makes it pretty simple, doesn't he? Walk with Him. Heed His words. Live according to what He teaches you. That is the wisdom from above that will preserve your life. In other words, walk with He who is wisdom for you, and stay as close as you possibly can.

Father in heaven, thank You for Your presence with me here today through Your Holy Spirit. Thank You for the words of life I read in Scripture. Please bring Your truth back to my mind as I walk through all the situations and conversations of this day. May your wisdom be evident to the people around me so that You will be glorified. In Jesus' name, I pray. Amen.

Steve Wingfield

Day 7

. . . you may be filled with the knowledge of his will in all spiritual wisdom and understanding, so as to walk in a manner worthy of the Lord, fully pleasing to him: bearing fruit in every good work and increasing in the knowledge of God.

—Colossians 1:9–10 (ESV)

Paul wrote a letter to the Christians in Colossae. As far as we know, Paul had never been in that city, but his letter is filled with heartfelt concern and intense encouragement. My prayers for you, my friend, even though we may never meet, follow Paul's model in the opening of his letter.

And so, from the day we heard, we have not ceased to pray for you . . . (Colossians 1:9a).

In Colossians 1:10, Paul encourages them to grow in their knowledge of the Lord, which will result in wisdom, understanding, and a life that is fully pleasing to the Lord bearing much fruit.

I pray that you get to know God better and better. I pray you know that Christ is worth everything, that He is the treasure far beyond anything else you will ever find. I pray you will live out your inheritance, showered by God's kindness. I pray the Spirit gives you His wisdom, leading you in wise and good paths to a life that is pleasing to Him as you represent Him well in this dark world.

Almighty God, fill me with the knowledge of Your will through all the wisdom and understanding that the Spirit gives, so that I may live a life worthy of You, Lord, and please You in every way: bearing fruit in every good work, and growing to know You, Lord. Thank You that You hear my prayers. In Jesus' name, I pray. Amen.

(Adapted from Colossians 1:9–10)

Notes and Prayers

_____

_____

_____

_____

_____

_____

_____

_____

_____

_____

_____

_____

_____

_____

_____

_____

_____

_____

_____

_____

Steve Wingfield

A FINAL WORD

In the first pages of this book, I listed the names of those generous souls who helped make GUIDING PRINCIPLES a reality. Even so, that list is not complete. I want to thank you, reader, friend, for your investment in these pages—for continuing with me day after day, week after week, for trusting me and allowing me this stage on which to speak. I pray now that every line, every prayer, every passage of Scripture, every benediction, and every bit of wisdom finds residence in the quiet of your heart, that you may know and enjoy true clarity in this complicated world. In Christ, our confidence, our hope, our guiding principle, amen.

—Steve Wingfield

LODESTAR
MOUNTAIN INN

Lodestar Mountain Inn is a non-denominational Christian retreat center situate on 524 acres in beautiful Smoke Hole in Upper Tract, WV. The majesty an serenity of the mountains, coupled with comfortable, rustic lodging, provide the perfect environment to connect with God on an intimate level an experience healing, hope, encouragement, rest, and recovery.

BUILD AMAZING
CHARACTER

TO LIVE, LEARN, AND LEAD

ENHANCE THE CULTURE OF YOUR ORGANIZATION OR HOME

- Businesses
- Civic Organizations
- Sunday School Classes
- Small Groups & Youth Groups
- Schools & Universities
- Families

Wingfield, Wingfield Ministries CEO:

thankful for Lodestar Guidance and the impact it has
in businesses, schools, and families, and I know it will do
me in your life. America is in desperate need of character
opment and a return to godly values. Lodestar Guidance
character by developing values using principles that are
ally based. I encourage you to invest in your family, local
ol, and business by using this program."

sit LodestarGuidance.com to
arn more about this valuable program.